ADOPTION FOR SINGLES: SECOND EDITION

Everything You Need
To Know To Decide
If Parenthood Is For You

VICTORIA SOLSBERRY
A SINGLEANDSATISFIED.COM BOOK
Arlington, Virginia

Singleandsatisfied.com Books   Arlington, Virginia
Author Head Shot August 2008 by Jonathan Timmes
ISBN: 978-1-453-69663-7

I dedicate this book to the memory of

My brother, Richard, who was my first friend,

And my father, Gene, who thought I could rule the world.

Contents

ACKNOWLEDGEMENTS

I would like to thank my friend and extraordinary coach, Carmen Bolaños, who took on the constant and overwhelming task of keeping me on track. Without her help, this book would not have happened. Really. You think I'm kidding?

I am grateful for the limitless support and love of my parents, Kay and Gene Solsberry, and their belief that I can do anything I set my mind to. Like many parents, I guess, but mine do it better than most. They each asked about my book every week for two years and never seemed to tire of the subject. My dad died in March, 2010, but asked about the book up to the end. Thank you, Mom and Dad. I love you both.

My friends were unfailingly supportive, as well, and are probably grateful to move on to my next obsession, uh, book. Thank you Brenda Blackburn, Glynn Cahoon, Gary Campbell, Melissa Chaffee, Camille Cocozza, Tracy Dieter, Renee Fluty, Jan Genevro, Margaret Gordon, Allison Hahn, Lisa McNellis, Christie Olsen, Gerrie Rodriguez, Janice Sanchez, Cameron Soulis, Laura Steele, Vicki Street (Sis), Ginger Sullivan, Kevin Thomas, Torry Thomas, Margaret Wood, my book group and friends for the last 14 years – Peggy Dahlquist, Michele Dausman, Jenny Reinhart, Carol Schwartz, Jennifer Schwartz, Nora Super, Muriel von Villas, Chris White, and Kim Witman, who like to critique books. Please go easy on me. And a special thank you to Kti Jensen and Katherine Nevius for their support and confidence in me.

I'd like to thank the young people who helped me with proofreading and computer work – Ariana Zaia, my nephew, Michael Solsberry, and Sophia Zaia. You caught many errors and changes and saved my behind.

And the rest of my family – Rich, who listened to me talk endlessly about the book and the future. Dave, my computer genius brother, who took the website off my hands, thank God. My sister-in-law, Heather, another Richard, my nephew, and Dan, his brother, who like the rest of the family, listened, gave me ideas, and supported me. Thank you all. I promise it's over. For now.

My interviewees – Thesia Garner, Margaret Schwartz, Ron Kolonowski, Art Engler, Natalie Newton, Patrick Mason, and Rita Soronen. You are the heart of the book. Thank you!

Last, but not least, the professionals – Kirk Schroder, my brilliant lawyer, and Jonathan Timmes, my fabulously talented photographer, thank you.

INTRODUCTION

Congratulations! The fact that you are reading this book means that you are clearly a very special human being. You think that you may want to be a parent even though you are unmarried. You believe that you may have room in your heart and in your home for a child who needs you, whether American, Ethiopian, or Honduran, a baby or a teenager.

You may have been thinking about this for a long time. Or it may be a new idea that came to you when a friend or family member asked if you would ever consider adopting, or when you saw a story in the news about a celebrity bringing home a child from abroad.

But, like others, you probably assumed that you couldn't afford it, or that you would be turned down because you don't own a home, or because you don't make enough money. Or you may have assumed that all available children have terrible behavioral problems, or are sick, or too young, or too old.

You will discover, however, that in most U.S. states and many foreign countries, you are not only acceptable as an adoptive parent, but actually sought after. Wendy's Wonderful Kids, the adoption arm of The Dave Thomas Foundation for Adoption, has social workers in all 50 states whose fulltime jobs are to recruit you and help you adopt. I will tell you more about Wendy's Wonderful Kids in Chapters 3 and 4, and you'll read the fascinating Q&A of Rita Soronen, the Executive Director of The Dave Thomas Foundation in Chapter 7. In the U.S. alone there are approximately 129,000 children whose parents' rights have been terminated who are waiting for someone like you to take them out of foster care forever. They are newborns to 17 year old orphans who desperately need a family.

Worldwide, it has been estimated that there are at least 5 million orphaned children in Ethiopia alone. Tracey Neale, a single woman and a former news anchor at the Washington, D.C. CBS affiliate, WUSA9, brought home 12 month old twins from Ethiopia in September of 2007. Go to www.veronicasstory.org, click on "Introduction" and "Meeting My Kids" on the left menu, read about her powerful journey, and see pictures of her beautiful son and daughter. Veronica's Story Foundation was named after a beautiful 18-month old girl named Veronica, who Tracey met in an orphanage in South Africa. She knew immediately that Veronica would be her daughter, and started the paperwork back in the United States to make that a reality. Most of the children that Tracey met that day in that orphanage had HIV/Aids, though, and Veronica soon died from the illness. Not all orphaned African children are HIV+, of course, but Veronica inspired Tracey to start a foundation to help orphans all over the world. Read her story.

Included in this book is a directory of all of the countries in the world – Appendix A – Intercountry Adoption Directory – with information gathered from the U.S. Department of State and foreign embassies about the adoption possibilities in those countries. Poverty and war have made literally millions of kids available for adoption by American singles.

Adoption for Singles: Second Edition is basically an overview of the adoption world and information about all aspects of the process so that you can try it on for size. It includes internet links to resources for further study, book lists, and referrals for baby, toddler, school-age and teenager parent coaches to help you with questions that you might have as you consider this big step. It also includes a link to a directory of adoption agencies prescreened for experience with or a desire to work with single prospective adoptive parents. It can be found on the book website, www.adoptionforsinglesbook.com. Housing this directory on the website instead of in the book makes it possible to keep the information more current and to add new agencies as they come to my attention.

Adoption for Singles: Second Edition was written to address a subject of increasing concern to single adults. In my twenties, singles didn't even buy a house without a marital partner, much less have a child. But single adoption is now legal in all 50 states and thousands more singles adopt every year. By the time we are in our late 30s and not married or engaged, many of us know that the panic about time passing so quickly is actually about children and whether or not we're going to have time to have them. We begin to think about doing it alone. But how?

Some people simply have kids the old-fashioned way. You get to experience pregnancy, delivery and know that the child is biologically related to you.

But you've bought this book, so raising a child that has already been or is about to be born may be a better fit for you. You may have political, religious or spiritual convictions about taking care of children in need of a parent, you may not feel comfortable going through pregnancy as a single, you may have religious beliefs that make unmarried pregnancy out of the question for you, or you may even be unable to conceive at the point that you've decided to go it alone. So you're thinking about adoption. Where do you start?

ABOUT THE BOOK

In this book, I will walk you through the process of making a decision about whether you even want to go forward. I'll tell you about the issues involved and what you need to know to make the decision.

In Chapter I, I will talk about the emotional issues that you must consider when thinking about adoption. In this chapter, I ask you to think about your personality, personal qualities, and attitudes that are optimal for good parenting. As you think more and more about the possibility of adoption in your life, I'd like for you to just begin to look at your relationships and behavior. This is not to discourage you or nail you on your weaknesses, but to help you appreciate where you are strong and where you could be a little more intentional in your preparation for parenthood. You've shown that you are a compassionate, altruistic person simply by deciding to look into adoption, so I'm sure that you want to be the best parent that you can be. This chapter contains many questions to help you start thinking about yourself in that context.

In Chapter II, you will learn about what it costs to adopt a child. The costs vary depending upon many variables – age, race, and nationality, and how many are available for adoption. I will discuss financial options and how others have found the money to adopt. I will also discuss the tax implications of adopting, that vary depending upon the child. Finally, you will learn about general costs of raising a child. What can you expect given the age and needs of the child?

Chapter III will address the next steps. You're thinking that this is something that you really want to do, so now what? What age child would be best for you? You will learn about the developmental stages that children go through as they mature, and what tasks and needs they have in each stage so that you can decide what age fits you and your lifestyle best. How do you feel about the race of the child? Can it be different from yours? What is available to you in terms of age domestically and internationally?

In Chapter IV, I will discuss the processes of working with an adoption agency, a private adoption lawyer, what they each offer, and how they differ. I will also discuss how you would go about adopting through the foster care system. Regardless of the type of adoption facilitator you choose, you will need a Home Study. What is it, and how can you prepare for it? What are the other steps necessary for adoption, and how long do they take?

Chapter V will address all of the things that you will need to consider once you've set the adoption process in motion. These are the things that we all think about when we take on a dependent – from health and life insurance, wills and trusts, to names and childproofing your home.

Chapter VI is for those of you who decide that adoption is not right for you. You may feel that you're not ready for such a permanent step, but you'd like to take time to prepare, or explore a less permanent relationship with a child. For you, this chapter will include information about mentoring and foster care. Others of you will decide that you really feel a need to try to have your own biological child, so this chapter will also include a link for information about assisted reproduction – artificial insemination and surrogacy.

As a disclaimer, I would like to say that I do not provide the link for information about assisted reproduction as a recommendation. I wrote this book because I believe strongly in adoption and I hope that you bought it because you do, too. I decided to provide the link rather than include the information in the book for two reasons. First, this is a book about adoption. Second, I am aware that some religions, including Roman Catholicism, have doctrines against assisted reproduction. Discussions of artificial insemination and surrogacy are by nature graphic, and I would not want to offend those of you with those religious beliefs. Otherwise, throughout the book, in the interest of helping all single adults – religious, nonreligious, gay, straight, conservative and liberal – I decided not to leave out discussions of lifestyles that may not apply to everyone. I hope you understand.

Chapter VII is a compilation of interviews with adoption experts – adoptive parents, a social worker, doctor and head of an adoption clinic, and the executive director of a national foster care adoption organization. I think that you'll find these Question-and-Answers to be fascinating and very informative. They're my favorite part of the book!

At the end of the book, you fill find Appendix A, a list of every foreign country recognized by the United States Department of State, and each country's policies on adopting to singles. This appendix is very time sensitive – in the last month of editing this book alone, more than a dozen countries had updates of changes made since the first of the year. To make it possible for you to stay on top of what's happening in the countries that you are considering, most entries include a web link to the latest information about the U.S.'s relationship to that country. Appendix B is a link to a list of prescreened American adoption agencies, along with contact information, a list of countries that each agency works with, and whether the agency is gay-friendly. As I noted above, throughout the book you will find links to organizations and websites that have been particularly useful in preparing this book. Many national organizations, the State Department, foreign embassies in the United States, the Internal Revenue Service, banks, and other resources will be given for you to use, as adoption laws change constantly! If you have purchased the eBook version of this book, as you read each chapter, you should be able to click the link if you'd like more information.

On the book's website you will also find several reproducible forms to use as you collect the information you need, interview agencies and budget for your adoption. If you purchased the eBook form of this book, I recommend that you print it out on three-hole punch paper and put it in a thick three-hole punch notebook. If you add dividers with checklists, folders and pockets for documents, and add pages for notes, you can use the book and forms as a workbook as you move through the process. It will be much less confusing and overwhelming if all of your information is in one place where you can pull it together when you need to.

Terminology

For the purposes of this book, what does "single" mean?

When you get to the Chapter VII, you will read several Q&As of men and women who have adopted children, both in this country and in others. Two of the adoptive parents are single women and two are men who have since been married in their home state of Connecticut, but were unmarried when they adopted their children. A friend and reviewer called to my attention that in a practical sense, the men's experience of adoption was different from the women's experience of adoption. Because the women were not in committed relationships they did not have a partner to support them, share in the endless tasks of preparing the adoption, and co-parent.

So let's talk about what it means to be "single," and later, what sexual orientation may have to do with adoption.

In the past several years the term "single" has come to mean someone who is available – that is, someone who does not have a girlfriend or boyfriend. When asked if they're dating anyone, young people now say, "no, I'm single." At a gathering last summer I told a new, young acquaintance about the book. She asked, "why would you focus on people who don't date?" I credit social media with this change, which regretfully muddies the waters of marital status communication. In this book the word "single" means not married. Period. Please feel free to date all you want. When you adopt, however, if you're not married, you have to do it alone.

For the purposes of consistency, I use the word "single" simply to connote someone, male or female, who is not either legally married, or allowed by law to adopt with another person. Single, therefore, may include people who have never married or are divorced and are *not* in a committed relationship, but also people who have never married or are divorced, and *are* in a committed relationship. These men and women may even live with their partners, and may have been with them for decades. If they have not been legally married in their state, however, they will have to choose one person to complete the adoption, and at the time of the adoption that person will be the child's legal guardian.

So in terms of legalities, this book describes rules for adoption for those people who are not in a position to adopt a child with another person, whether committed or not even dating. The emotional and practical tone of the book at times assumes that the prospective adoptive parent is looking to adopt and raise a child in a one-parent household. This simple reflects the fact that many men and women are choosing to adopt precisely because they are not in a relationship where they might have biological children with a partner.

If you are in a committed long term relationship, good for you! You will have the experience of approaching adoption as a team rather than as a singleton. The legal rules will still apply to you, but you'll have support and one person with whom to make all of those countless decisions. If you are not in a relationship, you won't have to compromise or negotiate, but will get to go forward in a way that feels perfect for you. Good for you, too!

Sexual Orientation

At the time of this writing, several states have prohibitions against adoptions to gays and lesbians. They are Florida, which will not adopt to gays and lesbians at all, and Utah and Mississippi, which will not adopt to any unmarried person who is living with a partner. A PBS documentary entitled NOW: Fighting for Family, which aired on April 7, 2006, looks at the subject of gay adoption in the state of Florida (www.ShopPBS.org, $19.95 for the DVD). In it are interviewed two men, one a lawyer and one a social worker, who have been fostering two little sisters for years. The girls have both had issues as a result of being moved from foster home to foster home before coming to the two men, and have needed counseling and lots of individualized care. They would like nothing more that to have a "forever home", but while the state of Florida says that the two men are fit to foster the girls, they believe that they are not fit to adopt them.

The documentary also describes a woman whose sister died, leaving children who needed a home. Because she was a lesbian, the children could not be adopted by her, someone who knew and loved them, but had to be given to a couple, strangers, for adoption.

Regardless of your feelings and beliefs about homosexuality, this type of thinking is inconsistent and irrational. The person who seems to suffer the most is the child, who longs for the certainty of never being removed from a home again. What is it that can potentially happen in an adoptive home that can't happen in a foster home?

Suffice it to say, if you're gay or lesbian, live in a state that prohibits gay or lesbian adoption, you have to decide whether it's more important to you to live in your state or adopt a child. Adoption legally happens in the state where the prospective adoptive parent resides, so you cannot go out of state to find a child and then bring the child home to adopt. However, if you lived in say, Massachusetts and adopted a child there, you can move to Florida and keep the child, of course. You wouldn't be the first person to leave your home state because of laws regarding your sexual orientation, should you decide that being an adoptive parent is more important.

Sexual orientation does come into play in intercountry adoption, where many countries state directly that they will not adopt to anyone but heterosexual men and women. China, when it adopted to singles, was one such country. If you're like me, however, you know a lesbian woman or two who has adopted a daughter from China, so clearly sexual orientation was not investigated during the adoption process.

When agency directors and social workers were asked directly about intercountry adoption and sexuality, many said that they take a "don't ask, don't tell" approach. One even said that it was really none of her business. Clearly, some religiously-oriented adoption agencies may take a more active stance in finding out about one's relationships and living situation, but it is clear that some agencies sidestep the question completely.

The Home Study will address the number of people living in your home, the number of bedrooms, and who will be around the child on a regular basis. I will leave it to your discretion to decide how to handle those questions.

In terms of sexual orientation and foster care adoption, gay men and lesbian women are not discriminated against based on their sexual status. Wendy's Wonderful Kids requires that the contracted social workers in each state, who usually are employees of agencies and social service organizations, treat gay men and lesbian women exactly the way that they treat heterosexual adults who are interested in adoption. Failure to do so results in termination of their contract.

ABOUT THE AUTHOR

Let me introduce myself. My name is Victoria Solsberry, and I am a Licensed Clinical Social Worker, having graduated from the National Catholic School of Social Service at the Catholic University of America in Washington, D.C. in 1980, and a Personal and Business Coach.

Adoption for Singles: Second Edition is the first of a series of Single and Satisfied books, all of which will address important issues of interest to single adults. As a single woman myself, I believe that whether or not you are actively pursuing a committed romantic relationship, and whether or not you even want one, the rest of your life can be so exciting and fulfilling that a partner would just be icing on the cake. Living as a single person is different from being married, in more ways than just the obvious. Everything from planning for retirement to adoption to taking care of all of the details of our busy lives requires a different eye. I hope to offer busy and happy singles the tools to make their lives easier. Stay tuned for my next book, *Retirement Planning for Singles.*

More about my professional experience. I've been practicing as a psychiatric social worker for 28 years and as a coach since 2003. Early in my career I worked at Chestnut Lodge (the psychiatric hospital in *I Never Promised You a Rose Garden*) as a Research Assistant on a major follow-up study, at the National Academy of Sciences Institute of Medicine as a Research Associate on a study named "The Human Health Effects of the Stress of Bereavement", and finally, as a psychotherapist and intake specialist at the Meyer Treatment Center at the Washington School of Psychiatry. I opened my private practice in 1982 and was in fulltime private practice by 1987.

After more than 20 years of doing psychotherapy, I decided to train as a personal and business coach, which is based on a positive psychology model and does not adhere to the medical model of mental illness. Rather than diagnosing psychiatric symptoms, positive psychology diagnoses strengths, which are then used to help my clients dream big, set and reach their goals, fill up their lives a little bit, and find richness – perhaps by adopting a child and becoming a parent! I hope that this book helps you decide to dream big, and that I can help you get a sense of what it will take to do that. Good luck on your journey!

Disclaimers

- I am not an attorney. Any information about the legalities of adoption was gathered from countless adoption websites, the U.S. Department of State, and the embassies of countries that adopt to American singles. Verify all information that I give to you with your adoption attorney and/or agency.
- I am not a physician. Any information about medical issues surrounding adoption was gathered from countless websites and Dr. Patrick Mason, the medical expert interviewed in Chapter VII, "In First Person." Verify all information that I give to you with preadoption medical specialists or a pediatrician of your choosing.
- I have not been able to visit every company or use every product that I cite in this book. Caveat emptor – let the buyer beware. I have researched the companies cited as thoroughly as possible on the internet, but you must make the final decision based upon your own research.
- I do not endorse or recommend adoption for everyone, nor do I think that every form of adoption is suitable for every prospective adoptive parent.
- Information gathered for this book was, by and large, accurate as of April, 2010. The adoption field changes very quickly, so please confirm any information given in this book. It was written to give you a starting place and a general overview of the very large field of adoption. You should not rely solely on the information, content or opinions expressed in this book.

- Web addresses were accurate at the time of writing this book, but web addresses change frequently, and even correct web addresses do not always work. If you purchased the ebook version of this book and a web link does not work, copy and paste into the browser window. If it still does not work, a search engine should be able to direct you to the new address.

Chapter I

The First Step in Deciding
Whether to Adopt As a Single:
Is This Something You Can Do Emotionally?

Well, you've bought this book, so we know that you are attracted to the idea of becoming a parent. You may have always known that you like children and that you want to have a family some day. The question that we're going to discuss first is: Is this the right time? Have you grown up sufficiently to parent a child? And, have you thought deeply about your feelings and relationships so that you are prepared for this new form of intimacy?

In this chapter we will discuss the qualities and experiences you will need to have to adopt a child. They are:

- Emotional Maturity: How responsible are you? How are you with conflict?
- Emotional Intimacy: How deep and committed are your relationships with family and friends?
- Empathy: Are you good at recognizing others' feelings?
- Flexibility and Adaptability: Can you accept change easily and go with the flow?
- Desire and Stability: How badly do you want this? Do you follow through with new ideas, or do you tend to lose interest in new activities?
- Parenting Skills: Have you thought about how you were parented and whether your style will be similar or different?
- Experience: Have you spent alone time with children the age you are thinking about adopting?
- Strengths: What do you have to offer a child?

The Style of This Chapter

Ideally, I would like to sit down with each person reading this book and have an in-depth conversation about your upbringing, your relationships with friends and family, your values and attitudes, your emotional style, and why you want to become a parent. That's impossible, of course, so this chapter will contain many of the questions that I would ask you if we had a month or so of face-to-face dialogue about you.

It may seem at times like a cross-examination, but I hope that you will hear these questions not as judgments, but as a way to begin to shape your thinking about your readiness to parent. In a typical family with two parents, there is a little more wiggle room for falling short—although it's not ideal even then. As a single parent, you will most likely be the sum total experience of a parent for your child. And since you are altruistic and loving enough to even consider providing a home for a parentless child, I'm sure that you want to be what that child needs to thrive if at all possible.

So take some time, think about the questions, and even perhaps journal your answers. You may find that you want to come back to a question as you live your life. For example, "How are you with conflict?" Begin to notice how you handle conflict at work, with friends, and with strangers. Write down the question along with your thoughts. Learning about yourself is good for you, good for the child, and will help enormously as you go through the adoption process. The home study will contain many of these questions. You'll be prepared!

But again, and I can't stress this enough, I ask you these questions to make you aware of your strengths and weaknesses as a potential parent, not to judge you. This is not a test. This does, however, give you a chance to make some changes in your behavior and attitudes, and to get some help if you need it.

So let's get started.

Emotional Maturity

What do you think and how do you feel when I ask you if you consider yourself to be emotionally mature? If you're like most of us, you probably think about how much you party, how much you drink, or how you spend your free time. And you may feel a bit defensive since to be accused of being immature is certainly an insult to an adult.

While your feelings about partying and going out with your friends are certainly important considerations when contemplating parenthood, we're going to look at some more specific qualities that may tell you if you're ready to take this huge step.

Responsibility

You probably already know that taking on the care of a child for the rest of your life is a huge responsibility. But what does that mean, exactly?

Do you keep your word? You're going to make many, many promises when you decide to become a parent. You are going to promise to house and clothe your child, to keep them as physically safe as possible, to make sure that they receive a good education, and to spend quality time together, among other things. Would your friends and family say that you are reliable? When you say you will do something for someone, do you usually do it? Would you rely on you? Could a child rely on you?

Are you financially responsible? How are you with credit? Do you pay your bills on time? Emotionally mature adults are able to delay gratification and save towards purchases that they can't afford right now. This kind of self-control with spending will mean that you will be able to say no to yourself because your child needs a band instrument or medication. It will also mean that you can scale back your lifestyle to make financial room for a new family member without feeling resentful. How does this feel to you?

What is your work ethic? Do you carry your weight at work and do whatever you need to do to get the job done? Emotionally mature adults have stopped looking for other people to do their work. They receive a lot of satisfaction from earning their pay and doing a good job. As you probably know, being a parent brings more work into your life. If you are really ready to do it, however, most of this work will be deeply satisfying to you. At night when your child is bathed, read to and asleep, and you settle down to relax for a little while before going to bed yourself, you will usually be exhausted, but hopefully, happy. Good parents feel good about the work of raising children. Not every task, of course, but in general, good.

Anger Management

How are you with conflict? How did you learn to fight in your family? How do you handle your anger? As a mental health practitioner I have seen every conflict style imaginable. Some people are frightened by conflict and as a result, are unable to tell another person when they have been hurt or offended. They walk through life never working things through with other people, either just "taking it," or walking away. Others have explosive anger responses and become insulting and frightening when they are offended or hurt. They've grown up believing that such behavior is normal, saying, "well, I was angry," when in fact, we call it dirty fighting. Yelling, name-calling, and belittling are emotional abuse, and unacceptable ways of showing anger, especially to your child.

Emotionally mature adults know how to tell another person that they are angry in respectful ways. As a parent, you will become more angry more often than you ever imagined. You will not be able to walk away from your child or ignore acting out behaviors. And of course, since you want to adopt to provide a better life and a loving home for a child, you do not want to be an emotional abuser.

Think about how your parents showed anger to you. Was it respectful? Did you feel frightened when one or both of them expressed anger towards you? Did either parent withdraw from you when angry? You may have a good sense of how you behave when you are angry, or you might need to ask family and friends to give you feedback.

One other piece of anger and conflict management: How difficult is it for you to apologize when someone tells you that you hurt or offended them? If you grew up in a home where adults did not apologize to children, you may have a lot of difficulty when called upon to apologize. When children are exposed to excessive anger when they make a mistake, they get the impression that mistakes are horrible things. It appears to change the way their parent feels about them, even if only temporarily. They learn to react defensively, or try to blame someone else, or tell a lie. Anything to get out of having to admit that they made a mistake.

Being able to apologize to a child when you make a mistake is extremely important. It tells the child that even adults make and admit their mistakes (kids know that you make them, even if you

4

won't admit it), and that there is reparation. If you are not emotionally-abusive when a child makes a mistake and you don't withdraw affection after the confrontation, **and** you admit and apologize for your own mistakes, your child will be less likely to tell a lie or refuse to apologize himself. Discipline becomes much more manageable and effective when the child comes to understand that **everyone** in the house admits and apologizes when they screw up. Do you do that?

If you discover or already know that you have a problem with anger and conflict, or that it is extremely difficult for you to admit when you're wrong, you'll probably need to do something about it before you become a parent. Read about it, talk to your friends about it, or get some help. You might consider reading *How to Disagree Without Being Disagreeable: Getting Your Point Across with the Gentle Art of Verbal Self-Defense* by Suzette Haden Elgin, or go to www.relationships911.org, click on Relationship Tools on the top menu, and then click on "Learn to Fight Fair Helpcard" on the left menu. The helpcard is an 8 1/2 by 11 card filled with information on what to do and what not to do when arguing ($10.95 for an electronic copy, $12.95 for a hard copy). If you decide that you need some help, I'm partial to social workers, but you can also find a counselor or psychologist to help out. Social workers and counselors will be the least expensive, followed by psychologists. There is no need to see a psychiatrist, who is an M.D. and will be the most expensive. You can find a good social worker at www.abecsw.org (click on Online BCD Directory), or a psychologist at www.apa.org (click on Find a Psychologist). Not only would that be good for the child, but for you in all of your relationships. Problems with anger hurt closeness. Period.

A close friend told me a story about becoming a mother for the first time. She said that soon after bringing the baby into her home she had an overwhelming feeling of responsibility for her daughter. Not as a burden, but as an awareness of the awesome power that she had to love and shape this little person. That she would not even be able to go to the bathroom without thinking about her daughter's safety. That until the day she herself died, she would be this child's mother – more concerned for her daughter's happiness than her own. That daughter is now a teenager and I know that my friend is just as committed to her safety and happiness as she was that day years ago. It takes emotional maturity to be a good parent and to love your child that much.

I believe that almost all parents **want** to be good parents, that bad parenting is rarely intentional, but instead the result of a lack of awareness of our own problems and issues. We all have the potential to figure it out. It's never too late to mature.

Emotional Intimacy

If and when you become a parent, it's going to be extremely important that you know how to be close to that child. We can get a hint of how you will be emotionally as a parent by looking at your existing relationships with family and friends.

Think about the people in your life that you consider to be in your inner circle. Some may be related to you, some are not. Why are they the most important relationships in your life? Are they your confidantes? Do they know you – both your good and bad points – the best? Do you feel the safest around them?

In part I ask these questions to find out how emotionally open you are. In part, to find out if you expect and require trustworthiness and nonjudgment in order for people to be admitted to your inner circle. Both are extremely important if you want to be a parent.

Emotional Openness

Do you consider yourself to be a pretty open person, or would you say that you are more closed, or "private"? If you've had a really bad day and a friend asks how you are, will you tell them? If not, why not?

I'm not talking about being that person that we all dread running into. The one who seems to have no boundaries and who will tell us more than we ever wanted to know, and we barely know them! I'm talking about authenticity. Letting people that we care about know who we really are, what's really important to us, what we love, what we can't stand. And how we're doing right now so that they can support us if we need it.

Unless you're planning to adopt a baby, you're going to need to deal with emotions right out of the gate. And if you are planning to adopt a baby, you'll want to be prepared to deal with emotions as the baby grows. I'll tell you why this is important.

Adults who were not taught about feelings as small children tend to be emotionally narrow. Some adults seem to have only one or two emotions available to them at a time – if it's a "bad" feeling, they feel angry, and if it's a "good" feeling, they feel happy. They were not taught the differences between "bad" feelings, so they can't identify disappointment, or sadness, or resentment, or frustration. All they know is that they feel something "bad", and that comes out as anger.

It's the parent's job to teach small children about the wide array of feelings that they might have. When the play date is cancelled because their friend is ill, we say "oh, I know you're really disappointed because you were really looking forward to playing with Peter." Or, when their favorite toy breaks, "I always feel so sad when my favorite things break. I bet you feel sad." It sounds like a parody of bad therapy, but for a child it is not corny or humorous. It is empathy and crucial teaching rolled into one.

You can actually buy posters with children's faces in all kinds of moods with the name of the feeling under the picture (www.Amazon.com – "How Are You Feeling Today?" or "Mood Swings", both by Jim Borgman, or www.TeachChildren.com – "How Am I Feeling? Emotions Board" (click on Teacher Supplies, then Character Education Items)). It may seem silly to make such a big deal over vocabulary, but it means more than that. It means that your child will not grow up to become angry every time something doesn't go right. Wouldn't you rather be around an adult who can say, "Ouch, that hurt," rather than get angry?

So, how are you with identifying and reporting your feelings? It's very difficult to teach a child about feelings if you don't recognize and know how to deal with your own. It's also extremely important to model emotional fluency and openness for your child. Just like the parent who can admit wrong and apologize, the parent who can say that she's sad or frustrated sets a powerful example. You can feel a lot of emotions, both good and bad, and yet you're still strong and can take care of the child. Most emotions really only scare other people when the emotional person seems out of control or unable to handle it. A person who can report a feeling and then work to make it better doesn't usually scare us. By modeling this emotional behavior, you teach the child that strong people have emotions and aren't ashamed of their feelings. And that people who express their emotions instead of acting them out are more predictable and easier to be around.

One last word about authenticity and emotional fluency: If you adopt an older child from foster care or abroad, you're going to be presented with emotions to handle right off the bat. Even if being adopted, or fostered, and becoming a member of your family is a very good thing, your child is going to feel sadness at the loss of other caregivers –perhaps a parent or grandparent, perhaps their culture, their last name, friends and foster siblings. They may be frightened about a new school, new foods, or having to trust an adult they barely know. They may be confused by the language, or the structure in your home and what you expect from them. Your ability to name and understand your new child's emotions will go a long way towards making you a safe and trustworthy person. And that will make it easier to eventually love you.

Friendship and Family Relationships

Go back to your inner circle. How do they handle it when you're vulnerable? Do they listen and ask a lot of questions to help you think about your situation, or do they essentially shut you down by telling you not to worry? Or worse – do they shame you or belittle you?

The people that you call your best friends need to be real friends. If you've analyzed your inner circle and have concluded that you can't be open with them because of how they handle it, you may need to rethink your idea of friendship. You're going to need a lot of support if you become a parent, and that means real friends who will listen and help. It will also model good friendship for your child and help you help them be a good friend and make good friends. You certainly want that for your child!

If you feel as though you have trouble making friends, that is another good reason to find someone to talk to. You want to make sure that you're not thinking of adopting a child simply because you are lonely, or because you feel as though no one really knows or loves you. That is too big a burden for a child. If you can figure it out before you adopt, then you'll have close friends **and** a child to love you. Who could ask for anything more?

Empathy

Empathy is the ability to know and understand what someone else is feeling, even if that feeling is different from your own. In order to be in a good relationship of any kind – and most importantly, with your child – we must be able to recognize and empathize with others' feelings. This is a variation of the emotional fluency we discussed earlier. First we have to know our own emotions, and because we recognize them in ourselves, we can recognize them in other people.

Part of empathy is also having a sort of sympathy for those feelings, giving them legitimacy and respecting them. We may not feel the same way in the same situation, but we can respect that the other person does.

This may seem obvious, but it's amazing how many people screw this up. Because I talk about feelings all day long, I may not be nervous about some situations that make some people nervous. For example, if I think I may have offended you, I will ask. That is fairly easy for me. But when a friend or client tells me that they think they may have offended someone else, but they haven't brought it up because they're uncomfortable doing so, I get it. Empathy means that I have to be able to imagine feeling that way and I have to get how scary it is. Even if it wouldn't be for me.

Part of good parenting is knowing that your child is going to feel things that you won't, and fully accepting those feelings as legitimate. Some people have trouble accepting differences. I once had an acquaintance who said she wasn't sure she could ever love a child who didn't love chocolate! Being alike makes us feel safe in the relationship because being too different from someone else may make them leave us. And it is fun to share a passion with someone, whether it is chocolate or something else that you love. But not respecting different tastes, interests, and yes, feelings, makes it hard for others to be in relationship with us. Something we definitely don't want for your child.

To recap: You need to be fluent in feeling and recognizing feelings in your child, and then you have to respect those feelings, even if you don't really get it. Now, that doesn't mean that your son is going to get his way just because you respect that he's upset.

You can say no to the tattoo and still truly understand how badly he wants it and that he's upset. That is simple respect.

Does empathy come naturally for you? If so, you're fortunate to have a great skill for parenting already down pat. If not, you can practice with everyone in your life. When someone tells you what they're feeling, especially if it surprises you, try to imagine having the feeling yourself so that you can connect with that person and their situation. When you notice that someone seems to be feeling something – upset, happy—ask them about it and listen carefully to the answer. And if you find yourself thinking "why in the world is she feeling that?", remind yourself that your experience is not the only legitimate experience of a situation.

Flexibility and Adaptability

Has anyone ever called you a "control freak?" Do you have a neat and orderly home with everything in its place? Do you make appointments and social plans days and weeks ahead of time and expect others to keep their appointments with you? And, do you imagine situations and then get discombobulated or disappointed when they turn out to be different?

This section is not going to try to convince you not to make plans with others, or to let your house go to the dogs. However, it will try to help you think about how you deal with change, interruptions, messes and playing it by ear.

When you have a child, or when you adopt a child, every day is an adventure! Kids have such an interesting way of forgetting things (her lunch), needing things (she develops a fever), and breaking things (the window) that we can never anticipate. Some of the change we certainly can anticipate, though, such as adding the child's schedule to our own, or turning the office into a bedroom. How does all that feel to you?

There are two main areas where your ability to be flexible and to adapt to new situations is important. They are in day-to-day living with a child, and in adapting to and learning to love a child who is not what you expected or imagined. Both are extremely important, although the latter is probably the most serious and needs to be addressed first.

When you first started thinking about adopting a child, like everyone else, you envisioned yourself taking care of and spending time with that child. It's a time to fantasize about the child and to enjoy the scenes that we create and the child that we want. In these fantasies we imagine a child who enjoys sharing our activities, our company, and whose personality complements ours.

When we have biological children, we usually have some reassurance that we'll have a lot in common with our child. While they may be temperamentally different from us, that difference is offset by the fact that they have our eyes, mouth, or hair. Or perhaps they look like our grandmother, but have the same quirks and tastes that we do. At the very least, we have the knowledge that we created this child from our own body, and that, for most people, brings with it a sense of attachment and nonjudgment.

When we adopt, right off the bat we are asked to think about a child being different from us. We may prefer a birthmother who looks like us, who has our coloring and height. Or we choose or reject the idea of a certain country because its native children are a different race than we are. It may sound petty, but I don't think my family has ever created a child with tight curly hair. While I would love to have a child with curly-curly hair, it would be different, not look like me in that regard, and require some experimenting to learn how to work with it – the hair, that is. No big deal in the overall scheme of things, but such differences can create "fish out of water" experiences and make us feel unsure. Too many of them may add up to too much discomfort and disappointment.

What this means is that you need to think about your expectations, and how you would react if the child you are given is not the child of your fantasies. Ask yourself how you would feel parenting a child who looks nothing like you. A child who is obviously not your biological child. Or how about a boy, when you envisioned a girl? Or a chubby child when you are thin? Or probably the most difficult to admit, a child who is not good-looking?

Oftentimes, when I discuss adoption with a prospective adoptive parent, I hear questions about all of the potential problems and difficulties that may arise with that child. "But what if the child has learning disabilities, or needs counseling, or is malnourished when I get it?" "Or what if the child is very shy, or what if I'm not drawn to that child for whatever reason?" What then?

For some reason, questions like these don't seem to deter people from getting pregnant. The possibility of having a baby who might become a child with learning disabilities, or a child who may later develop diabetes or asthma, probably would not stop most people from conceiving. But for some other reason, it may put off someone considering adoption. Think about the fact that there are no guarantees with any child. Parents whose children make it to adulthood with no problems are very, very lucky. And if a child is going to need help to have the best possible outcome, imagine how much they would need the love and care of a parent. Could you do that?

So, fantasies and expectations need to be acknowledged. For most of you, the fantasy and the expectation are not irrevocably linked. That is, you may envision a "mini-me" in looks and personality, but after consideration realize that that is not very important to you at all. For others, it may be a deal-breaker. There is no right or wrong here, ultimately, as long as you figure it out for yourself and act accordingly.

The second type of flexibility and adaptability is less important for most people – that is, the unpredictability that comes with life with a child, and the changes you have to make to be a parent.

As single people, most of us are used to making decisions with only ourselves in mind. At the end of the work day, we are usually free to make last-minute plans to meet a friend for dinner. We may be free to take a vacation during the first weeks of school in September when prices go down. And we never have to leave work because someone else gets sick.

Now is the time to start noticing how you react to changes in plans. Do you just move on to Plan B, or do you get angry or wonder what you're going to do next? The other day I was noticing that I generally do things in the exact same order when I get up in the morning for work. I never bring the newspaper in before I leave for work, and I never eat before I shower. If I had a 5 year old in the house, who knows what the routine would look like? I might have to shower at night. I know I would have to make breakfast even when I'm not hungry! This is all pretty obvious, of course, but worth thinking about. Watch the routine of a friend with a child. Notice the limitations and structure of that person's life.

Please don't get the impression that you have no control and that kids rule. Your life will be a middle ground between your life now and a life where you obey your child's every command. However, good parents don't carry on as usual, expecting their children to accompany them through an adult lifestyle. About half of your activities may be of little interest to you. Can you live with that?

Bottom line: 1. It is extremely important to ask yourself if you may be only capable of parenting the "perfect" child of your fantasies, or if you could parent a wide range of children in terms of looks, personality, and maybe, age or gender. And 2. Are you willing to play it by ear and create a new structure for your life – one that takes into account both the child's needs and interests, and your own?

Desire and Stability

This one is pretty easy to describe and determine. How much does everything you've read so far discourage you? Have you always known that you needed to be a parent? Or is this perhaps a curiosity that may go away in a few months?

If you are not absolutely sure that adopting or even parenting a child is not for you, put it aside for awhile. There is no hurry. And, again, there is no right or wrong about whether to raise children. Not all of us are cut out to be parents, and many of us have other contributions to make to the world that might not be possible if we had a child at home. Just remember: If you adopt and it is not right for you, ultimately it will be the child who suffers. And if it is right for you, you will eventually know.

And here's a little exercise to help you determine whether you are stable enough to do this: Think about all of the ideas that you've had for your life. Have you generally picked a path and stuck with it? Have you changed jobs or careers a number of times? Had a lot of boyfriends or girlfriends? Do you own the equipment for a number of hobbies, or projects that you've started, but not finished? Answering "yes" to one or more questions doesn't necessarily mean that parenthood is not for you; it simply means that you may need to live with the idea for awhile to make sure it's right for you.

Parenting Skills

We've all seen the funny movies and television shows where a bachelor or single career woman somehow inherits a baby or child without warning and clumsily, but hilariously, finds a way to parent the child. The key words here are "without warning," and if you'd like to adopt, now is the time to prepare.

The first thing you need to do is to set aside some time to think about how you yourself were parented. You may already know that there are some things you would do differently, or you may have never even thought about it. You will want to be the kind of parent that matches your core values and that may mean making a few changes from the way you were raised. Think about each of these areas, how your parents did it, and what feels right to you.

- Discipline: Were you spanked, and how do you feel about that? Were your parents consistent in their discipline – in other words, did you always know what behavior was unacceptable? I recommend that you watch a wonderful television show currently running to get an idea of good disciplinary tactics. It's called "Supernanny" and stars a British nanny named Jo who models appropriate boundary and limit-setting. It airs on ABC at 9 eastern/8 central on Wednesday evenings. See what you think of her techniques and compare them to the way you were disciplined. I think that you will see an enormous respect for the child coupled with firm, no-nonsense reaction to acting out. You may also want to read the book *1-2-3 Magic,* or one of the other books listed later in this chapter to see how they compare to your ideas about discipline.
- Affection: How often did you hear the words "I love you" from your parents or parent? It never ceases to amaze me how many people I've worked with who never heard those words growing up. It is extremely important that you be able to offer genuine affection to

your adoptive child as soon as you feel it. It is also extremely important that you not withdraw this affection when you are angry with your child, or following discipline. If showing affection is difficult for you, you may want to think about why it is difficult, whether or not you would be comfortable doing it anyway, and, if not, get some help to prepare yourself to parent.

- Communication: How much time did your parent or parents spend talking with you and listening to you? Were you offered a safe place to discuss your concerns? What do you imagine your communication to be like with your child?

- Homework: This may be a curious parenting skill to you, but were you "helped" with your homework as you were growing up? I don't ever remember having a parent sit with me as I did my homework or studied, but I have clients that spend hours with their kids every night, preparing them for school the next day. How do you feel about that? Have you ever discussed the topic with your parent friends?

- Activities: I know parents that spend late afternoon every weekday and all weekend taking their kids to lessons, team sports, and play dates, while others limit extracurricular activities and encourage their kids to entertain themselves or play outside. This will directly impact how many of your own activities you'll be able to continue and how dramatically your life will change. Do you see your life being completely changed by having a child, or do you see a compromise where both you and your child get some of the free time for hobbies, interests, and other people? How did your parents handle this?

- Chores: How much work around the house and yard were you expected to do growing up? Did you get an allowance and what were you expected to do for it? Find out what parents around you expect from their kids, and why. As usual, there are extremes to be found here. You'll wear yourself out if you do everything for your child, and you'll also raise an adult who not only doesn't know how to care for her home, but feels entitled to someone else doing it. But on the other hand, a child's life is not supposed to be all work, so…

In addition, there are wonderful resources out there to help you with your parenting skills. In addition to a number of books on parenting, I can enthusiastically recommend individual and group parent coaching, most of which is done on the telephone or by internet. Until you get a child or know what age child you're going to get, you probably won't need coaching. But most of the coaches that I recommend have websites, publish newsletters, teach classes and run groups for prospective parents. Go to their websites and sign up for any information that's available. Here is a partial list of coaches that I can recommend:

1. **Camille Cocozza**, L.C.S.W., is a Personal and Family Life Coach and is dedicated to the emotional, physical and spiritual well-being of families. She focuses on parents of toddlers and preschoolers and parents of young children with developmental delays, including social/emotional and behavioral issues. She has a professional background in foster care and adoption. Camille provides individual coaching, parent support groups, and educational teleclasses and workshops. Go to www.openwaycoaching.com where you can sign up for her free newsletter and classes on parenting. Watch for her upcoming book on how to choose a daycare center to enhance your child's emotional growth.

2. **Laura Steele**, M.A., M.S., N.C.C., is a practicing parent coach and psychotherapist/play therapist. She specializes in helping families with children birth to age 10 with behavioral, developmental and social/emotional challenges. Her expertise includes families experiencing dramatic change such as separation, divorce, loss, or adoption. In addition to more than 30 years of experience working with and for families and children, she is a parent and grandparent. She can be reached at Lsteele66@verizon.net.

3. **Cathy Rodrigues** specializes in coaching parents of children with special needs from birth through adulthood. She also develops training programs and innovative groups for parents of foster, adoptive and medically complex children. Currently, she runs weekly telephone groups for mothers of young children with special needs. She can be reached at Cathy@CathyRodrigues.com. To learn more about Cathy's services, visit her website at www.cathyrodrigues.com or comment on her blog at www.parentingthespecialneedschild.com. Cathy strives to help with the life transition to parenting by accessing strengths and identifying resources toward creating a nurturing and supportive family.

4. **Toni Schutta**, M.A., L.P., is a Parent Coach with 14 years experience helping families find solutions that work. Toni helps families with children ages 3-12 who don't need therapy but could use a little help with parenting challenges like: getting your child to listen the first time, creating a positive discipline plan that works, reducing bedtime, morning, homework hassles and anger outbursts. For details go to: http://www.familiesfirstcoaching.com/ or http://www.getparentinghelpnow.com/.

5. **Chuck Adam,** MSW, has 33 years experience as a family therapist, and 5 years as a parent coach, educator, and consultant, with a special interest in parents of teenagers–including adoptive, foster, and step-parents. He believes that our society and our children are so different from when we were kids, that new approaches are needed by parents, and particularly parents of teens. Chuck offers parenting classes, coaching, and consultation over the phone, and can be reached by email at chuckadam@sbcglobal.net. His website is www.chuckadamcoach.com, and his blogsite, containing dozens of articles on parenting, is www.parentchildharmony.com.

You may also want to do a little reading to see what styles of parenting resonate with you. Here is a list:

1. *Parenting from the Inside Out*, D. Siegal and M. Hartzell, Penguin Books, 2003.
2. *1-2-3 Magic*, T. Phelan, Parent Magic, Inc., 2003.
3. *Touchpoints*, T. Berry Brazelton and J.D. Sparrow, Perseus Books, Cambridge, Massachusetts, 2001.
4. *Your Baby & Child from Birth to Age Five*, P. Leach, Borzoi Books, Alfred A. Knopf, New York, 1977.
5. *Playground Politics*, S. Greenspan, Da Capo Press, 1994.
6. *The Optimistic Child*, M. Seligman, Houghton Mifflin, New York, 1995.
7. *Everyday Blessings: the Inner Work of Mindful Parenting*, Kabat-Zinn, M. and J., Hyperion, New York, 1997.
8. *Too loud too bright too fast too tight*, S. Heller, Quill Harper Collins, New York, 2003.

Experience

Have you ever spent time alone with a child? Played with one on a regular basis or babysat for a weekend? Do you have nieces or nephews and know what it's like to take care of them?

It is important that you have some knowledge of what this is like before you bring a child into your home. There are many ways to do this. You can ask your friends if you can spend time alone with their kids on a regular basis, which has the added benefit of giving your parent friends time away. You can be trained to be a respite foster parent – foster parents who keep a foster child for a day or a weekend to give the regular foster parents time off. You could coach a team, become a Brownie or Cub Scout leader, teach Sunday School at your church or synagogue, or become a mentor at school or in a program such as Big Brother/Big Sister (see Chapter VI for information). Ask your friends. They might have all kinds of ingenious ideas.

The purpose for gaining this kind of experience is for you to find out how it feels to be alone with a child or children for awhile.

You may discover that you don't really enjoy any age, which is in itself, important, or that you enjoy all ages. It will also help you identify your fears and discomforts and give you an opportunity to figure them out. Do you perhaps feel overly responsible for children and worry that a child in your care may get hurt? Whatever you discover about yourself when you're around and responsible for children will be important grist for the mill in your journey towards parenthood. You can then discuss these fears with your parent friends, your counselor, or even your parents, to see how others handle them.

But most important, being alone with kids will allow you to try on the parent role to see how it feels. This will help you determine if you're perhaps considering parenthood because someone else thinks you should, or because you think you should. If you enjoy the kids, you'll know you're on the right track.

By now you're probably thinking that I think you have to be almost perfect to be a parent. That is not so! It's been my experience, however, that if we are completely unconscious about what it takes to be a good parent or just a good human being, we're likely to miss the mark more often. Thinking about our own personalities, maturity level and emotional readiness helps us to prepare and clean house of bad habits in our relationships with other people and to learn new skills. At least then we can be more intentional in our decisions about our child and in our own behavior with her.

As I have mentioned several times earlier, you can show your seriousness about being a good parent by thinking about your problem areas and getting some help, if necessary. I can assure you that a counselor would be totally impressed by a single man or woman who wanted a few months' help exploring their personality to prepare for parenthood. We do the best we can with what we know, and when we know more, we do better. Learning about yourself – perhaps your inability to apologize, or to say "I love you" – can only help your life. (www.abecsw.org and www.apa.org)

Strengths

Learning about your personal strengths is an amazing and gratifying thing to do even if you're not planning to become a parent. There are several ways to do this, and the first involves simply sitting down with some paper and a pen and taking careful stock of your own thoughts about your best qualities and skills.

Make a list. Think about what you value about yourself, and what others have said about you. Are you the go-to person when your group needs something done? Do people confide in you? Are you organized, a great cook, a talented painter, singer or dancer? Are you deeply spiritual, easy-going, calm, energetic, reliable, honest, funny?

Ten or fifteen years ago I was going through a valley in my life, and I asked a close friend to share with me why he appreciated and loved me. He took on the request enthusiastically, and we planned to go out to dinner near my birthday so that he could tell me what he had come up with.

Over champagne, filet mignon and chocolate mousse, he pulled out his notes and told me why he was my friend. Some of what he said was familiar, but some other things he named came as a complete surprise to me. Needless to say, it improved my mood and made me feel like a more valuable human being than I had felt when I asked for the favor. It was a profoundly loving gift.

Consider doing this with your closest people. Others see you in ways that you might not see yourself. If you can't imagine doing it as formally as I did, then at least consider asking family and friends what they see as your best qualities some day when you are in conversation about the possibility of adopting. Tell them that you will need to discuss your strengths in your autobiography and in your home study. It may be fascinating to hear what they have to say.

Another way to find out about strengths that you may not put on your list is to take a test that was created by Martin Seligman, Ph.D., Fox Leadership Professor of Psychology and Director of the University of Pennsylvania Positive Psychology Center. Dr. Seligman is the father of the positive psychology movement, which studies positive emotions, strengths-based character, and healthy institutions.

Dr. Seligman believes that rather than diagnosing our weaknesses, which is common in the medical model practice of psychology, we should diagnose our strengths. This has the two-fold purpose and effect of allowing us to be proud of and appreciate our personal gifts, and also to allow us to develop them and use them more purposefully.

At www.authentichappiness.com, Dr. Seligman offers a test that will determine your top strengths. He has identified 24 main strengths that humans possess (even if you are mentally ill or in prison, you have strengths), and this test not only allows you to see your top strengths, but also your "less-strong" qualities. The 24 strengths are:

1. Appreciation of beauty and excellence
2. Bravery and valor
3. Capacity to love and be loved
4. Caution, prudence, and discretion
5. Citizenship, teamwork, and loyalty
6. Creativity, ingenuity, and originality
7. Curiosity and interest in the world
8. Fairness, equity, and justice
9. Forgiveness and mercy
10. Gratitude
11. Honesty, authenticity, and genuineness
12. Hope, optimism, and future-mindedness
13. Humor and playfulness
14. Industry, diligence, and perseverance
15. Judgment, critical thinking, and open-mindedness
16. Kindness and generosity
17. Leadership
18. Love of learning
19. Modesty and humility
20. Perspective (wisdom)
21. Self-control and self-regulation
22. Social intelligence
23. Spirituality, sense of purpose, and faith
24. Zest, enthusiasm and energy

When I first took this test years ago, I had to laugh out loud about some of my "signature strengths". One of my top strengths was "Curiosity and interest in the world." I had always thought that I was just nosy, and all along it had been a strength. Another was "Capacity to love and be loved." That put a whole new spin on the people I had scared away in my pursuit of friendships and love relationships as an adult. I am "mushy" and pretty open about what I appreciate in other people. But if a potential friend scored very low in that strength, meaning that they were not good at receiving affection, we were doomed. How fascinating! It made me feel so much better about my "mushy" style and the friendships that didn't happen.

You too may find that your top (and bottom!) strengths explain a lot about how you function and how your life has gone so far. Again, go to www.authentichappiness.com and take the test. It's called the VIA Signature Strengths test, and should take about 40 minutes to complete. Print out the complete list and see where you are the most and least strong. It can be very telling in terms of your preparation for parenthood. Scoring low on your ability to love, or hope and optimism may indicate that you need to figure yourself out before you adopt.

Dr. Seligman has written a number of books about positive psychology, strengths, and gratitude. His views on our skills and how to raise a child who is optimistic is fascinating and might be interesting reading for you. Check out *The Optimistic Child*, M. Seligman, Houghton Mifflin, New York, 1995, and *Authentic Happiness: Using the New Positive Psychology to Realize Your Potential for Lasting Fulfillment*, M. Seligman, The Free Press, New York, 2002.

Conclusion

I hope that you have begun to think about yourself, your emotional life and relationships and that you are encouraged about your ability to parent. The truth is, even people who've worked in the field for 30 years know that we are works in progress and don't get it right a lot of the time. But we do know what is ideal, and now you do, too. If you discovered an area where you know you need work, I encourage you to get some help. Remember: We can change anything about our beliefs, attitudes and behaviors that we want to. You are going to grow in ways you never imagined once you have a child, so why not start now?

Resources

- To learn how to fight fairly, *How to Disagree Without Being Disagreeable: Getting Your Point Across With the Gentle Art of Verbal Self-Defense*, Suzette Haden Elgin, Wiley, March 1977 www.Amazon.com, or
- The "Learn to Fight Fair Helpcard" at www.relationships911.org (click on Relationship Tools at the top, then the helpcard on the left menu
- To Find a Counselor, The American Board of Examiners in Clinical Social Work www.abecsw.org
- The American Psychological Association www.apa.org
- "How Are You Feeling Today?" or "Mood Swings," both by Jim Borgman www.Amazon.com, or "How Am I Feeling? Emotions Board" www.TeachChildren.com (Click on Teacher Supplies, then Character Education Items.)
- Camille Cocozza, preschool and developmentally delayed parent coach www.openwaycoaching.com
- Laura Steele, preschool coach www.Lsteele66@comcast.net
- Cathy Rodrigues, special needs parent coach www.cathyrodrigues.com or www.parentingthespecialneedschild.com.
- Toni Schutta, school age parent coach www.familiesfirstcoaching.com or www.getparentinghelpnow.com.
- Chuck Adam, teenager parent coach www.parentchildharmony.com
- For VIA Signature Strengths test www.authentichappiness.com

Books:
- *Parenting from the Inside Out*, D. Siegal and M. Hartzell, Penguin Books, 2003.
- *1-2-3 Magic,* T. Phelan, Parent Magic, Inc., 2003.
- *Touchpoints,* T. Berry Brazelton and J.D. Sparrow, Perseus Books, Cambridge, Massachusetts, 2001.
- *Your Baby & Child from Birth to Age Five,* P. Leach, Borzoi Books, Alfred A. Knopf, New York, 1977.

- *Playground Politics*, S. Greenspan, Da Capo Press, 1994
- *The Optimistic Child,* M. Seligman, Houghton Mifflin, New York, 1995.
- *Everyday Blessings: the Inner Work of Mindful Parenting,* Kabat-Zinn, M. and J., Hyperion, New York, 1997.
- *Too loud too bright too fast too tight,* S. Heller, Quill Harper Collins, New York, 2003.
- *Authentic Happiness: Using the New Positive Psychology to Realize Your Potential for Lasting Fulfillment*, M. Seligman, The Free Press, New York, 2002.

Chapter II

The Second Step to Adopting as a Single: Is This Something You Can Do Financially?

After you have decided emotionally that the time is right for you to adopt a child, the next step is to decide whether this is something you can do financially at this time. As you can imagine, considering the financial aspects of adopting a child is a very important part of the adoption process. Evaluating your financial situation now will give you input into the type of adoption you should pursue, and also give you a chance to work on how you handle money, and if needed, eliminate debt to prepare for new expenses. Or, for some of you, analyzing your finances may suggest that it's time for a new, higher-paying job, or time to cut back on an expensive lifestyle.

Figuring out now how you can afford to adopt and raise a child will also help you later in the process when you are interviewed for the required adoption home study (a detailed report about you and your circumstances that is prepared by a social worker); your early preparation will indicate to the social worker that you have evaluated all aspects of this very important decision and are prepared and serious about pursuing the adoption. To help you gain a sense of how much the adoption process costs and how much in general it takes financially to raise a child, this chapter will address the following:

- How much does adoption cost?
- A general overview of the basic costs associated with adoption, specifically foster care adoption, other types of domestic adoption, and intercountry adoption.
- What funding opportunities are available for adoption?
- Once the child is home, what are the general costs of raising a child? What things should you consider?

How Much Does Adoption Cost?

General costs for all types of adoption

The Child Welfare Information Gateway, a service of the Children's Bureau, Administration for Children and Families, U.S. Department of Health and Human Services, states that the cost of adoption can range from $0 to $40,000+. This range seems very broad, but the cost of adoption all depends on what type of adoption you pursue—foster care adoption, private agency or independent domestic adoption, or intercountry adoption.

Common costs are associated throughout each of these types of adoption, however. One common expense is the home study which all prospective parents are required to complete (see Chapter IV for more information). The cost of a home study can range anywhere from $300 to $3,000. Another common expense, no matter what type of adoption you pursue, is legal fees. The Information Gateway states that "all domestic adoptions and some intercountry adoptions must be finalized in a court in the United States ... The cost for court document preparation can range from $500 to $2,000." The National Endowment for Financial Education (NEFE) states that legal fees are usually only a small portion of the total adoption costs, except if you pursue an independent adoption—more on that later in this chapter and also in Chapter IV.

The NEFE reminds us, though, that it is important to look at everything included in the adoption agency's fee if you decide to work with one. Adoption agencies will sometimes include the cost of a home study and legal expenses in their overall fee, which is why it is necessary to review exactly what is included when shopping for an agency. The Agency Interview form, downloadable on the book's website, has spaces to record what each agency offers so that you will remember to ask when you talk with the agency representative. Since agency coverage varies widely, it will also help you to remember who offers what when you are comparing agencies to make a decision.

Another factor to consider is the incidentals that come with any type of adoption. For instance, you will be photocopying a ton of records and paperwork, paying for transportation costs to and from either the agency or lawyer you choose to work with, postage and overnight delivery costs, authentication fees to the State Department, copayments on physicals and psychological evaluations, just to name a few. Incidentals can add up quickly, so you will need to budget for them.

As I've already stated, except for these common costs, the cost of adoption all depends on what type of adoption you pursue. Next I review the general costs associated with the different types of adoption.

Foster care adoption

According to the Information Gateway, the cost of adopting a child through the U.S. public foster care system ranges from $0 to $2,500, which includes attorney fees and possible travel expenses. Because public social service agencies want to encourage foster care adoptions, fees are often low or even nothing in some cases.

There are two separate issues related to the costs of adopting a foster child. The first has to do with the costs of the adoption itself, and the second has to do with financial help that is available for the care of the child once you've adopted her. This financial help was created to take away the hardship of moving from fostering a child to adopting it. The monthly stipend and free medical care available to foster parents who might not otherwise be able to afford a child used to make it impossible for some foster parents to adopt the child and leave the foster care system. For many people, a monthly stipend, grants, and continued coverage by Medicaid for healthcare makes it financially doable.

The cost of the adoption itself is negligible. My friends, Art and Ron, are now raising three children placed with them through the foster care system. The oldest is now 6, and the youngest are 2 year old twins, a brother and sister, born prematurely in December of 2007. They adopted Joshua, their oldest, in 2006 and fostered Benjamin and Anna until they were adopted in April, 2009. The following is an estimation of the costs of adopting their first child.

Ron Kolonowski and Art Engler's Foster Care Adoption Expenses		
Service	**Amount**	
Informational Open House at Department of Children and Families	$	0.00
Up to 33 Hours Preservice Training	$	0.00
Statement of Health from Medical Doctor	$	0.00
FBI Check	$	0.00
State Police Check	$	0.00
Local Police Check	$	0.00
Fingerprinting	$	0.00
Protective Services Checks	$	0.00
Pre-licensing Assessment Group Sessions	$	0.00
Up to 4 Home Study Interviews	$	0.00
Legal Fees	$	0.00
Adoption Assistance Program	$	0.00
Health Insurance for Child	$	0.00
College Assistance/Post Secondary Education Assistance (tuition, room, board, fees equivalent to University of Connecticut rates)	$	0.00
Subsides for Child's Care, average $9,700 per year	$	0.00
Total	**$**	**0.00**

As you can see, it cost Art and Ron **nothing** to adopt Joshua. They were even provided with free childcare during required parent training classes and reimbursed for mileage to and from the agency!

In addition, they receive a monthly stipend for Joshua's care until he is 18, free state health insurance, and free college tuition, in-state!

Many of you may feel in your heart that you are more suited for an older child or are too old for a baby or toddler, but are worried about the short amount of time you would have to save for the education of an older child. More and more states are passing laws to provide for the college education of adopted foster children. As you can see from the chart above, Joshua's college education, including room, board and fees, will be paid at any public university in the State of Connecticut, or he will receive the equivalent of University of Connecticut rates to use at private or out of state schools. Also, see my interview with Rita Soronen, Executive Director of The Dave Thomas Foundation for Adoption and Wendy's Wonderful Kids, found in Chapter VII, "In First Person." Wendy's Wonderful Kids is a fabulous organization devoted to the goal of 10,000 foster care adoptions by 2010, and they do everything in their power to help people like you become parents. Rita and her adoption social workers can give you up-to-date information about current and upcoming laws on in-state college tuition and other financial help for adoptive parents. www.thedavethomasfoundation.org

The following is an overview of financial help available for kids adopted through foster care.

The majority of children available for adoption through foster care are *special needs* children. Each state defines *special needs* slightly differently, but in general *special needs* means that the child is school-aged (6 and up), part of a sibling group, has a physical or developmental disability, may have been neglected or abused, or simply is a minority, even if a newborn. In some cases, children have a combination of these factors (see Chapter III for more information on special needs).

Adoptive parents of a child with special needs "may be eligible for a one-time payment of nonrecurring adoption expenses incurred in connection with the adoption of a child." www.childwelfare.gov These expenses (adoption fees, court costs, attorney fees, required health and psychological examinations, transportation) are expenses directly related to the adoption. The Federal Title IV-E adoption assistance program can award up to $2,000 on a nonrecurring basis for children who are determined to have special needs. For children who are not eligible for the federal reimbursement, i.e., do not have special needs, state assistance programs can also reimburse up to $2,000 of these nonrecurring expenses. Natalie Newton, a senior social worker who specializes in adoptions in Fredericksburg, Virginia, says that Fredericksburg will go as high as $2,000 (for more information, see Natalie's interview in Chapter VII, "In First Person"), although some states set reimbursement amounts lower than $2,000. You should check with your public agency to find out which expenses are covered and how much reimbursement your state allows, or go to www.childwelfare.gov/adoption/adopt_assistance/. Go to Option A and select your state.

Sometimes special needs children require ongoing care for physical, mental, or emotional needs. The child being adopted may be eligible for ongoing government subsidy payments either through the Federal Title IV-E adoption assistance program or through state adoption subsidy programs. The Federal Title IV-E program mentioned above was enacted by Congress in 1980 to remove financial barriers to the adoption of special needs children. Eligibility for recurring (ongoing) monthly payments requires that the child have special needs, but he or she must also satisfy one of four requirements, including receiving AFDC (Aid to Families with Dependent Children), or Supplemental Security Income from the Social Security System. Your financial situation has no effect on your child's eligibility for Title IV-E adoption assistance, although it will be used to determine the amount of the monthly subsidy. Federal law states that the monthly payment cannot exceed what the state would have paid for maintenance of the child in ongoing foster care. Go to www.hunter.cuny.edu/socwork/nrcf cpp/downloads/foster-care-maintenance-payments.pdf to see what the monthly maintenance payments are for your state.

Children who qualify for Title IV-E subsidies are eligible for Medicaid benefits as well (see Chapter V for more information).

Children not eligible for the Federal Title IV-E program may be able to receive funds through their state's adoption subsidy program. Each state's program is different, but in general, state subsidies can provide funds for medical assistance, maintenance assistance to help pay for the child's living expenses, or special services (one-time payments to cover a child's emergency or extraordinary need). Newton explains that her social services agency agreed in one case to pay daycare for an adopted child. Newton says that they also sometimes provide a *conditional subsidy,* which is given to the adoptive parents if the child develops any issues or special needs that were not present at the time of adoption but are caused by things that happened before the adoption (for example, a birth injury or separation anxiety).

Private Agency Adoption

The Information Gateway estimates that the cost of working with a domestic licensed private agency can range from $5,000 to $40,000. These agencies will help you through each step of the adoption process and will work to match you with a child available for adoption (these agencies help you adopt children of all ages). The fees often include services for home study, birth parent counseling, adoptive parent preparation (classes and counseling), post-placement supervision, and a portion of agency costs for operating expenses.

To help you gain a sense of how much domestic adoption through an agency costs, the following is a breakdown of placement-related fees charged by a domestic adoption agency that specializes in newborns in the Commonwealth of Virginia. Note that the fees do not include attorney fees and a home study update after the adoption is finalized. In this scenario, the agency provides an estimate on how much their services will cost.

Domestic Agency Placement-Related Fees	
Service	**Amount**
Application Fee (due with application)	$ 250.00
Home Study Fee (due at beginning of Home Study)	$ 1,500.00
Clearances	$ 66.00
Educational Credits Required (30 in Commonwealth of Virginia	$ 300.00
Placement Fee (for Caucasian newborn, for Bi-racial newborn, $15,000, for African-American newborn, $8,000)	$ 18,000.00
Post-Placement Fees (due at time of supervision, 3 @ $250.00 each)	$ 750.00
Finalization Fee	$ 150.00
Total	**$ 21,016.00**
Estimated Additional Costs:	
Attorney's Fees (approximately $350-$1500)	
Home Study Update ($250. If required)	

One way to save money when working with a domestic adoption agency is to locate your own birthparent through marketing or word-of-mouth strategies, which we'll describe in the next section when discussing independent adoptions. Some agencies will offer reduced fees if you find your own birthparent and use the agency only for counseling, adoption facilitation, home study, and supervision services. Some agencies provide sliding-scale fees based on the prospective adoptive parent's income. When researching adoption agencies, inquire about whether or not they offer sliding-scale fees.

It is extremely important to interview a number of agencies before you choose to work with one. This will give you a chance to comparison-shop and get a feel for the range of fees charged by different agencies. Ask about payment plans. Some agencies will let you pay for their services over time, even after the adoption is complete. Never pay the full fee up front. At the very most, pay for each service as it is provided. When you are interviewing agencies and references, ask if there are additional charges besides the ones in their package. Question fees that seem much higher or lower than other agencies.

As I mentioned earlier, I have designed an Agency Interview Form that can be printed from the book website. All of the questions that I've raised in this section are included on the form. Download it, make a number of copies on 3-hole punch paper, and put them in your adoption notebook as you interview agencies and fill them out. I can't stress enough that organization is extremely important during this process. You're going to be dealing with so much paper that to lose something that you worked hard to get or create could be really bad news. You'll get peace of mind knowing that everything is in one place.

On a side note, remember when researching adoption agencies that it's not all about the cost and services provided. You also need to feel comfortable with the people who work there. You will be working very closely with them throughout the entire adoption process and you want to make sure you feel safe with the people who will be helping you. So while it's important to gain a sense of what the agency is charging, it's also important to gain a sense of how you feel about the agency and the individuals who work there. There is a place on the Agency Interview Form for you to write your impressions.

Independent domestic adoption

When you pursue an independent adoption, you do not work with an agency. Instead, a lawyer handles the adoption process while it is your responsibility to find a baby to adopt. Independent adoption costs range from $8,000 to $40,000 (average is $10,000 to $15,000). The costs associated with an independent domestic adoption vary depending on a number of factors—legal fees for representing both you and the birth parent, advertising expenses, and medical expenses for the birth mother. This effort sometimes involves placing advertisements in magazines and newspapers stating that you are seeking to adopt a baby.

A friend of mine recently completed an independent adoption. She placed ads in all of the local newspapers and received a call from an expectant birthmother looking to place her child for adoption. My friend also placed ads online and sent information sheets to her friends and family and asked them to distribute them to everyone they knew. She ultimately ended up adopting a baby who she learned about from a friend of a friend. Her advertising and word-of-mouth efforts paid off.

When pursuing an independent adoption you need to remain flexible with how much you may have to spend. Sometimes unexpected costs such as medical expenses for the birthmother may occur, although some state laws do restrict these costs. You also may have to spend more on advertising for an expectant mother if your search does not go as quickly as planned. Again, though, there are restrictions in some states on how much you may be able to spend on advertising, which may range from $500 to $5,000.

Intercountry adoption

International adoptions start at about $7,000 and can go as high as $30,000, sometimes higher. This cost depends on a number of factors, including what country the child is being adopted from, what is required by the adoption agency or facilitator you choose to work with, and the country's requirements. You most always have to work through a licensed adoption agency that handles international adoptions, as that's the only way the majority of countries will adopt to U.S. citizens.

Other costs associated with international adoption include dossier processing, passport fees, translation fees, visa processing fees, travel expenses, and in some cases foreign attorney fees. The cost may also include a donation to your child's orphanage. When budgeting for international adoption, make sure to also include incidental fees such as obtaining shots and passports, and taking time off from work for international travel. Some countries require that you make two trips to the country before the adoption is finalized. See Appendix A for a directory of all of the world countries, their policies on adopting to Americans and singles, requirements for travel to the country, and required residencies (time in country) for the adoption.

Victoria Solsberry

Thesia Garner, a single mother and a friend of mine, adopted her child from China in 2003 when a single person was allowed to adopt from China. [In May 2007 China changed its policies to disallow adoption to single adults. Her story is told because although Chinese adoption is no longer an option, any foreign adoption through an American adoption agency will be remarkably similar. Agency fees vary minimally for different countries.] In total, she spent approximately $25,000 on the adoption, which included $2250 for the home study fees and $7500 for travel costs—to and from China. Here I provide a summary of her costs (this list is not all-inclusive but does cover the major expenses and gives you a good idea of what to expect). For more information and for a full interview with Thesia, see Chapter VII "In First Person."

Thesia Garner's International Adoption Expenses	
Service	**Amount**
Application Fee (due with application)	$ 100.00
Home Study Fee	$ 2,250.00
International Flight, Insurance and hotel*	$ 7,500.00
Program Fee	$ 2,000.00
Dossier Processing Fee	$ 2,500.00
State Department Authentication Fee	$ 120.00
In-Country hotel stay, food, and airfare	$ 3,600.00
Donation to Chinese Orphanage	$ 3,000.00
Follow-Up Home Studies once home in U.S.	$ 3,600.00
Total	**$ 24,670.00**

Note:
This line item includes travel and hotel costs for Thesia, a friend and return trip for her daughter.

What Funding Opportunities are Available for Adoption?

As you read this chapter you may be thinking to yourself, "I had no idea adoption was that expensive! I can't afford this!" But before you abandon hope of adopting a child, take a deep breath and relax. There are ways to help defray the costs and make adoption *affordable*.

Here I present a sampling of funding opportunities to support you and your dream of becoming a parent.

Adoption grants

Search for "Adoption Grants" on Google and you'll find that the Internet is full of grant opportunities. For example, one website, www.affordingadoption.com/grants.php, contains a list of grants. The best thing to do is search online for opportunities...you will find a lot. A few examples include:

- **Gift of Adoption Fund (www.giftofadoption.org):** This organization awards grants to "pre-approved adopting parents who demonstrate an unusual degree of financial hardship." Grants range from $2,000 to $5,000 and according to the organization's website, the grants "are often the last rung in the ladder of an adoptive parent's journey to reach their dreams." When I wrote to the organization they confirmed that they do provide grants to singles interested in pursuing adoption.
- **National Adoption Foundation (www.nafadopt.org):** The mission of the National Adoption Foundation is "to grow families in America." The foundation helps remove financial barriers and provides information, services, and a supportive community to adoptive families. The Foundation's programs are available to any family whether they are adopting an infant, a child from abroad or a child from foster care. The grant program is open to all legal adoptions including public or private agency adoptions, international, special needs or adoptions facilitated by an attorney. There is no income requirement. There is a simple one- page application and the only requirement to apply is a home study, or one in progress. When I wrote to the organization, they also confirmed that they award grants to singles. In collaboration with their corporate partners, the foundation has created additional programs such as credit cards, insurance, and 529 College Savings Plans that grandparents, aunts, uncles and friends may access to support the cause.

Tax breaks

The IRS offers tax credits for adoption expenses such as adoption fees, court costs, attorney fees, travel expenses, and other expenses directly related to adopting a child. The Adoption Tax Credit in 2010 is $13,170 per child, not per year, for parents earning under $174,730 per year. This tax credit decreases on a sliding scale as your income increases from $174,730. At an income of $214,730 the tax credit disappears. If you adopt from foster care, and you adopt a minority child, a child aged 6 and up, a sibling group, or a child with any kind of disability, you will be allowed to claim the $13,170 tax credit, per child, even if the adoption cost you nothing! For those adoption expenses that you might incur with any type of adoption, the IRS will also allow you to exclude adoption expenses reimbursed by your employer from your gross income. Download IRS Form 8839 – "Qualified Adoption Expenses" and the form's instructions to find a list of expenses allowed to be covered by this tax credit. For specific eligibility requirements, visit the IRS website at www.irs.gov, www.irs.gov/taxtopics/tc607.html.

Many states also have adoption tax credits, although some are restricted to foster care adoption. Be sure to check out state tax credits as well. Tax rules are complicated and not everyone will qualify for a tax break, but be sure to check with an accountant to see what you are eligible for.

Employer benefits

Some employers provide benefits to adoptive parents, including leave, paid or unpaid, when a child arrives home, or reimbursement of some portion of adoption expenses, in some cases as much as $10,000. Don't forget to look into this…you may be surprised what assistance your employer provides. According to NEFE, approximately a quarter of U.S. employers offer adoption benefits to their employees (this was based on a 1995 study, so hopefully more employers offer adoption benefits today). Many universities, for example, offer their employees adoption assistance. NEFE says that some employers offer direct reimbursement for specific adoption expenses, pay for the medical expenses of the birth mother (in the case of a domestic adoption), or offer adoption seminars and information classes.

Ask your employer what adoption benefits they provide and if they don't, ask them to consider offering adoption benefits, especially if others in your company are also interested in adoption. For more information, a good resource is The Adoption Friendly Workplace, a signature program of The Dave Thomas Foundation for Adoption (see Chapter VII "In First Person" for an interview with Rita Soronen, Executive Director of The Dave Thomas Foundation for Adoption). The Foundation is honoring America's Best Adoption-Friendly Workplaces with special recognition for the top 100, the best small, medium, and large employers and industry leaders. The foundation offers a comprehensive step-by-step guide for employers to establish adoption benefits and one for employees to propose them. To order the toolkit, visit www.adoptionfriendlyworkplace.org/afw/ afw_index.asp.

Loans

Some banks offer special adoption loans. Start by calling your bank to see what loans they offer, and then shop around to see what other banks offer. For example, Old National Bank, a bank with branches throughout Illinois, Indiana, and Ohio offers a "Building Families Adoption Loan Program," which provides assistance to cover adoption expenses through two loan programs: A home equity line or a personal loan. With the home equity line, you can borrow up to 90% of your home's value, less any other mortgages, and take advantage of a line of credit to help manage your expenses. For parents who are in the process of building equity in their home, the Building Families program also offers personal or unsecured loan options at preferred rates. With this type of loan, you can borrow up to $10,000 to help cover adoption expenses. While this loan offer only applies to prospective adoptive parents living in Indiana, Ohio, Illinois, Kentucky, and Tennessee, it provides a good example of what loan options are available. For more information on the Building Families Adoption Loan Program, see www.oldnational.com/, click on Loans and Credit Cards, and then Adoption Loans.

When the first edition of this book was written, most national banks offered unsecured adoption loans. As you know, however, we have recently gone through an economic crisis in this country, and to our dismay, as of April, 2010, we could not find one single national bank that still has adoption loans. I would suggest that you check with your bank, especially if it is a smaller regional bank (like Old National Bank above). If you are a longtime customer, and have a good credit rating, it is possible that you could still get a loan.

Many organizations that used to advertise unsecured adoption loans now advise potential clients to apply for a credit card for the purpose of paying adoption expenses. For example, The National Adoption Foundation sponsors a Visa card with "very high approval rates," and says that they have helped over 4,000 people adopt this way. If your adoption will cost $20,000, though, a credit card with a $2,000 credit limit will be of limited help to you. Obviously, the higher your credit score, the more likely that you're going to get approved for a higher credit limit. If this is an issue for you, take a few months, get copies of your credit reports, pay off some bills, and take care of any problems that you find on those reports. You may find mistakes that are affecting your score, or outstanding debt that you didn't even know you had. Credit scores are very fluid and can move upwards with even the smallest debts paid off. www.nafadopt.org

Certain foundations also provide adoption loans. For instance, A Child Waits Foundation provides low-interest (5%) loans to individuals pursuing international adoption. Their loans, up to $10,000, require a co-signer and you can take up to 5 years to pay it back. An application can be found online at www.achildwaits.org. The loans provided by the organization are (in their words) "not a low cost alternative to other financing options; rather they are a last means of financing for those who have already exhausted all other possibilities and funds." The Foundation provides loans for the final costs of the adoption. In other words, if the adoption will ultimately cost $20,000, they expect that you will have provided the first $10,000 at the time of your application. They also require that you are in the process of adopting through a licensed adoption agency in your state, and will ask for copies of your home study, tax returns, and a financial statement, including a monthly budget.

Currently, the most obvious ways to borrow money for your adoption are with a home equity loan or on a credit card that you already have. So if you own a home or condo and have lived in it for a few years, ask your bank how much equity you have in your home and how much they might lend you. If you have a credit card with a high credit limit, look for the checks that come with your statement. Those are usually for a low-interest loan for amounts up to your credit limit. If you don't have those checks because you always shred them as soon as they arrive, call your credit card company to find out what promotions are current. They will send you checks if there is a promotion that sounds good to you.

Fundraising

People who love you will most likely want to do all that they can to support your dream of adoption. You probably have a good sense of the financial situations of your grandparents, parents, siblings, aunts and uncles and friends. Who might be able to give or lend you $500 or even more? Do you have knowledge of money that you're going to inherit from someone who might give it to you early?

The adoption website www.precious.org offers a number of creative funding options that you may not have thought of from payment plans (offered by some adoption agencies) to non-profit adoption foundations that provide grants up to $2,000. In addition, don't forget fundraising events like garage sales and car washes and bake sales. Even though it may seem that those types of activities don't draw in much money, you'd be surprised at how quickly the funds add up. Advertise it as an "Adoption Yard Sale" or "Help Me Adopt An Ethiopian Orphan Car Wash." It sounds hokey, but people love to feel like they're helping you achieve your goal of adopting a child. Creative fundraising options can be found online at www.precious.org/blog/category/adoption-infor mation/adoption-financing/. In addition, the National Endowment for Financial Education publishes a booklet "How to Make Adoption an Affordable Option" online at http://www.smart aboutmoney.org/nefe/uploadfiles/ AdoptionOption.pdf.

Adoption travel

Finally, a break for prospective adoptive parents that other people don't get! Here are four travel agencies that specialize in adoption travel:

- **Fellowship Travel International** (www.Fellowship.com/ - click on Why FTI? on the top menu, then Adoption under Special Interest). Air travel, hotels, travel insurance, visas. Contact Denison Borges at 800-235-9384 or 804-550-0121.
- **Velocity Adoption Travel** (www.velocitytours.com - click on Adoption Travel on the left menu). Air travel, hotels and cars. Contact Trent Hendrickson at 801-296-8687.
- **Azumano Travel** (www.Azumano.com – click on Adoption Travel on the top menu). Air travel only, but part of American Express Travel, so you can use your American Express Membership Rewards Points for air travel. Contact Nancy Parrot at 503-221-6101.
- **Golden Rule Travel** (www.GoldenRuleTravel.com – click on Adoption Travel on the top menu.) Air travel only. Contact Eldo Miller at 888-950-3273.

The beauty of these adoption travel specialists is that they have special relationships with the airlines and therefore can accommodate the unknowns of adoption travel. Some are travel consolidators and others negotiate special fares for prospective adoptive parents. And, sometimes you only get a few days or few weeks notice that you need to travel across the country or around the world. No problem. These travel agents are used to that. And all stay in touch by email while you are traveling to make last minute changes if you need to stay longer than originally anticipated, or if things go really well and you can come home early. In addition, they handle the fact that you're going to have a child or children who only fly one way, and if needed, arrange for bulkhead seats to accommodate a bassinet. Some also handle hotel reservations, travel insurance, and visas for countries that require them.

When you think about all that you have to do to get yourself to a new place to meet your child, what a relief to know that someone is very experienced in the intricacies of adoption travel, can anticipate what you'll need, and can respond to changes so that you don't have to spend time talking to airlines from Ethiopia! Wonderful!

What are the General Costs of Raising a Child?

In addition to costs associated with the immediate adoption, it is important to consider the cost of raising a child in general. When you are considering adopting a child, make sure to consider whether or not you will have a similar quality of life after adopting a child without incurring so much debt that you will not be able to support the child. But also keep in mind the ongoing financial help that you can get from the Federal government or state with foster care adoptions.

The first thing you need to consider is all of the upfront costs you are going to have to incur before the child enters your home. Are you going to need to move to provide a bedroom for the child? Do you have a place for the child to sleep – a crib for a baby or toddler bed for a three-year old? Or a desk and bookcase for a teenager? Do you have clothes for the child? Toys, a bicycle, or computer? You will need all of these items once the adoption is complete.

Don't feel that you have to go out and buy out BabiesRUs or Old Navy, though. You know so many people with kids that I'm sure that some will want to help you. When a colleague of mine adopted a newborn 2 years ago, word got out to her clients and she received bags of beautiful dresses and onesies. Let your friends give you an adoption shower and accept a used computer or bicycle for your ten year old. Shop at consignment shops for clothes and go on Craig's List for furniture, or even www.freecycle.org for free things that people don't need anymore. Just put out the word that you're adopting and could use some help, and see what happens!

After that, you will have annual expenses for the child. A terrific resource to help you gain a sense of how much it will cost to raise a child is an annual report published by the United States

Department of Agriculture (USDA), titled "Expenditures on Children by Families, 2006" www.cnpp.usda.gov/Publications /CRC/crc2006.pdf. According to the report, it costs a single-parent family who brings in less than $44,500 annually (before-tax income) $136,200 to raise a child from birth through the age of 18. The report breaks down how much it costs annually to raise a child at different ages, as well (for example, $6,820 a year for a child aged 0–2, or $568 a month). In some ways, the younger the child, the more expensive they are. Once a child enters school, daycare stops, saving you hundreds of dollars a month. Older children have more activities that have costs associated with them, but not usually hundreds of dollars a month!

The USDA groups expenses associated with raising a child into seven categories: housing, food, transportation, clothing, healthcare, childcare and education, and miscellaneous expenses. The USDA estimates that healthcare, for instance, will cost a single-parent family $9,120 for a child from birth to the age of 18, or $506 per year. The USDA estimates that annual healthcare expenses will range between $280 and $640 depending on the age of the child. This estimate is based on a single-parent home with a before-tax income of $44,500. Check to see how much your insurance premium will increase to add a child. And see Chapter V "Homecoming" for more information on health insurance and other expenses such as daycare.

For clothing, the USDA estimates that it will cost a single-parent family $8,610 for a child from birth to the age of 18, or $478 per year. The USDA estimates that annual clothing expenses will range between $310 and $780 depending on the age of the child (again, this estimate is based on a single-parent home with a before-tax income of $44,500). Obviously, to save money in this area you can always rely on hand-me-downs from helpful friends and family. As your child ages, though, and clothing becomes a more important part of his or her life, you'll have to get creative to outfit your child in the latest fashions that all teens seem to want.

For food, the USDA estimates that it will cost a single-parent family $27,750 for a child from birth to the age of 18, or $1542 per year ($128 per month). The USDA estimates that annual food expenses for your child will range between $1,140 and $1,900 depending on the age of the child. But unless you're adopting a 15 year old football player, making spaghetti for two instead of one is not a huge stretch financially. Besides, you'll be eating at home more now that you're a parent, and we all know that the cost of a restaurant meal or two (or more) a week can pay for a lot of groceries! Yes, some of your expenses will go down! Be sure to take that into account when you plan your budget.

The USDA estimates that it will cost a single-parent family $11,910 in childcare and education costs on a child from birth to the age of 18, or $661 per year. The USDA estimates that annual childcare and education expenses will range between $410 and $720 depending on the age of the child. It's important to note that this estimate, in particular, can vary widely when you have an infant or preschooler. While this is the U.S. average, in certain areas childcare alone, which is almost always needed by a single parent, can run hundreds of dollars a month per child. You probably have a sense of your area of the country and whether it is particularly expensive or not. You also know if you have a family member or two who would love to keep your small child while you work. Or if you have parent friends who could share the cost with you. If your child is school-age, these costs go way down.

I'd like to remind you not to forget the adoption subsidies that are available from your state if you cannot afford the estimated $500-600 per month that it costs to raise a child. Talk to your adoption social worker about what's available for you.

Do your research

Hopefully I've provided some helpful guidance in this chapter on what to expect financially when it comes to adopting a child. The bottom line is you must do your research and take your time when looking into the financial aspects of adopting. It is an essential part of the adoption process and you and your child will benefit greatly by taking steps to ensure financial security.

Resources

- A Child Waits Foundation: www.achildwaits.org
- Azumano Travel: www.Azumano.com
- Affording Adoption: www.affordingadoption.com Child Welfare Information Gateway "Costs of Adopting" Fact Sheet: www.childwelfare.gov/pubs/adoption_gip_two.pdf Child Welfare Information Gateway "State Regulation of Adoption Expenses": www.childwelfare.gov/systemwide/laws_policies/statutes/expenses.cfm
- Dave Thomas Foundation for Adoption: www.adoptionfriendlyworkplace.org/afw/afw_index.asp
- Fellowship Travel International: www.Fellowship.com/
- Gift of Adoption Fund: www.giftofadoption.org
- Golden Rule Travel: www.GoldenRuleTravel.com
- Adoption Financing. www.precious.org/blog/category/adoption-information/adoption-financing/
- Internal Revenue Service: www.irs.gov/taxtopics/tc607.htm
- iVillage "How Much Does it Cost to Adopt?": www.parenting.ivillage.com/baby/badoption/0,,69p0,00.html
- National Adoption Foundation: www.nafadopt.org
- National Endowment for Financial Education "How to Make Adoption an Affordable Option" and "Myths about Adoption" and "State Laws and Fees": www.smartaboutmoney.org/nefe/uploadfiles/AdoptionOption.pdf
- For information on state foster care maintenance schedules, go to www.hunter.cuny.edu/socwork/nrcfcpp/downloads/foster-care-maintenance-payments.pdf
- Free items, such as cribs, changing tables, bicycles, computers, clothing, toys, etc. www.freecycle.org
- USDA "Expenditures on Children by Families, 2006": www.cnpp.usda.gov/Publications/CRC/crc2006.pdf
- Velocity Adoption Travel: www.velocitytours.com

Chapter III

So You've Decided This is Something You Can Do—Now What?

So, you're beginning to think that this is something you can really do. Maybe you've been talking about it for years and everyone in your life knows that you want to be a parent. Maybe it's a relatively new idea that you floated past family and friends as a possibility because you were unsure. But now you've decided that you're going to move forward and if everything goes well, you'll become a parent. It's time to come out of the closet as a prospective adoptive parent!

You probably got an idea of how the people in your life feel about you adopting when you told them you were thinking about it. People either responded enthusiastically and with excitement, or they were surprised, maybe stunned. Some may have even been critical or skeptical. But now is the time to tell them that you're moving forward with the decision and that you'd like their support. It's time to think out loud with the people closest to you about how you'd like to proceed. To think about and decide what age child you see yourself adopting, and then, where you might go to find this child.

In this chapter we will address those decisions:

- What age child do you want to adopt?
  - o An overview of the developmental stages of childhood and what you could expect from each stage
  - o Children with special needs – what are they and could you handle those needs?
- Do you want to adopt domestically or internationally – what is available?
  - o Domestic adoptions – agency, private adoption and foster care
  - o International adoptions – what ages are available?

What Age Child Do You Want to Adopt?

Close your eyes now and picture yourself as a new parent with your new child. What do you see? What do you envision when you think of being a parent, and what have your fantasies been when you've thought about being a mom or dad? Do you see yourself holding an infant, carrying a diaper bag, furnishing a bedroom with a crib and changing table? Do you see yourself explaining the world to a toddler that you can still carry around? Do you envision an older child, one you can teach to throw a baseball, or perhaps a preteen, with whom you can talk about boys and girls and becoming an adult? Or even a teenager that you might only have in your home for a few years, but who will be your child as they find a career, get married, and have your grandchildren?

Is it important for you to be the only parent your child remembers? Is it important to you to watch your child grow from infancy to adulthood? Or are you the type who could have parental feelings for any child that needs you?

If you'd had a baby yourself, is there an age that you would have looked forward to? When you notice or interact with children, do you find that they are usually of a similar age?

I love teenagers. I was a youth worker in a church in my early twenties, an outreach worker at high schools in my late twenties, and even today, have teenagers in my life that I adore and find completely entertaining. Playing with Legos on the floor would have been something I would have done to please my child, but talking about the explorations of adolescence, the opposite sex, what you want to be when you grow up—that's really satisfying for me.

For others, the best part of parenting comes with the "lap ages," that is, birth to about five, when the child is carried, held on one's lap, taught all the words for items in everyday life, taught to feed and dress himself. The child at this age is very physically and emotionally dependent, and many enjoy those stages the best.

What about you?

Determining the age child that makes the most sense for you will inform your decisions about where to adopt. For instance, if you really want the experience of a days-old newborn, you will need to adopt domestically. Internationally, even babies who are given up for adoption at birth are held in orphanages and/or foster care throughout the process of terminating parental rights, or investigating and determining orphan status. The youngest babies from out of country tend to be 8–10 months old by the time they are eligible for adoption.

Conversely, if you have your heart set on a child from a particular country, the child may have to be a certain age for you to be eligible to adopt. For instance, if you are of Greek heritage (Greece gives preference to prospective adoptive parents of Greek descent) and would like to adopt from Greece, the child can be no less than 18 years younger than you are. In this case, country of origin may be a more important variable to you than age.

One way to decide, if you are truly ambivalent or feel that you could parent any age child, is to consider the needs of the child at each stage in life, and how they match up with your own needs and your lifestyle. When we think about taking care of a child at any age, we tend to think about what we call "maturation," that is, physical growing – size, sleeping and feeding needs, talking, ambulation (walking), and levels of independence–can the child dress himself or go to the bathroom by himself.

Erikson's Stages of Psychosocial Development

In each stage of growing up, there are also psychological benchmarks, and we refer to this form of growth as "development." In other words, what emotional and psychological issues is the child dealing with at each age? What is he or she learning – or as mental health people refer to them – what are the "tasks" of each stage?

While a child's intelligence and physical health are for the most part determined by the time you take him or her into your home, the child's socialization and personality development will ultimately have a lot to do with your parenting style and how well the child navigates the tasks of each stage. Erik Erikson (1902-1994), Danish by birth but Viennese by training, studied at the Psychoanalytic Institute in Vienna with Anna Freud in the 1920's, and through his work with children in a school setting, set forth what he called the Stages of Psychosocial Development. These stages focused on the main concerns that the child has in each stage, and depending upon how well the child is supported and parented in each stage, the child will either enter the next stage optimally – that is, having achieved the best possible outcome – or at a deficit. The process concerns the child's developing identity and self-esteem.

Here are the stages of development as put forth by Erikson. We will discuss what the child's main tasks are in each stage, and what you can expect that the child would need from you for the optimal outcome. See how each one feels to you, and try to imagine whether you can see yourself being the parent that they need at each age.

Trust vs. Mistrust

From birth to about 18 months, while the child starts as a cognitive blank slate, she is a bundle of emotional and physical needs. All that matters in the first few months of life is feeling firmly held, warm, dry and sated, which translates to feeling generally "safe." The breast or the bottle is an extension of the child – that is, the infant is incapable of knowing that the parent is a separate person, that the bottle is inanimate, and the baby is incapable of manipulating the adult or adults that care for her. She cries because she is hungry, tired, wet, cold or uncomfortable, and it is here that the trust or mistrust begins. When these needs are met in a timely and loving way, the baby begins to trust in relationships. It requires consistent attention from the parent to ensure that the child learns that when she asks to have a need met, someone will be there to take care of it. If the need is repeatedly not met, the baby will learn that people are *not* there for her, and she will not learn to rely on people in a healthy and normal way.

Some of you may have been taught that you need to "train" a baby to live in your world or else it will become "spoiled" and come to expect that you will give it everything it wants. As noted above, new babies are incapable of thinking that way, and hence, are incapable of manipulating you. They are simply eating, breathing, eliminating, and sleeping little organisms that respond to physical needs. Please believe that a month-old baby is not looking for ways to get attention.

There is something to be said, though, for children in the last months of this stage needing to begin being taught how to soothe and entertain themselves, so if you sit and watch in order to anticipate their every want, they will be slow to learn to play alone or put themselves back to sleep when they wake up in the night. Meeting a baby's real needs does not mean holding them all the time. They simply need to feel physically comfortable and to know that they are safe because you or another familiar, responsible adult is nearby. It sounds complicated, but most parents learn how to do this pretty quickly.

Throughout this 18 month stage, which ends when the baby begins to separate from the caregiver in dramatic and physical ways, the baby is largely immobile, and unable to meet any of its own needs. Adults are everything to the baby.

After she leaves the newborn period, she begins to be able to tell one adult from another. Halfway through her first year, she begins to grasp, pick up small objects, and responds with smiles and laughter when adults smile and laugh with her. She sits up on her own, and gets a new view of the world from an upright position. She also may begin to express fear and discomfort when away from the primary caretaker. This is called "stranger anxiety" and typically begins between 7 and 10 months. Adults that she previously went to happily will be unacceptable to her, and life will become temporarily difficult for the parent who finds that he or she is unable to get a break, and who has to make dinner with a baby on the hip!

At approximately 12 months, the baby will begin to walk and experience the sensation of being upright and being able to move from one point to another. From that time until 18 months, she becomes increasingly independent, wanting "down" from a lap more and more, and wanting her needs met even while she is seemingly less involved with the parent and less clingy. For some parents, it becomes more difficult to meet the baby's needs when she doesn't want to cuddle, be held, or even have her hand held when she walks! It requires a sound knowledge of the normal development of a baby at this age, and the commitment to be consistently available so that the child doesn't have to be overly fearful or feel abandoned. If she does feel abandoned, she will grow to feel insecure and anxious and to feel that the world is a dangerous place.

Autonomy vs. Shame and Doubt

From approximately 18 months to about 3 years, the main task of the child is to become more and more independent. She becomes more and more sure on her feet, and "the world becomes her oyster," a marvelous place to explore and discover new and wonderful things. It is important that she is allowed to go away and come back when she needs to, and that the parent is ready and available when she does. This coming and going characterizes this developmental stage, and being welcomed back each time makes the child feel loved and safe.

If the child feels punished for separating, and not welcomed back when she needs to be comforted or cared for, she begins to learn that separating is a bad thing. She may lose her zest for exploration and cling to you so that she doesn't lose you, or become overly self-sufficient to avoid your emotional punishment. She may also begin to doubt her worth. If she is not praised and supported in her attempts at independence, she may feel inadequate and falter, like the cartoon roadrunner that only falls when he looks down and realizes that the road is gone. The toddler pushes forward, trying new things, and needs ongoing praise, support, and reassurance that things are good, that life is fun, and that Mom and/or Dad is always ultimately available.

Potty training typically begins during this stage, and is fraught with more control and competency issues. Starting too soon and then expecting too much, criticizing and trying to control can cause shame and more feelings of inadequacy in the child, and she further doubts her own abilities.

Initiative vs. Guilt

The next stage begins at about age 3 and continues until age 6. Self-initiative is the main task of this stage, and involves making more and more decisions for herself such as what to wear every day and what to eat, being creative with imaginative play, learning how to lead and how to entertain herself. This is the age where the child may insist on wearing a costume every day, or insist that she be called by another name ("no, I'm Princess Ariel"), or that you play make believe with them ad nauseum ("no, you're the daddy and I'm the mommy"). The parallel play of the toddler (toddlers tend to play side by side rather than with each other) gives way to the give and take of games and organized play. Preschool will begin to socialize them to the rules of childhood – sharing, sitting still, taking one's turn, raising one's hand. During this stage of development, the child begins to have confidence in her ability to make decisions and to influence others.

Parents may criticize and try to control a child who seems too strong-willed, however, resulting in feelings of guilt in the child. The challenge for parents of a child between 3 and 6 is to give her freedom and space to initiate, create and be as dramatic and imaginative as she wants to be without embarrassing her or making her feel overly criticized. Most important, though, is that the child feels liked and that her exuberance is enjoyed and encouraged. She will soon come out of the stage with new tasks and concerns, and you won't have to buy costumes and role play forever!

Industry vs. Inferiority

The next stage basically encompasses elementary school, or the ages of 6 to 11. As you might imagine, the main task of this stage is to learn, and the child begins to develop a sense of pride in being able to do so and in accomplishing whatever is expected of her in school. It is during this stage that her special talents may be discovered. She begins to study music, or ballet, or drawing, or soccer. She is identified as a tomboy, or an artist, or a scientist, and her talents are probably different from yours and other children in the family. It becomes important to her to become good at what she does and to fully develop her talents. She will need your support, even if you have no idea why she wants to do what she wants to do, and your praise as she becomes more skilled and competent in her talents.

She will spend more time away from family, and teachers and classmates become more important. She'll want to spend social time with friends, and less time with you. She'll have her first overnights, and learn that it's safe to be away from home without you. She'll learn to bathe herself, wash her own hair, and basically, become more and more able to take care of herself. Many parents miss the physical contact and the near-constant interaction of the younger

51

ages, and find it hard to let go of the child so that she can experience other people and activities. But if you support those activities, yet welcome her back when she wants to be with you (many parents feel guilty when they realize that they enjoy their child's sick days!), she'll know that you believe in her competence. Try to hold her too close, give her too little independence, or criticize and fail to praise, and she will develop feelings of inferiority. After all, if you don't believe in her, she's not all that. Right?

Identity vs. Role Confusion

This stage is adolescence, the time when your child solidifies her sense of self by experimenting, finding her group, and developing the skills that she will need in adulthood. If she has been supported in her explorations up until this point, she will begin to have ideas about what she wants to do career-wise, where she'd like to live and go to college, and what kind of intimate relationships she'd like to have. She'll find or continue activities in high school, and make more friends through these activities. She may also try things and do things that you'd rather she didn't. And again, just as in the stage before, she's probably not going to want you around her friends very much, but for you to be completely available when she needs you. Structure and consistency are extremely important to keep her safe, and of course, your complete enjoyment of her personality and talents to keep her self-esteem healthy.

A Few Words About the 11–17 Year Old

Teenagers tend to have a bad reputation. Ask any parent of a young child how they feel about the prospect of that child becoming a teenager, and typically you will get a look of pure anxiety and dread.

Maybe it's because we remember our own teenage years – years when we started to keep secrets from our parents and turned increasingly to our friends for advice and support. Years when some of us acted out, got into trouble and spent time grounded – or worse, arrested! Years when some of us hated the social milieu of high school as we tried to fit in and tried to be cool, but inevitably got hurt or felt humiliated.

Being different was not okay. It made us feel vulnerable and disconnected from other kids. I remember insisting on buying, making and wearing the styles that all the other girls were wearing, even when I knew deep down inside that they didn't suit me and perhaps even made me look a little silly (think the babydoll look of the late 1960s on a 5'9" girl). Being one of the truly popular girls wasn't even a goal. I simply didn't want to be so uncool that I stuck out. Blending in took all the energy I had.

Some of us coped with the social pressures by opting out of the social scene altogether. We had a few close friends, hopefully, but didn't go to parties or dances, date, or run for student government. Some of us found our niche as good students, getting positive attention from teachers and risking that curious rejection that comes from other kids when we got the highest grades on tests, or received praise from an adult.

Then on top of the social, emotional, and academic pressures we endured, add the physical changes that our bodies went through! Puberty can be downright embarrassing. You start growing things, perhaps your voice changes, and you become capable of procreating, with all the discomforts that come with that. Our hormones were wearing party hats! Our mood swings made us look manic-depressive, and sulking drove our parents crazy. It was really difficult!

Occasionally I work with an adult who truly believes that high school was the best time of life – so good that they're wondering if any other stage could possibly be as fulfilling. But most people I know look back on their high school experience with a combination of affection for their teenage selves for trying so hard and being so brave, and a cringing relief that they never have to go through that again!

Now take all of these issues of adolescence and imagine a child having to go through them without a parent. If the orphaned child is very lucky, they've been in the same foster home for a long time and will be there until they reach adulthood – that is, 18. If they're lucky, they've been loved and supported by those foster parents.

But perhaps they have been in two, or three, or six foster homes, and perhaps they don't feel very special or loved by those foster parents. Then adolescence becomes filled with landmines and is a truly scary journey for the child.

If you were to consider adopting a child in preadolescence or adolescence, you could expect a little more intensity than you'd get with the average baby or 8 year old. But the unconscious (and sometimes conscious) yearning for cherishment, or the "expectation to be loved" (*Cherishment*, Young-Bruehl and Betheland, The Free Press, 2000) is just the same. This yearning can be covered over with an unreceptive attitude that makes it seem like the child wants to be left alone. But I don't know a single adult who doesn't want to be loved, so how much more true must that be for a child, especially one whose parents have failed them.

Adolescence is a time when the human being has a second chance to complete some of the tasks that were left incomplete in earlier developmental stages. Teenagers have a second chance to deal with the separation and individuation issues of the toddler. They have a second chance to develop the passions of the 8 year old. A good home and a loving, consistent parent who is committed and permanent can make the difference between a severely troubled young adult and a normal young person. Just knowing that someone, an adult, wants to be related to them for the rest of that adult's life is a powerful security blanket, and helps take the shame out of being unclaimed.

Yes, occasionally a teenager who is adopted from foster care will act out and need help. But you could have a baby yourself, or adopt a 2 year old and that child may act out and need help as a teenager. One advantage that the adoptive parent of a teenager has is the involvement of social services and the availability of counseling and other kinds of help. All of these services would be explained to you when you talk with the adoption social worker.

Of course you're going to take into account your own personality, limitations, and desires when deciding what child to adopt. I know that I could handle a shy, insecure, or even a depressed teenager, but would have difficulty with one who has a history of intense anger. Others wouldn't know what to do with the sad, withdrawn teenager. These are issues that you would discuss thoroughly with your placement social worker. No one expects you to go into adoption blind or with no say in the type of child you could optimally parent. Everyone wants to make it work, and a failed placement is in no one's interest.

But, that said, if you like and are comfortable with teenagers, especially if you are a little older, say, 50+, think about it. Not only would you provide a grandparent for that child's kids, but that child would provide grandchildren for you. And, again, risking beating a dead horse here, imagine being 30 or 40 or 50 and having no family. It's sobering.

What are special needs children?

We've already briefly mentioned the term special needs in Chapter II. In some countries single adults are only allowed to adopt children with special needs. And if you decide to adopt an older child through the foster care system here in the United States, most of the children available for adoption are termed special needs. The term has different meanings depending on the context.

In the United States, the term *special needs* has a fairly broad definition. It includes:

children aged six and up
children with handicaps or chronic medical issues
minority children of any age, including newborns
siblings who cannot be separated

By definition, then, a child has a special need simply by being diabetic, or being older, or being a racial minority.

Internationally, special needs usually means a medical condition that could be better treated in the United States, such as a child needing surgery for a club foot, or a reparable heart problem. Ongoing medical issues such as diabetes, asthma, and the like are also considered a special need, because an adoptive parent with one or two children could give it the day to day attention that it needs. A special needs child may not be sick at all, but may need special accommodations, such as a deaf child who needs a home where the parent knows American Sign Language.

The term special needs may sound overwhelming and heavy to some of you. It brings up visions of constant care, doctors, social workers, problems. For others, those of you who need to be needed and are more comfortable with lots of responsibility, it doesn't sound so scary. There is no right or wrong here. It amazes me how many people volunteer to foster very medically-fragile children who really do need constant attention. Other people would be terrified simply to have so much ride on their ability to care for those children.

Keep in mind, though, that special needs can be as benign as a healthy 6 year old, a brother and sister team, or a racial minority child of any age, even infancy. And that handicaps and chronic medical issues can be non-life threatening and the child can live a normal life. If you are a prospective adoptive parent with a chronic medical condition yourself – diabetes, asthma, severe allergies to name a few – you would know how to handle the same issue with a child.

Some kids take more time because of their special needs, and only you have a sense of how much time your career and other responsibilities take. If you expect your adoptive child to get most of your free time, you may be right for a kid who needs Attention Deficit Disorder medication and more help with homework, and may be willing and eager to embrace that. You know who you are.

Again, the idea here is not to shame you into adopting a child that you're not comfortable with. The idea is to encourage you to look at your strengths, weaknesses and gifts, and to perhaps look past the "special needs" label and find that it might be right for you. We want the right kids with the right parents. Your adoption social worker can help you sort this out.

Domestic or International? What is Available?

Domestic

When I started researching singles' adoption for this book, I assumed that it would be nearly impossible for a single adult to adopt a newborn in this country. Of course I knew about Rosie O'Donnell, Sharon Stone, Sheryl Crow, and other celebrities who had adopted newborns, but assumed that it was one of those things that happen to the rich and famous that seldom happens for the rest of us. I was wrong.

I found out, however, that it is completely possible for a single adult to adopt a newborn. There are several ways to do it. While compiling the agency directory found on the book's website, I found that while most agencies reported that they were willing to work with single prospective adoptive parents wanting a newborn, most said that their Caucasian birth mothers rarely, if ever, chose a single parent for their babies.

By now you've probably thought long and hard about your feelings about race and your adoptive child. You know your world, your family, your conviction, and your capacity for parenting a child who is a different race than you. Or a child who might be isolated as the only minority in your rural community or neighborhood.

The simple truth, however, is that it is a matter of supply and demand, and there are fewer Caucasian babies available for adoption than any type of minority baby – African American, Hispanic, Asian, Native American or mixed-race. If you are determined to adopt a Caucasian newborn, you may need to go the route of advertising for a teenager or woman willing to give you her baby for adoption. It may be a little harder, and may take more time, but it can happen.

If you are a minority yourself, or if you've decided that the race of the child is not so important to you, you, of course, have more options. Many agencies will be able to find a minority newborn for you in a relatively short period of time. There is also foster care, where it might take longer than with an agency, but it is possible and would cost much less.

Let me talk again about my friends, Art and Ron. Art and Ron decided that they wanted to raise a family several years ago and decided to go through the foster care system to adopt. They contacted the Department of Child and Family Services in January of 2005 and received Joshua in June of that year when he was 14 months old. A year later, when Joshua was 23 months old – June 15, 2006 – the adoption was finalized. When you read the Q&A in Chapter VII, "In First Person," you will see that Art and Ron waited quite a while for another child because they were committed to adopting through the Connecticut foster care system. (Note: Wendy's Wonderful Kids can help you adopt from out of state, which can happen more quickly.) On December 13, 2007, however, they received a call from their social worker at DCF asking if they would be interested in premature newborn twins, a girl and a boy. They gladly accepted, and now Benjamin and Anna are 2 years old and part of a wonderful, loving, growing family!

Adoption from foster care is regulated by your state department of social services. According to the U.S. Children's Bureau, the Administration for Children, Youth and Families, 55,000 children were adopted from foster care in FY2008, up from 51,000 in FY2005. In the same year, 123,000 children were waiting to be adopted in this country, up from 114,000 in FY2005. The adopted children ranged from infancy to age 17, with about 4-5% under the age of 1, and for each year up to 17 (i.e., 4-5% were 2, 4-5% were 3, etc.). Waiting children are only counted up to age 16, so 123,000 does not include the 17 year olds.

Permanency is the big word in older child adoption these days. Social workers and adoption advocates use the word to look forward way beyond age 18, when the child becomes a legal adult. We've begun thinking about the long-term implications of adopting even a 17 year-old, who may only be in your home for a year.

Foster children phase out of the system at 18. In Vermont, the state legislature is considering a bill that would extend foster care, with the approval of both the foster child and the foster parents, to age 21. Imagine your average high school senior or new graduate. At 18, most are not mature or experienced enough to completely take over physical and financial responsibility for themselves. Foster kids leave the system with, at most, several thousand dollars to find a place to live, get health insurance and a job and to try to begin college while they work to support themselves. It's one thing to work fulltime and take college courses when you're 30. It's quite another to do that at 18.

Money, a place to live, and ongoing education are just part of the challenge, however. Imagine having no family for Thanksgiving. No grandparents, aunts and uncles, cousins for your children. We tend to think in terms of care and some semblance of a family home for minors. But having no family affects the rest of your life at every age.

While researching this book, I attended an adoption expo at a hotel in Washington, DC. It was clear from the booths that had crowds in front of them, that many prospective adoptive parents wanted small children, "the younger the better." Galleries with pictures and bios of local kids awaiting adoption had postcards for attendees to take if they were interested in a specific child. Without exception, postcards for boys and girls under age 5 were depleted, and postcards for older kids were hardly touched.

At this expo, there was a booth specifically for teenage adoption. On display behind the booth was a poster with the heading, "Ten Reasons to Adopt a Teenager." It had been designed to make you smile, with such reasons as, "We sleep through the night," "We're potty-trained," "We know how to use and program your electronic equipment," and poignantly, "We're leaving soon." It broke my heart to think about being 13, or even 17, and trying to convince people to consider me and not just the cute 3 year olds. To give me a Mom or Dad who will be my parent forever.

Although some social workers report that most kids adopted from foster care are adopted by long-term foster parents, there are clearly thousands who are not. Here in the Washington, D.C. area, on Sunday mornings, the NBC affiliate, WRC, airs a segment titled "Wednesday's Child," featuring one or two children in the District of Columbia who are looking to be adopted. The program is sponsored by the Freddie Mac Foundation and additional information can be found online at http://adopt.org/Wednesdays child/home/contact-page.htm. Perhaps your local television station does the same. These kids are available right now, and a phone call to indicate your interest would start the ball rolling for you.

To get an idea of the kids available for adoption in this country, go to www.Adoptuskids.com or www.childrenawaitingparents.org, where you'll find pictures of hundreds of children waiting for parents. You will find kids representative of every culture in our country. And you will also find every age imaginable.

Children available for adoption through the foster care system are there for every reason you can think of. Some, of course, have been abused and/or neglected and their parents' rights have been terminated for that reason. Some have been orphaned, especially if they were being raised by a grandparent or other older family member, and simply need a new home. Some are children who have been in foster care for a long time, and desperately want a "forever home" and a "forever mom or dad," and their foster parent is unable to adopt them for some reason.

One of the advantages of adopting an older child domestically is that unlike international adoptions, you get more reliable information about the child's physical health and behavior. There are school records, doctors' reports, and the experience of the foster parents and social workers who have worked with the child. You can have more of a sense of what the challenges are going to be with such a child. But you also will have more of a sense of the child's personality and the unique specialness that each one brings. On "Wednesday's Child" the kids are interviewed and taken to an activity that addresses their special interests. A musical child might be given a drum lesson from a professional drummer, or an athletic child, a visit to a coach. I have a musical background myself, and as silly and superficial as it may sound, I find myself drawn to every musical child that they feature on "Wednesday's Child." What a joy that would be!

International

Most of you reading this book probably know someone who has adopted a child from out of country. Make it a point to read the Q&A of Thesia Garner, a friend of mine who adopted an adorable little girl from China. You will see that it was a complicated and sometimes emotionally draining experience, but clearly worth every second of it. I think you'll also be interested in the Q&A of Margaret Schwartz, who adopted two toddler boys from Ukraine. Her book, *The Pumpkin Patch* tells about her journey from thinking about adoption to living with her energetic sons. It's a wonderful story.

Over the past number of years, different countries have come to the forefront for international adoptions. When China decided to limit births to one per family, and most families wanted a son, girls were abandoned and hence, put in orphanages by the thousands. In FY2005, 7,906 Chinese baby girls were adopted by U.S. citizens. In December of 2006, however, China made the decision to close adoptions to single adults. How tragic for the baby girls who will not benefit from having a mother like Thesia.

I believe that Africa will be the next big push for international adoption. Recently, Madonna adopted a 12 month old little boy from Malawi, and in the summer of 2005, Angelina Jolie adopted a 7 month old girl from Ethiopia. I like to think that she used her celebrity and chose Ethiopia to bring attention to the dire situation there. And as I told you in the Introduction, Tracey Neale, a former local news anchor, adopted 12-month old Ethiopian twins this past fall (www.veronicasstory.org). There are currently 5 million Ethiopian children orphaned and needing a home.

As I stated earlier, it is not possible at this time to adopt a newborn from out of country. I read recently that thousands of abortions are performed every year in India on women who have learned that they are having a girl when they want a boy. I have the fantasy of someday helping to set up an adoption service to help these little girls be adopted internationally at the time of their birth. A little farfetched, perhaps, but a way to start the adoption process before the baby is born so that it is possible to take her home as a newborn. Maybe someday.

For the time being, though, the youngest babies that you will be able to adopt will be 8 to 10 months old and from such countries as Ethiopia, Honduras, and Russia. Children are available from some countries all the way into their teenage years. Many countries will allow adoptions of special needs children only, meaning that they will probably be older. Appendix A is a directory of most every country in the world and their policies on foreign adoption as of Winter 2010. If you are interested in an out-of-country adoption, read it with an eye to the countries that appeal to you and then check with the State Department website for any recent changes. Each State Department internet link is included with the country's description in Appendix A.

Conclusion

I hope that this chapter has given you a general sense of what children are out there and what they need at every stage of growing up. You may now have a better idea of what is right for you and where you need to look to find that child.

To summarize, children from birth to age 17 are available for adoption. Children age 6 and up, or those in a sibling group, or a minority, are considered "special needs," as are those with a specific physical or emotional issue – everything from learning disabilities to severe food allergies. You will not be able to adopt a newborn abroad, and not all countries adopt to singles. Some countries allow singles to adopt only their "special needs" children.

Other countries, like Ethiopia, have millions of children available to single adults. The U.S. Foster Care system has more than 129,000 children available for adoption today. So if you thought it was going to be hard to adopt, you now know that there is a desperate need for people like you. What a wonderful feeling to know that you can make such a difference in a child's life!

Resources

- An academic discussion of the need to be loved: *Cherishment*, Young-Bruehl and Betheland, The Free Press, 2000.
- Kids available for adoption through foster care: www.adoptuskids.com, www.childrenawaitingparents.com
- Tracey Neale, former news anchor at WUSA9 in Washington, DC, and her adoption of 12 month old Ethiopian twins: www.veronicasstory.org
- Freddie Mac Foundation (Wednesday's Child): www.adopt.org/wednesdayschild/home/contact-page.htm
- U.S. Department of State (Information about intercountry adoption): http://travel.state.gov/family/family_1732.html
- Wendy's Wonderful Kids www.thedavethomasfoundation.org

Chapter IV

The Adoption Process:
A General Overview of What to Expect

As I've already discussed, there are a number of ways to go about adopting a child—whether you pursue foster care adoption, domestic adoption through an agency, domestic independent adoption with the help of an adoption lawyer, or international adoption through an agency. Each of these adoption processes can be painstaking at times due to the sometimes roller-coaster world of adopting, but the end result—a child to love and care for—is worth it!

In this chapter I present an overview of the different types of adoption to give you an idea of what to expect. By no means is this a thorough step-by-step guide, which would be impossible since each adoption situation is different. This overview should provide you with an idea of what each type of adoption entails. This chapter will address the following:

- What do I do first? What can I expect in terms of the process?
- What does the home study entail? What should I expect?
- What do I need to know about foster care adoption?
- What do I need to know about domestic adoption?
    Private agency
    Independent
- What do I need to know about intercountry adoption?

What do I do first? And what does the process look like?

First, let's talk about your home, space requirements and what you'll need to do to adopt. If you're pretty certain that you are going to pursue adoption, you may need to change your living situation before you start the process. Here is information that is true in most states:

- If you adopt a newborn or an older infant, the baby may sleep in your room, in a crib, until his or her first birthday.
- Giving the child the bedroom in a one bedroom apartment or condominium (while you sleep in the living room) is not permitted.
- Any child past his or her first birthday must either have its own bedroom or share with a child of the same gender, as long as both children are under the age of 18. Some states limit the number of children in a room to two.
- The shared bedroom must be at least 75 square feet for the first child, and an additional 45 square feet for each additional child.
- The adopted child must have his or her own bed.

What group of people is most likely to live in one bedroom apartments and condominiums? Singles, of course! Many, many single men and women have looked into adoption, only to find that their home didn't have enough rooms to be approved. And many, many single men and women have gone out and rented or purchased two bedroom apartments and condominiums in order to be eligible for adoption. Check with an adoption agency in your state just to make sure that the general laws apply where you live. You can go to the directory on the book's website, or to www.childwelfare.gov/nfcad/, choose your home state and then check one or more of the following boxes: Private Domestic Adoption Agencies, Public Foster Care and Adoption Agencies, Private Intercountry Adoption Agencies, and Foster Care and Adoption Resources in Your State or Territory. Call any agency and ask them about bedroom requirements in your state. Knowing ahead of time that you're going to need to move will mean that you won't start the Home Study only to find that it has to be suspended for months while you find a new place to live.

Later on in this chapter I will tell you about how to find an agency for intercountry or domestic adoption if that is your choice. And I will also describe the ways that you can go about finding a foster child to adopt. But first, here is an overview of the steps that you will probably need to take to adopt.

First, when you start calling adoption agencies, many of them will invite you to come in to talk with them about your interest in adoption. If you do this with every agency that you call, you will spend a lot of time at orientation meetings, picnics, and private meetings with representatives of all of the agencies. Many a prospective adoptive parent has spent the afternoon at an agency event, only to decide that they don't like the programs or the attitudes of the employees. If you follow the process described on the Agency Interview Intake Sheet found on the book's website (www.adoptionforsinglesbook.com), you can get an idea of the feel of the place, how your questions are answered and how your concerns are addressed. When you like what you hear and how you've been treated, then it makes sense to spend an evening or afternoon at the agency to learn more.

Most agencies will ask that you attend the orientation, where you will be walked through their processes. The order of the next steps may vary by agency, but if you want to adopt from foster care, you will be required to take a course on parenting and adoption that will meet weekly for a month or more. For instance, the Children's Home Society and Family Services of Minnesota requires 18 hours of classes on such subjects as abuse and neglect, cross-cultural parenting, attachment, loss and grief, and question and answer sessions with professionals and other adoptive parents. These classes are designed to help you decide the type of child you could best parent. Other agencies, especially those working in intercountry or domestic newborn adoptions, may require fewer, if any hours at all, of education. All types of adoption require the Home Study, however, and the next section will explain that process for you.

The home study

The adoption home study, one of the first steps in the adoption process, is required for any adoption, whether it is from foster care, intercountry, or domestic newborn. It is basically "a written description of you and your family prepared by an adoption agency or private adoption professional" www.nefe.org. In most cases if you are working with an agency for a foster care, domestic, or international adoption, the agency will provide a licensed social worker who will conduct your home study. If you are working with an attorney for a private adoption, or if the agency does not provide a social worker, you will have to hire a social worker to do the home study. Most adoption attorneys and agencies will have a list of experienced home study social workers and will be able to refer you to them. It will then be your responsibility to set up an appointment to begin the home study, and in this case, you will probably have to pay the social worker directly. For home studies that are not included in an agency fee, the price ranges from $500 to $3,000.

The home study can be scary for anyone who is preparing to become a new parent … *Will the social worker think I'm going to be a good parent? Is my house safe enough? Will they think I'm financially stable enough to adopt?* These fears are common, but relax and be yourself. As you've read through these chapters I've asked you to consider many things when thinking about adoption—what it takes to be a good parent, what it will cost, how you can pay for it, what children are available and what they may need from you—so you have already put a lot of careful thought into this major decision. That will be obvious when it comes time for your home study, and you will be prepared for all of the questions that you will need to answer.

You will have to fill out forms and gather documents such as your birth certificate for the home study. You will also have to undergo criminal background checks and child protective service checks. You may also be asked to fill out questionnaires that will inquire about (among other things) your family, how you feel about discipline, or your favorite childhood memory (www.about.com). You will be asked by the social worker to describe your environment, what area schools are like, and the nature of your relationship with neighbors. You will probably also be asked to write your autobiography, including why you want to adopt a child.

Thesia Garner, a single mother who adopted a baby from China before the rule change that now prohibits single-parent adoptions from the country, says that the social worker conducting her home study visited her on three occasions. The number of visits a social worker makes will depend on the home study requirements for the state you live in and the country you are adopting from if you are pursuing an international adoption. Thesia says that each home study visit had a different focus. The focus of one of the visits was Thesia's readiness to be an adoptive parent. Another visit focused on safety and lifestyle issues, so the social worker looked at Thesia's home. And the third visit focused on Thesia's financial situation and the social worker reviewed the current status of all of Thesia's debts and assets. For more information about Thesia and her experiences with international adoption, see Chapter VII, "In First Person."

When evaluating your readiness to become a parent, the social worker might ask you why you want to adopt and might interview you about your values and your hopes and expectations for the adoptive child. The social worker might also ask you about how you handle crises and change and where you'll get support or professional help. During this interview process the social worker will try to gain a solid understanding of your values and the reason you want to become a parent. You may also have to take a physical exam, a Tuberculosis (TB) test, or have a chest x-ray. The social worker will want to know if you have any serious health problems that may affect your life expectancy. You may have to present medical reports from your physician.

In Thesia's case, the social worker evaluated her home to make sure the environment was safe and healthy for a child. The social worker will want to make sure you have a room planned for the child. During one of the home visits the social worker might check to make sure you have fire extinguishers and smoke alarms in your home and might ask about nearby medical facilities and fire stations. The social worker might also offer advice on how to childproof your home. For information about childproofing your home, see Chapter V, "Homecoming," for a complete list and resources to help you get started.

One of the roles of the social worker in a home study is to help answer any questions parents might have about bonding/ attachment issues, childhood development, and childhood behaviors. View this as an educational opportunity; this is an excellent time for you to get more information about the age child you wish to adopt and to learn about the agency's resources for teaching parenting skills.

Another important aspect of the home study is to verify that you will be able to care for a child with your current income. During the home study you will have to verify your income with paycheck stubs, a W-4, or income tax forms 1040 or 1040 EZ. You may also be asked to show additional financial information such as bank statements, proof of insurance, and any investments that you might have.

During the home study you will also need to provide the contact information for three or four references. Choose people who have known you, at least, for several years, know your family, and have seen you in a variety of situations. These references will be asked about your strengths and weaknesses and what kind of parent they believe you will be. Obviously, it is important to choose people who know you well enough to have opinions about your readiness to parent, and knowledge of your values and temperament. And even more obviously, choose people who like you!

The home study can take several months to finish. According to the Information Gateway, "most families who have adopted say the home study process was beneficial. It allowed them to consider their individual feelings about adoption and to explore their readiness for a child."

The next sections of this chapter will focus on the specific types of adoption and what you might expect in terms of process. We'll start with foster care adoption.

Foster care adoption

If you are interested in adopting from foster care, you have two options as first steps. Three or four years ago I would have told you to contact social workers at your local county government Department of Child and Family Services, because at that time it was the only option. It can't hurt to do this just to find out if there are any local children available for adoption. If there are, the social worker will set up an appointment with you to discuss the program.

For state-by-state contact information for a variety of adoption-related organizations and services, including public and licensed private adoption agencies, visit www.childwelfare.gov/nfcad/index.cfm.

When the index screen comes up, first choose your state of residence, and then select the type of information you desire. Click on "Public Foster Care and Adoption Agencies." This will lead you to a list of adoption social workers in each district of the State Department of Social Services.

As I noted earlier, though, in 2010 there is an organization named "Wendy's Wonderful Kids" that is part of The Dave Thomas Foundation for Adoption. If that name sounds familiar, it is because it is the same Dave Thomas who started Wendy's Hamburgers (hence the name Wendy's Wonderful Kids!) and was himself an adopted child. You may also remember seeing him in commercials promoting the idea of adoption. He has since died, but his legacy is The Dave Thomas Foundation for Adoption and adoption even more than hamburgers! I imagine that he would be thrilled with what is being done in his name.

For more detailed information about Wendy's Wonderful Kids, see Chapter VII, "In First Person," for an interview of Rita Soronen, Executive Director of The Dave Thomas Foundation for Adoption. For purposes of this discussion, however, let me tell you a little about the program.

Wendy's Wonderful Kids started with the goal of having 100 social workers in all 50 states hired to do nothing but recruit adoptive parents and facilitate adoptions. When talking to social workers in the area, it was extremely frustrating to find that they had such overwhelmingly heavy caseloads of children and families in foster care that they had no time and little interest in helping someone who wanted to foster to adopt only. Several social workers were actually quite irritable when asked how they would respond to a phone call from a single adult asking about adoption. One got the impression that an end-result of adoption was seen as a reward for foster parents who had put in many years fostering a series of kids and being a lifesaver for the social worker. When asked directly about people who didn't want to be long term foster parents because they were looking for permanency, the answer was that that rarely happened. That when a child became available for adoption, i.e., the parents' rights were terminated by the court, that child would go to someone who had, in essence, paid their dues. Not all social workers were like that, of course. See Chapter VII, "In First Person" and read the interview with Natalie Newton, a senior social worker for the Fredericksburg City Department of Social Services in Fredericksburg, Virginia.

The old system also meant that all kids in need of adoption were only offered to local families. The Dave Thomas Foundation saw the holes in the system – foster care social workers who were not adoption social workers, no way for a prospective adoptive parent in Arlington, Virginia to adopt a child from Montana, and few people actually glad to hear from you if you wanted to adopt! And Voila! Wendy's Wonderful Kids, a brilliant idea aimed at finding homes for the almost 129,000 kids awaiting adoption.

Having a national system makes it possible for you to adopt from another area of the country if you are unable to find an appropriate child in your jurisdiction. A Wendy's Wonderful Kids social worker in your state is able to contact the WWK social worker in the state where the child resides, and is able to help facilitate the interstate adoption.

Having a national system also takes into account cultural differences in feelings about certain types of adoptions in this country. Prospective adoptive parents in urban areas are more used to diverse families and seeing Caucasian parents with children of color. Percentages of prospective adoptive parents willing to take only babies of their same race appear to be lower in more diverse areas. That is my opinion, of course, but is based on what I see here in the Washington, D.C. area compared to towns that I visit often in other areas of the country. At any rate, having a national system means that I can look at and inquire about children from all over the country, because the WWK's social workers work together if your local area has no children for you.

Here's how it works: In your state, 1, 2, or 3 social workers at pre-existing agencies have been contracted to recruit and work with prospective adoptive parents. Their sole responsibility is to help children find permanent homes. Go to www.davethomas foundation.org, click on Wendy's Wonderful Kids on the right side of the web page, then click on "Recruiters" to bring up the WWK locations available to you. In more populated states you will probably have more than one city to choose from. Click on the city that you prefer to get the recruiter's name and telephone number. Contact that person to find out how many and what kinds of kids are available in your state. Also, go to www.adoptus

kids.org and www.childrenawaitingparents.org where you can find pictures of children of all races, ages, and needs from all over the country. It is sobering to look at face after face of babies and kids who need us. But do it and you may find a few that speak to you somehow. Your Wendy's Wonderful Kids social worker can help you if you do.

If you start with your local social service agency, here's a little bit about what you can expect.

Some, but not all, localities require that prospective parents interested in adopting a child through their system become foster parents first. For instance, the Fredericksburg City Department of Social Services in Fredericksburg, Virginia, allows singles to adopt a child but requires that they and all prospective parents foster a child for at least six months before pursuing adoption. The child you foster may not end up being the child you adopt. Newton says, "Our foster parents often foster a number of children before they foster the child they eventually are able to adopt. This happens for a few reasons, such as the child may return home, may go to live with a family member, the family may not be able to meet the child's needs, or the child may be at an age of discretion and wish not to be adopted."

This may be useful for you if you really need some time to explore the idea of adoption, so that being a foster parent to kids who move on or go home would give you a chance to see how individual, and different from each other, kids are and what it is like to parent different types and ages.

Newton says, though, that in Fredericksburg it is very likely that the child a family fosters will be the child they end up adopting. She attributes this to the fact that her agency conducts a special training program on fostering-to-adopt. In a typical foster-to-adopt program, the training can run around eight weeks or so, three hours each week. In Fredericksburg, a home study and complete background checks are conducted on prospective parents during the course of the training. "Once the training is complete and the background checks have been approved, we try to figure out what kind of child would best suit the person or family as well as what kind of child they can handle—what behaviors they can handle and what they can't handle." says Newton. "Once a child is placed with the person or family, the child has to live in the home for six months. Again, we require all of our potential adopters to foster a child first for at least 6 months. This foster-to-adopt requirement ensures that the match is a good fit for both child and parent."

Another option is to volunteer and be trained as a foster parent for your county. In most counties that can lead to the possibility of an adoption if the child is not returned to his or her parents. Here in Arlington County, Virginia, where I live, however, most children's parents do not have their rights terminated, and there are very few foster children available for adoption. Those who are available are usually adopted by their foster parents, but volunteering to be a foster parent here needs to be something you do because you want to be a foster parent! It would be a long shot that the child you're taking care of would be adoptable some day. Check with your local county Department of Social Services to see what the statistics are on foster care adoption and to see if prospective adoptive parents are desirable. Clearly if there are 129,000 children nationally available for foster care adoption in 2010, my county is not typical. Check it out.

Again, at the risk of sounding like a broken record, in most local social service agencies, adoption is not the goal of the agency. At Wendy's Wonderful Kids, it *is* the expected outcome. Explore both and see what works for you.

Domestic adoption

Two additional ways to adopt a child domestically in addition to working with the foster care system are through domestic private adoption through an agency or an independent adoption, where you work with a lawyer. Here are the pros and cons of each:

Agency:

- You will be entering a process that you don't have to manage yourself because the agency takes care of all aspects of the adoption, including government requirements
- Will probably involve a longer wait for a Caucasian baby, sometimes up to several years. Depending upon

the agency, will involve a much shorter wait for minority babies

Lawyer:

- If you are looking for a Caucasian newborn, your wait will probably be much shorter because he or she will help you actively advertise and look for pregnant girls or women who will give their baby to you

Whichever you choose, you're going to end up with a newborn baby and you will have made it through every step required to get there. So your choice will probably be made based on your financial resources, the time you have to wait to get your baby, and your willingness to consider all newborns regardless of race. Agency adoptions involve getting everything done and then waiting. I have friends who have waited for months and months, and then the phone call comes—they've been chosen by a birth mother who read their bios and saw their pictures. And then they wait until the baby is born and live with the possibility that the birth mother will change her mind. With private adoptions through an attorney, your ads are put out into the world and you wait for a phone call from a pregnant woman or girl who wants to find out more about you. You are doing the looking and you are not waiting to hear from an agency that a baby is forthcoming. Which you choose is just a matter of style, your financial situation, and your temperament.

Domestic private agency

If you decide to work with an adoption agency whether for a domestic or international adoption, the first thing you need to do is make sure the agency is accredited. Agencies that have received a license from any state to do adoptions have met numerous requirements for staff, procedures, and policies. For example, the State of Georgia's Office of Regulatory Services does an annual review of adoption agencies in that state, and issues a license for one year. Agencies must comply with state law in providing such things as a written manual of policies and procedures, maintaining and storing records, staff requirements such as trained and state-licensed social workers, and a formal complaint process for clients. In some states a team from the government goes through all of the agency's files to make sure that they are meeting standards. Because of these strict standards, your best bet is to go with a licensed non-profit adoption agency. To check an agency's license status and to see if they are in good standing, contact your state's Human Services licensing department. You can also check with the Better Business Bureau to see if there have been any complaints again the agency you're considering.   Go to www.search.bbb.org/   to inquire about any agency you're considering.   Another website to check for complaints about agencies: http://www.adoptachild.org/ICAR/Adoption-Registry.aspx.

Once you have found a few accredited agencies, you will begin your intake interviews. These initial agency interviews provide a chance for you to ask questions of them and for them to learn about you. As I mentioned in Chapter II, it is extremely important that you interview a number of agencies before you choose one. Not only will it give you a chance to compare costs, but it will also give you a chance to request and check references, and get a feel for the attitudes of the people who would be working with you. For instance, in my research I found that some agencies were very negative about the possibility of a single person adopting a newborn, while others said that it was completely doable. You don't want to commit to an agency that acts as though only married couples are appropriate parents for babies. That attitude would directly affect how they talk about you to birth mothers and make it a long shot that you would get a baby. Attitudes such as these may not be immediately apparent in the interview, but if they are unable to give you a single parent-newborn reference, take that seriously.

Again, I have designed a form for you to use when you interview and weed out agencies. Begin using it with the first telephone contact you have with an agency representative. By walking through the steps you will be less likely to forget to ask an important question. Continue to use the form when you attend an agency orientation or talk with a reference. Collecting so much information about a number of agencies can be overwhelming and confusing, and it will be helpful to have it all organized. It will also help you make comparisons when the time comes to make a decision. It will all be there right in front of you in black and white! You can find a copy of the form on the book website. www.adoptionforsinglesbook.com

After you have decided that you are going to move forward with a particular agency, the agency will give you an application to fill out to begin your process of adoption. One major component of that application is the "Dear Birthmother" letter—a document that uses words and photographs to create a picture of your life, hobbies, and dreams of parenting. This letter is shown to potential birthmothers who will be choosing their baby's adoptive parents. For helpful advice on how to write a "Dear Birthmother" letter, see http://adoption.families.com/blog/how-to-write-a-birthmother-letter.

As I've previously mentioned, the agency will also either begin the home study or recommend to you social workers for your home study (some agencies include home studies in their fees, some do not). That process may take as long as six months, but in some cases can be completed in two months.

Once your home study and your application are completed and Dear Birthmother letter is written, depending upon the agency and your preference as to race, you may have to wait for a birthmother to choose you. Once that happens, the agency will help facilitate the birthparent(s) relinquishment of rights and will advise you on the steps you need to take for post-placement home studies. The agency will also advise you on what legal documents need to be completed through the help of a lawyer to finalize the adoption.

During the adoption process, most agencies also provide a number of services such as monthly support group meetings, individual and family counseling, and parenting classes. Take advantage of these resources!

Independent domestic adoption

If you decide not to work with an adoption agency but instead pursue an independent adoption you will need to retain the services of a good lawyer. The most important advice I can give you when choosing an attorney for an independent adoption is to make sure the attorney is a member of the American Academy of Adoption

Attorneys (www.adoptionattorneys.org). Adoption law is very complicated and state specific and you want to make sure the attorney is well-versed in the adoption laws of your state.

In fact, you may find that independent adoption is illegal in your state. According to Mark T. McDermott, J.D., past president of the American Academy of Adoption Attorneys, and an adoptive parent himself, independent adoption is legal in all states except Colorado, Connecticut, Delaware, and Massachusetts. If you live in a state that allows independent adoption and would like to look into it, go to www.theadoptionguide.com/options/articles /independent-adoption to read McDermott's article entitled "Independent Adoption." In it he says that "in a typical independent adoption, the prospective parents take an active role in identifying a birthmother, usually by networking advertising, or by using the Internet." He also says that if the prospective adoptive parent and the birthmother live in different states, it is important to have an attorney that understands the Interstate Compact on the Placement of Children. In independent adoptions, it is common to meet the birthmother early in the process, and also to be present at the hospital when the baby is born.

On its website The American Academy of Adoption Attorneys provides the following tips for choosing an adoption attorney:

- Contact an attorney as early as possible in the decision-making process.
- Know what the attorney charges and how the fees are structured. Make sure they are affordable.
- Learn about the specific types of adoptions and services that the attorney provides. Ask what percentage of the practice is dedicated to adoption and how many adoption proceedings the attorney has handled.
- Ask for references. Ask a lot of questions, share your concerns, and provide the attorney with all relevant documents.
- Choose an attorney who is experienced in the type of adoption you are considering.

After finding an attorney and learning about the adoption laws in your state, your next job is to find a birthmother who is planning to place her baby for adoption. As already discussed in Chapter II, your state law might limit the amount of advertising you can do to find a birth mother. Once you are aware of what your state will and will not allow, you can begin your search. Place ads in newspapers and on the Internet. Let all of your friends and family know that you are pursuing an independent adoption. As I mentioned earlier, a friend of mine made a flyer with her picture and information about herself for friends and family to distribute in case they heard of a birthmother wanting to put her baby up for adoption. You can also contact local obstetricians or pregnancy crisis centers to pass on your information to prospective birthmothers.

Kathe Gallagher, a social worker and author for *Healthwise*, writes that once you find a birthmother the next step for you and your attorney is to develop a legal agreement with the birth mother and father (if known, he must be included). You will be responsible for her legal expenses and it's also common for adoptive parents to pay for a birthmother's health care and living expenses.

International adoption

The general process

Once you have chosen an agency to help you with your intercountry adoption, the steps are predictable and similar. They are:

- Complete the Home Study
- Submit the I-600A Application for Advance Processing of an Orphan, used when you plan to adopt abroad and have not yet identified the specific child that you will adopt. In essence, you get permission from the United States to find a child to adopt.
- Include with the application proof of U.S. citizenship, proof of divorce, if applicable, an FD 258 Fingerprint Chart (another official form), a Home Study, and a $525 filing fee. This may be covered in your agency fee.

- Receive I-171H, Notice of Favorable Determination Concerning Application for Advance Processing of Orphan Petition. This approval is good for 18 months.
- Complete dossier for the country where you'll be adopting. The dossier contains
    - A physician's report on his letterhead
    - Financial information, usually from your bank
    - The adoption petition (provided by your agency)
    - The I-171H (provided by your agency)
    - The post-placement agreement (provided by your agency) which details reports that are made back to the adopting country, usually annually until the child reaches 18.
    - Certified copy of birth certificate
    - Certified copy of divorce decree, if applicable
    - Certified copy of death certificate of former spouse, if applicable
    - Proof of home ownership or a lease if you rent
    - Employment verification on company letterhead, including salary, length of tenure, even if self-employed
    - Home study
    - Copy of your agency's license
    - Criminal background check from local police department
    - Copy of passport photo
    - Letters of reference (can be the same ones used in the Home study)
    - Copy of most recent federal income tax return
    - Power of Attorney for agency
    - Photos of you, your family, pets, neighborhood, etc.
- Wait for a child to be chosen for you, or in some instances, go to the country, visit orphanages, and see which children are available
- Receive referral documents and evaluate – many countries send medical information, sometimes a video of the child. If you are adopting from Russia, you will be making two trips to the country and the goal for the

first trip is to meet the child and start the legal process of adoption. During that first trip it is wise to take a camcorder to make your own videos of the child. Once you have the referral, medical records, and/or a video, this is the time to consult with a pediatrician who specializes in adoption.

- Make decision about whether you will accept the child chosen for you. In some countries you will be sent another referral if you refuse the first one. Your agency will have that information. Also, see Appendix A, the Country Directory, for specifics about the country you choose.

- Depending upon the country, submit I-600 Petition to Classify Orphan as an Immediate Relative, which indicates that a specific child has been chosen. Some countries require that this petition be made at the U.S. Embassy in the country. The petition includes the child's birth certificate, documentation that the child has been placed for adoption by the parent or has been proven to be orphaned, and a health examination of the child.

- If you're not already there, travel to the country to meet your child. Most countries will complete the adoption there.

- Apply for Immigrant visa at the U.S. embassy in that country. U.S. officials will review your documents, including the child's health examination.

- Bring your child home!

Many of these steps will be completed by the agency, and you will be supported as you collect the required documentation and compile it to submit to the country you've chosen. In other words, you're not compiling and checking off the list by yourself, and you don't submit the dossier yourself. The agency will receive your documents, check to make sure everything is there, and submit the dossier for you.

Finding an agency

Personally, especially after making the list above, I think that attempting an intercountry adoption without an agency would be incredibly difficult and unnecessary. While some countries allow you to hire an attorney in-country directly, others require that you use an American adoption agency both licensed in your home state and in the adoption country. American agencies have ongoing relationships with foreign governments, specific orphanages in those countries, and lots and lots of experience facilitating intercountry adoptions.

Once you have perused the country list in Appendix A, have made a list of the countries that appeal to you, and have checked for recent updates with the State Department, go to the Agency Directory on the book website, www.adoptionforsinglesbook.com. The Agency Directory is a list of adoption agencies, by state, that have been prescreened for experience with and a desire to work with singles. Each agency indicates whether they work in domestic and/or intercountry adoptions, and they will list the countries that they represent. The directory will also include each agency's contact person and address.

Since April 1, 2008, when the United States began implementing The Hague Convention for Intercountry Adoptions, adoption agencies working abroad have needed an additional license. The State Department maintains a list of "Hague-Accredited" agencies, which are those agencies that have completed the reapplication process to be allowed to work abroad. This means that they have proven that they have put processes in place to fulfill the new requirements as set out by the Hague Convention. Go to www.travel.state.gov/family/adoption/convention/convention_4169.html# to see a list of Accredited, Temporarily Accredited, and Approved Hague Adoption Service Providers. You can also ask the agencies that you call if they are Hague-Accredited. As time passes, most agencies that worked abroad before the Hague Convention went into effect on April 1 will catch up and get the additional accreditation.

The agency directory is located on the book website in order to keep it as current as possible. Note that a survey of 1024 licensed adoption agencies in all 50 states did not yield responses from every state. Having the directory on the website will allow additions when I hear of your positive experiences with agencies in your state. Please let me know if you use an agency not in the directory and have a good experience so that I can contact their representative to see if they'd like to be listed. For those of you living in states not represented in the agency directory, I'm sorry your local agencies didn't respond! Your search will have a few extra steps. Go to www.childwelfare.gov/nfcad/, select your home state, and check the box of the type of adoption you're considering. You will get a list of licensed agencies that specialize in that type of adoption in your area.

For some countries, such as Russia or Ethiopia, you will probably have a number of agencies to choose from. Less popular countries, such as Poland or Jamaica, will be represented by fewer agencies in the United States, but they do exist! Make a list of agencies that you'd like to interview and you can get started.

As noted previously, when interviewing agency contacts, I would also recommend asking for references so that you can speak directly with other singles who have used the agency to adopt. Ask them how the process went, and how much support and compassion they got from their social workers at the agency. Ask if they would use the agency again if they wanted to adopt another child. Technical expertise is certainly important when it comes to adoption, but we get to be as high-maintenance as we need to be when we are going through this process, so understanding, kindness and hand-holding are a must.

Choosing a country

When I talk to singles about intercountry adoption, many people express concern about health issues that may not be disclosed by the orphanages. It's not unusual for an orphanage to offer you a child who needs some kind of medical care in order to be healthy. Most of the time it is some kind of surgery for a cardiac problem that can be repaired, or a cleft palate, or a club foot. At other times, however, you may take your child home before you realize that there is a problem, and rarely, it may appear after months or years. To get the real story about what you can expect, read the Q&A in Chapter VII by Patrick Mason, MD,

Ph.D., a pediatric endocrinologist and a member of the Executive Committee of the American Academy of Pediatrics' Provisional Section on Adoption who runs a preadoption medical clinic at Inova Fairfax Hospital in Fairfax, Virginia. In his interview, Dr. Mason gives his opinions about what to expect when adopting from specific countries.

Dr. Mason says that illnesses such as malaria are not unheard of, but that once they are treated, the child is normally healthy. Reactive Attachment Disorder is a serious psychological condition that is caused by inadequate emotional care during the first months of life, and while it is very dramatic and is to blame for stories about adopted children becoming violent, Dr. Mason says that the chances of getting a child with RAD are not great. Fetal alcohol syndrome can be an issue in some countries, but working with a medical expert early in the adoption process can help you learn to recognize the symptoms. If you live in the Washington, DC area and would like to contact Dr. Mason at the International Adoption Center at Inova-Fairfax Hospital for Children, go to www.adoptionclinic.org/index.htm. If you live in other areas of the country, you can find adoption health clinics and professionals at www.comeunity.com/adoption/health/clinics.html or www.med.umn.edu/peds/iac/otherprofessionals.html. Click on adoption health services, and then click on your state for a local listing.

An issue of great importance to anyone hoping to adopt from out of country right now is the 1993 Hague Convention on Protection of Children and Cooperation in Respect of Intercountry Adoption, called the Hague Adoption Convention, for short. The purpose of the creation of this convention was to insure the safety and rights of every child put up for adoption in the world, namely that they are in fact available for adoption by virtue of being orphaned or legally put up for adoption by a biological parent. This is in response to the growing problem of children being stolen and sold for adoption in some countries.

The United States finally ratified the Hague Adoption Convention in December, 2007. It had become mired in legal issues in Congress for many years, but legislation was finally signed by President Bill Clinton on October 6, 2000, and it took the United States over seven years to implement the terms of the convention. As with all treaties, it must be ratified by all nations that agree to work under and abide by its rules. U.S. ratification could not happen until structures were put in place to ensure that these rules will be followed.

The Hague Convention will affect adoptions from all countries who are a party to, but who have not yet ratified the convention themselves. One worrisome and prominent example is Guatemala. Although Guatemala deposited its accession instrument (became a party) to the convention in March 2003, they have not yet changed their adoption practices to come in line with the requirements of the Hague Adoption Convention. Until they do, they will not be able to ratify the treaty themselves, and adoptions are not possible to prospective adoptive parents from countries that have ratified the treaty. So on April 1, 2008, when the Hague Convention began to be implemented in the United States, adoptions from Guatemala were closed.

State Department officials are hopeful that Guatemala will do whatever it needs to do to reopen adoptions to U.S. citizens, and any adoptions that have begun by the time we ratified the convention will be grandfathered in. The United States has been a major resource for Guatemalan orphans—in FY 2005 there were 3,783 American adoptions from Guatemala. It is in their best interest to ratify the treaty quickly to keep this valuable resource available.

Several other countries are not available for adoption at this time, some for Americans in general, and some just for singles. Korea, which released 1,630 children to U.S. citizens for adoption in 2005, does not adopt to singles (or interestingly, to overweight people!). Ukraine closed adoptions to Americans, because of what they perceived to be abuses of the system when American parents did not submit post-adoption reports as required by the Ukrainian government. Although adoptions to Americans recently reopened, on April 28, 2008, a new law was signed that closed adoptions to singles who are not citizens of Ukraine. Closing adoptions to unmarried individuals is a new and worrisome trend, so if you are interested in a foreign adoption, it is in your best interest to move quickly before your chosen country changes that law. Most of the time prospective adoptive parents who are in the pipeline when the law changes are allowed to complete their adoptions.

Vietnam cut off adoptions to Americans in early 2003 after being a major source of adoptive children (766 were adopted in 2002), but entered into an agreement with the U.S. on June 21, 2005, and recommenced American adoptions in January of 2006. On April 25, 2008, however, the American Embassy in Hanoi issued a scathing report about the abuses in the Vietnamese adoption system. In response, the Vietnamese government closed adoptions to Americans on April 28 of that year. It is the hoped that the United States and Vietnam can repair this relationship and that adoptions will reopen, perhaps in a few years.

Muslim countries do not allow adoption at all because it is not allowed by Islamic law.

Conclusion

As you can see, each form of adoption has its own sets of benefits and challenges. The key is to figure out what is best for you—whether it is adopting internationally through an agency or adopting domestically through an agency or foster care. What we've described in this chapter is a summary of some of the main aspects of each adoption process—you may find that your experiences are different. In any case, it's important to conduct as much research as possible before beginning the adoption journey.

Resources

- About.com "What is an Adoption Home Study?" http://adoption.about.com/od/adopting/a/homestudy.htm
- ADOPT: FAQ about Adoption: www.adopting.org
- Adoptions.com "Legal Issues of Independent Adoption": www.adoptions.com/aecindependent.html
- Adoptive Families: The Adoption Guide. "Independent Adoption" Mark T. McDermott, J.D.: http://theadoptionguide.com/options/articles/independent-adoption
- AdoptUSKids: http://www.adoptuskids.org/
- American Academy of Adoption Attorneys http://www.adoptionattorneys.org
- Child Welfare Information Gateway (National Foster Care & Adoption Directory Search): http://www.childwelfare.gov/nfcad/index.cfm
- Families.com "How to Write a Birthmother Letter": http://adoption.families.com/blog/how-to-write-a-birthmother-letter
- Healthwise "Types of Adoption" Kathe Gallagher, MSW: http://health.yahoo.com/ency/healthwise/tn9011
- Wendy's Wonderful Kids: www.davethomasfoundation.org

Chapter V

Homecoming

Wow. By this time you've been through a lot. The journey has been long, complicated, intense, vulnerable and personal. After months of gathering information about yourself, writing your autobiography, being studied, fingerprinted, background-checked, referenced and physically examined, you've done all you can do. Now it looks as though it's going to turn out the way you want it to. Either sooner – you've been notified that a baby or child is available to you, or later – you passed all the tests and now just need to await your child, you will be bringing this new family member into your life and your home. The wait probably seems interminable. After all the work of getting this far, you are restless and feel impatient to get going. Good news! There is much more to do!

Can you imagine what all you would have to do if you or a partner were giving birth? All of the legal and practical things you would have to do to become a parent? Equate your adoption process up till now with getting pregnant and carrying the child to term. The work now becomes preparing for your new arrival.

If you or a partner were pregnant and awaiting a birth, you would be assured of starting with a newborn. Since you are adopting, you *may* start your parenting journey with a newborn, but it may also be an older baby, or a toddler, or even a teenager. We will discuss the preparations that you will make regardless of the age of the child, and also some preparations that are specifically for younger children.

In this chapter, we will look at:

- Names and the adoption
- Health insurance
- Social Security Number
- Life insurance
- Wills and trusts
- Religious Ceremonies and Godparents
- Family Medical Leave Act

- Flexible Spending Account
- School or Childcare
- Childproofing and safety issues

Naming the Child

If you were giving birth to a child, you would have started thinking about a name for your child soon after finding out that you were going to be a parent. Maybe there have been names that you've loved your whole life. Maybe you would spend hours looking through name-the-baby books, compiling lists of names that catch your fancy. And maybe you would start listening to the name of everyone you meet, or read about in a novel, or hear about in a movie. Soon you will begin to narrow it down and find yourself coming back to the same name or names over and over again. Finally, you have a name. It is your child!

When you adopt, naming your child may or may not take the same path. If you are adopting a domestic newborn, yes. It you are adopting an Ethiopian 18 month old, a Russian 12 month old, or an American teenager, however, it may be a little more complicated. Let's think about it.

In *The Pumpkin Patch*, Margaret Schwartz goes to Ukraine not knowing if she'll bring home one or two children, exactly how old they'll be, and whether they'll be boys, girls, or both. Adoptions happen in-country in Ukraine, and Margaret had just days to name two little boys so that their Ukrainian birth certificates could be reissued with her as their mother. The boys had been named by the birth parents or by the orphanage, names that she might not have ever chosen, left to her own devices. These two boys were nineteen and 27 months old when she chose them as her sons, and had certainly come to regard the names by which they were identified and were called as their own. When they were spoken to by name, they reacted and knew they were being addressed.

In this case, Margaret had a sense that she didn't want to take their birth names away from them completely. I'm sure that she had thought about names that she liked, family names that had meaning to her for both boys and girls, and she certainly would have had no way of knowing the names of the children she would eventually choose. In this case, she gave one of the boys a new first name, preserving his Ukrainian name as his middle name. The other boy retained a version of his Ukrainian first name, but was given a new middle name. In addition, both boys received second middle names when they were baptized 6 months later.

Older children will have long become used to their names, and common sense tells us that to change the name after years of identifying with it could be unwise. For children who have been in foster care for years, living with an adult or adults and perhaps other children with a different last name, just the fact of changing their last name to match the new parent is significant by itself. It is a sign of having a "forever" family, and for a child who hasn't lived with a biological parent since being very young, it may be the first time that they've shared a last name with a caregiver. As we can all imagine, the emotional impact on an older child of having a family with only one last name could be considerable.

Since the older child is being adopted and changing his or her last name, it is a perfect opportunity to change other names – first or middle – if the child desires it. Maybe he or she has unpleasant associations to their name, or has never liked it, or perhaps would like to start afresh with a new name in a new life. The important key here is, of course, that this must be the child's wish, and not yours. As a longtime mental health professional, I have seen just about every self-centered thing that an adult can do, so I feel compelled to spell out what is probably obvious to you. For every child who wants to change what they've been called up till now, there are many more who won't want that, so as a new parent, it will be important that the child doesn't discern that you don't like their name. Letting them know that it's a possibility without suggesting it is important. And forget imposing the name you would have picked for a newborn. It the child wants to change her name, she chooses the name.

Health Insurance

Whether you are bringing home a domestic newborn, an older baby or toddler from abroad, or a local foster child, you are going to need health insurance coverage for the child from the moment you take custody and assume financial and legal responsibility for the child.

For a domestic newborn, this will start with the child's birth expenses in the hospital (he or she has a separate hospital account from the birth mother, for whom you may not be responsible). For intercountry adoptions, this may start with an illness that the child has even as you pick them up in their country of birth. You may recall that Angelina Jolie took her then 7 month old daughter, Zahara, to the hospital for malaria within days of her return home from Ethiopia. And for older children, this may start with a check-up at your own pediatrician once the child is adopted.

Very fortunately, laws have changed in the past 30+ years to make it possible, in most cases, to get this coverage for your child. In 1974, ERISA (Employee Retirement Income Security Act) Section 609 (c) changed federal law mandating that group health plans provide the same coverage for adopted children as for "natural" children, to begin "when the children are placed for adoption." At that time, there were exemptions for government employees and employees covered by church-sponsored plans because those plans were regulated at the state, not federal, level.

In 1985, COBRA (The Consolidated Omnibus Budget Reconciliation Act) made available to all employees leaving a job for any reason except gross misconduct, the opportunity to stay in the employer-sponsored health plan for up to 18 months (sometimes longer) as long as the employee paid the premium. One problem for prospective adoptive parents, though, was that if they were in the adoption process when they left the job and began COBRA, if the child was adopted during that 18 month period, he or she was not covered.

HIPAA (The Health Insurance Portability and Accountability Act of 1996), Public Law 104-91, closed that gap. Children adopted during the COBRA coverage period are now eligible for coverage.

In addition, HIPAA made other changes regarding health insurance coverage and adoption that are extremely significant and valuable for new adoptive parents. They are:

- Insurers may not impose a pre-existing condition clause or waiting period on a child under the age of 18 who is adopted or waiting for adoption if enrolled within 30 days of adoption or placement for adoption.

- Coverage is retroactive to birth, adoption, or placement for adoption.
- If eligible, you and your child may enroll in your company's health plan upon birth, adoption, or placement for adoption within 30 days, and not be treated as a "late enrollee" (i.e., you, as the adoptive parent may not be penalized with a longer waiting period for preexisting conditions, usually 18 months, but a maximum of 12 months in this case). This is called "special enrollment" and you may enroll at any time during the year, regardless of your company's period of "open season." I can't stress enough, however, that you must enroll within 30 days of birth, adoption, or placement for adoption, or you will be denied enrollment until open season. www.dol.gov/ebsa /pdf/consumerhipaa.pdf

For those of you who are self-employed or who may have individual health insurance policies because your employer does not offer health insurance, the laws are not so clear. Individual health insurance plans are regulated by each state, so federal laws for group plans do not apply. The good news is that as adoption gets more and more attention from lawmakers and from the press, state legislatures are stepping up to the plate and requiring that insurers who cover individuals offer coverage for children that come into the insured's (in this case, the prospective adoptive parent's) life after the policy has been issued. States such as California, New York, Alaska and Arizona already have laws addressing individual insurance policies and adoption. To find out whether your state has passed such laws, go to www.healthguideusa.org/state_insurance_departments.htm to peruse the list of all 50 states. Clicking on your home state will take you to the state insurance department or board for your state. Oftentimes you will be able to find the information on the website, but if not, all of the websites have "Contact us" information.

Children who are adopted from foster care are usually covered by Medicaid at the time of their adoption. The Adoption and Safe Families Act of 1997, which was designed to help older children get adopted by providing financial help to adopting families, extends Medicaid coverage to children with state-level adoption subsidy agreements if the child has special needs for "medical or rehabilitative care." Title IV-E mandates that Medicaid transfers with the child to any state of residence. If your older adopted child does not have special medical needs, or if you don't need state subsidies in order to adopt and support the child, you will probably want to cover the child with your own health insurance. Many experts advise, however, that since at the time of adoption of an older child there is no way of knowing what physical and emotional effects of foster care may come down the road, you may want to apply to keep the Medicaid coverage in addition to private health insurance. Should the child need ongoing counseling or treatment for a chronic condition, double coverage would help with copayments and deductibles each year.

Social Security Number

You may wonder why a child, especially a newborn, would need a social security number so soon. As you probably know, you now need a social security number for each child claimed as a dependent on your income taxes. In addition, if you plan to open a bank account for your child, perhaps to save for college, you will need a social security number to do so. And should your child need government services of any kind, a social security number is necessary.

If you are adopting a newborn, it is much easier to get a social security number for the baby at birth than later on. In fact, you can apply for it in the hospital when you apply for the birth certificate, and when the state is issuing the birth certificate, they will forward the information on to the Social Security Administration for the assignment of a social security number.

But once the adoption is final, if the child does not have a social security number, it will be a little more complicated to get one, but just as necessary. You must fill out Form SS-5, Application For A Social Security Card online or at the local social security office, and provide original documents proving the child's

1. U.S. Citizenship
2. Age
3. Identity

Documents accepted to provide U.S. citizenship include:

1. U.S. Birth Certificate
2. U.S. Consular Report of Birth
3. U.S. Passport
4. Certificate of Naturalization or Certificate of Citizenship

To prove age:

1. Birth certificate or passport

To prove identity:

1. U.S. Passport
2. Adoption decree
3. Doctor, clinic or hospital record
4. Religious record such as Baptismal certificate
5. Daycare center or school record
6. School ID card

All of the documents presented must be originals or copies certified by the issuing agency, in other words, no photocopies or notarized copies will be accepted. You must provide two separate documents.

As the adoptive parent, you must also prove who you are, since you will be listed with the Social Security Administration as the child's parent. You may provide two of the following:

1. Driver's License
2. Passport
3. State-issued non-driver's license ID
4. Employee ID
5. Health insurance card (not Medicare)
6. U.S. Military ID
7. Adoption decree
8. Life Insurance Policy

If your child is in your home awaiting adoption, it may be easier to wait until the adoption is final to apply for the Social Security Card for the child. This way you can have it issued in the child's new name, and have yourself listed as the child's parent with the Social Security Administration.

For tax purposes, however, a waiting child for whom you provide more than half financial support, is considered a dependent, and may be listed as one on your tax forms. Go to the IRS website and find IRS form W-7A, Application for Taxpayer Identification Number for Pending U.S. Adoptions, along with instructions. www.irs.gov/pub/irs-pdf/fw7a.pdf.

Life Insurance

If you're like many singles, you have had no dependents up till now, and have probably assumed that your savings and investments would pay for your funeral and pay off your debts when you die. Leaving money for the ongoing care and upkeep of another person hasn't been an issue that you've had to worry about.

With adoption, of course, that all changes. You now have to start planning for the future costs of raising your new child should something happen to you. You may also want to think about life insurance for the child, which I will explain later.

I recommend that you find a good financial planner, perhaps someone that a friend or family member has used and felt good about. But let me give you a brief overview of how to choose the type and amount of life insurance you need to buy.

Term vs. Whole Life: This is a somewhat controversial decision to make. Basically, term life insurance is the simplest form and is usually the least expensive. With term insurance, you pay premiums for a specific length of time, i.e, the "term," which can be from 1 to 10 years and your beneficiaries would receive the death benefit if you die during that term. When the term is over, there is no cash value. Some policies have options for renewal at the end of the term, but premiums typically go up when the new term policy is written. Most companies will not write term policies for people over 65, and at about age 50, premiums may become prohibitively high. That's where whole life insurance comes in.

Whole Life is usually more expensive and includes a "forced savings" called "cash value." After a few years, should you win the lottery or find a better deal, the cash value is the amount of money you would receive back if you cancelled the policy. You can also borrow from that cash value while the policy is in effect.

Universal and Variable Life Insurance are simply whole life policies where you earn more or have some control over the investing of your cash value.

Suze Orman, one of my favorite financial gurus, says, "I hate whole life insurance. I hate universal life insurance, I hate variable life insurance. The only type I like – for the purposes of insuring your life – is term insurance!" www.SuzeOrman.com She believes that there are much better ways to save and invest and that life insurance should be used only for the death benefit.

If you'd like to do some research, go to her website, www.SuzeOrman.com, or www.Smartmoney.com (click on Personal Finance in the left menu, then Insurance, and then "Term or Whole Life?" under Life Insurance in the middle of the page) or read an article on MSN Money, (Go to www.MSN.com then click on "Money," "Insurance", "Life Insurance," and then "Expert Advice – The Raging Debate Over Term vs Whole Life") and decide for yourself.

Most experts agree, though, that as long as your child is under 25, is still a student, or has special needs, you need to prepare for the care of that child in the event of your death. Term insurance can be purchased for that time period (say you adopt a newborn – elect a ten year renewable term, or a 15 year old, a ten year term). Whole Life, of course, might be the insurance of choice if you adopt a handicapped child that will need help all of his or her life, so that if you die at 80 and the child is 40, there will be a death benefit paid to the child.

How much life insurance should you buy? Sit down and think about how much it will cost to support yourself and your new family. Both Suze Orman and Smart Money have online calculators to help you determine how much money it would take for someone to raise your child. Go to www.SuzeOrman.com, and find Resource Center on the left side menu. Then click on "Insurance", and then "Online Calculators". There you will find both the Kiplinger Insurance Calculator and the CNN and Money Magazine Insurance Calculators. Or go to www.Smartmoney.com (click on "Personal Finance" in the left menu, then "Insurance", and then "How Much Do You Need?" under Life Insurance at the top of the page).

At www.SuzeOrman.com 's Resource Center, you can also find links to Insurance Rating Services such as Standard and Poor, or Moodys, which will tell how financially sound each insurance company is (they have ratings based upon their ability to pay claims). Also check out her link to Insurance Quote Services to compare rates.

More information you need to know: Your credit rating affects your insurance rates, so that is another reason to pay attention to your money. Smoking and being overweight can double your annual premiums. And ask about all discounts. Some are rather strange and you would never think of them. Look at the companies that you might already use to insure your house or car. They may offer discounts to persuade you to let them cover your life, as well.

About insuring your child. There are, as usual, two sides to this issue. Babies and children are very insurable and premiums tend to be very low for their policies. Because they don't have dependents, however, some financial advisors question the need for life insurance on them, saying that once they reach adulthood and have kids of their own, they can buy their own life insurance.

But adopted children are more likely to have special needs and may not be able to get life insurance at a reasonable price, or at all, when they're older. And some teenagers do become parents, as we know, so having a dependent does not necessarily mean being grown. It's something to consider and make your own decision about.

Wills and Trusts

You may already have a will, that document that expresses your wishes for disposition of your estate when you die. Now is the time to add your child to your will to make sure that your planning for the child is spelled out quickly should you die suddenly.

You've already taken out life insurance to ensure that your child's expenses will be provided for. The will will give instructions as to how that will take place.

One very serious issue to consider is the establishing of a trust to provide for a seamless availability of money to care for your child. These trusts are called "Living Trusts" or "Revocable Trusts," and not only help your child and other family members avoid estate taxes on your possessions (which will include your home, investments, savings, and pensions), but will also avoid probate – that is, going to the court to get permission to carry out the wishes you expressed in your will. Probate can be a lengthy and expensive process, and in the meantime, someone will need to feed and house your child.

While your life insurance death benefit is usually tax-free, most insurance companies advise that you set up a trust for the proceeds so that the child's guardians can have access to the money to support the child. The guardian and successor trustee can be the same person. Keep in mind that in probate, the court can control the child's money until he or she is 18, and that includes life insurance proceeds.

If your estate has to be settled in court, which can take as long as several years, your beneficiaries will have to pay income tax on the estate during that time while not having access to your money. Trusts do not involve the court at all. The person you appoint to be your Successor Trustee (you are the Trustee when you are alive) will be able to spend money on the child's behalf immediately. Just think about it. You can read about the differences between wills and trusts at www.completetrusts.com/trust_vs_will.html.

Be sure to read "Marcia's Story" to get an idea of what can happen when property is left to a child in a will rather than in a trust.

Have you given some thought to who you would like to take your child should something happen to you? I'm going to talk about how wills and trusts will affect your choice of who will raise your child if you die.

In your will, you will make your wishes known as to who should raise your child should you die. If you are in a committed relationship, that person may be an obvious choice for you. If you are unattached, however, you will need to think about all of the friends and family members who are committed to you, and who would be the best person for your child.

First, make a list of all of the people who come to mind. You will want to think about their lifestyles, their values, both personal and religious, and whose parenting style would most likely be closest to yours. You will want to consider who would be able to take on the responsibility in terms of time and interest, and who is emotionally most equipped to be a parent to your child. Do they already have children, and would there be room emotionally and physically for another child? Does the child like or love the adult that you're considering, and does the adult like or love your child? Where does the adult live and what would that mean to your child?

Once you've picked one or two adults who you think would be good parents to your child, sit down and talk with them. They might enthusiastically say yes, or no, and give you more of an idea of how they would be with your child. Finally, pick an adult or couple and put your choice in your will. You might also need to choose a second person as an alternate in the event that circumstances may change for your first choice over time.

Unfortunately, since a will is viewed legally as nothing more than an expression of your wishes, you cannot be sure that the person you choose to be a legal guardian of your child will in fact be appointed if your will has to be probated. The court is allowed to decide what they consider to be in the best interests of the child, and that may be someone completely different in their eyes.

This is especially important for those of you who are gay or lesbian. In most states you will not be legally married to your partner if you have one now, or if you settle down with someone in the future and that partner may or may not adopt your child while you're together. This is called "Second-Parent Adoption" and is not legal in all states.

Of course you would want your child to stay with his or her other parent, your partner. The trauma of losing one parent is bad enough, without having to face losing both parents. But if your will, which would include your child, ends up in probate, conservative courts could determine that it's in the best interests of the child to be raised by someone heterosexual. A trust does not guarantee that your family might not use legal means to try to take the child, but at least without probate, your partner won't have to be scrutinized by the courts during the probate process. Again, check it out and think about it. www.Completetrusts.com/trust_vs_will.html where you'll find a lot of information about trusts in the Frequently Asked Questions, or www.janetdlaw.com, click on "Resources", then "Trusts", "Estate Taxes", and "Wills and Probate."

Religious Ceremonies and Godparents

Priest: *Dear Friends: It has pleased God our heavenly Father to answer the earnest prayers of Katherine, member of this Christian family, for the gift of a child. I bid you join with her in offering heartfelt thanks for the joyful and solemn responsibility which is hers by the coming of Brian to be a member of her family. But first, our friends wish us, here assembled, to witness the inauguration of this new relationship.*

Priest: Katherine, do you take this child for your own?

Parent: I do.

[Then if the child is old enough to answer, the Priest asks]

Priest: Brian, do you take this woman as your mother?

Child: I do.

[Then the Priest, holding or taking the child by the hand, gives the child to the mother..., saying]

Priest: As God has made us his children by adoption and grace, may you receive Brian as your own son.

[Then the parent says these or similar words]

Parent: May God, the Father of all, bless my child Brian, and I who have given to him my family name, that we may live together in love and affection, through Jesus Christ our Lord. Amen.

Priest: May God the Father, who by Baptism adopts us as his children, grant you Grace. Amen.

Based upon "A Thanksgiving for the Birth or Adoption of a Child," The Book of Common Prayer (of the Episcopal Church of the United States of America), p. 440.

This section discusses religious rituals, including baptism, and the choosing of godparents and how they may differ in role from guardians. The above ritual is from the prayer book in my church, and is done during a service soon after the child is brought home to live with you. Most religions have similar rituals that may be performed to welcome your child into your spiritual community and to bless your new relationship. Some are called Naming Ceremonies, others are called Dedications of a Baby or New Child. If you are a member of a religious community of any kind, you are probably familiar with what is offered. Talk with your clergyperson about what may be available for you and your child.

The most common religious ceremony observed after the addition of a new child to your family is baptism. Baptism is generally seen as the initiation of the child into the Christian faith and into the Christian family, and is usually performed in liturgical churches (Roman Catholic, Orthodox, Lutheran, Episcopal, Anglican, etc.) in infancy. Other Christian denominations perform baptisms when the individual is old enough to embrace and accept Christianity on their own. This section will address the former – infants or small children whom you decide will become members of your church through baptism. What do you need to do?

As soon as you find out that you will be a parent is a good time to begin talking to your clergyperson. Many denominations require that parents take a class to learn about the ritual and to discuss the theology of their church surrounding baptism. This will give you a chance to think about your own religious beliefs and to confirm that this is something that you really want to do. If you are unsure, it will give you time to talk with friends, family members and clergy to answer your questions about your religion, and to be able to make the right choice for you and your child.

Many adults who were raised in a particular denomination may find that after they left home they fell away from the religion in which they were raised. It may not have even been a question as they lived their single lives. But many find that becoming a parent makes them start thinking about religion and the church for the first time in years. They remember the religious rituals of their childhood and begin to think that it may be something that they want to give to their child. Some believe that baptism is the only way to ensure the eternal safety of the child, and others just find that they are feeling more religious and spiritual when they think about the enormous responsibility that they're taking on.

If you've made the decision to adopt, and if you would say that you are a spiritual and/or religious person, you may want to start thinking about the rituals of the religion you choose.

Once you've talked with a clergyperson or taken a class at your church, you'll probably want to start thinking about choosing godparents for your child. Depending upon the denomination, you may need to consider the religion of the people that you're considering. Some churches, such as Roman Catholicism, require that the godparents be baptized Roman Catholics to be eligible. Others require that the godparents be Christian of some form, and others have no requirements about religion. It is generally believed, however, that the people that you choose will be spiritual guides for your child, and will ensure that they are raised in a religious or spiritual home.

In the Episcopal Church, godparents are called sponsors, and are asked during the Baptismal service, "Will you be responsible for seeing that the child you present is brought up in the Christian faith and life?" And the sponsor responds, "I will, with God's help." They are then asked, "Will you by your prayers and witness help this child to grow into the full stature of Christ?" The sponsor answers, "I will, with God's help." Finding out what your denomination requires will help you decide if the people that you have in mind could answer the questions that are asked by your church.

Generally, you will want to make a list of people that would want to be involved with your child throughout their growing up. We can assume that family members feel this way already, and will be involved with our child anyway. One thought is that asking people outside of your family brings more adults into the child's life in a significant way, and adds to the positive attention and love that he or she will get as they grow up. It is worth considering.

Some people consider Godparents to be more than spiritual guides for their children, and assume that they are choosing people who would raise their children should something happen to them. And that might be true for you.

Legally, people who would raise our children should we die are called Guardians, and are either appointed by you in your will or trust, or by the court should you die without indicating who you would like to take over your role as a parent. If you decide that one of your child's godparents will also be the person who would raise your child after your death, in addition to including them in the Baptismal service, you also need to put them in your will as Guardian. If necessary, reread the above section on Wills and Trusts to see what steps you need to take to make this possible.

Flexible Spending Account (FSA)

In Chapter II, we discussed the financial side of adoption in terms of the costs associated with the adoption itself. You also need to think about the ongoing costs of having a child, and so now we're going to talk about a way to lower the health care and childcare costs for your new son or daughter.

Most of you are probably familiar with the Flexible Spending Account (FSA), and if you work for a government or for a medium to large company, may already have one. But in case you don't yet have one, or don't know the ins and outs of getting one and what they actually do for you, here goes. FSAs allow you to designate a pretax amount of money up to $5,000 per year per account to be deducted from each paycheck and deposited into a savings account to be used for specifically allowed expenses.

The beauty of an FSA is that you actually get to pay your medical, dental, and vision care bills with pretax money. Say you are in the 25% tax bracket once you are a parent, and therefore, "head of household" – that would be taxable income between $42,650 and $110,000 per year, and your state and FICA (social security) taxes add approximately 11-12% (state, on average of 4% and FICA, 7.65%), you are effectively in a 37% total tax bracket. On $5,000 of income, that is a $1,850 tax break that can be used for medical care of you and your child, something to write home about!

As you know, the Federal government has a 7.5% threshold on Adjusted Gross Income for medical expense tax deductions, meaning that if you were to decide to itemize medical expenses rather than use an FSA, the first 7.5% of your medical costs would not be deductible. And, all Health and Dependent Care FSA deposits, in addition to being federally tax-free, are also exempt from FICA (social security) taxes, a deduction not available on your tax return.

The most common form of FSA is the Health Savings Account (sometimes called Medical FSA, Medical Expense FSA, or Health FSA), and is used in conjunction with a high deductible health insurance plan to pay deductibles, copayments, and most wonderfully, for over-the-counter medications (wonderful because the federal government does not recognize the cost of over-the-counter drugs as tax-deductible expenses). The expenses must be for an illness or medical condition (in other words, not for cosmetic surgery), for you or your dependents. For a list of allowable expenses, go to www.irs.gov/publications/p502/index.html.

The rules for establishing a Health FSA are that your health insurance deductible must be higher than average (High Deductible Health Plan, or "HDHP"), a minimum of $2,100 for family coverage (you and your child), and the allowable maximum annual out-of-pocket expenses before the health insurance company pays 100% can be no higher than $10,500. This is for in-network coverage.

Self-employed adoptive parents can set up a Health FSA called an Archer Medical Savings Account (MSA) through a bank or insurance company (authorized by the Health Insurance Portability and Accountability Act of 1996, January 1, 1997). Like a regular FSA, it also requires a High Deductible Health Plan (HDHP), and for family coverage requires a minimum annual deductible of $3,650, a maximum annual deductible of $5,450, and maximum out-of-pocket expenses of $6,650 before the health insurance company pays 100%. See www.irs.gov/publications/p969/ ar02.html.

A second type of FSA is designated for dependent care, such as daycare, before- or after-school care, and summer day camp, for children aged 13 and under, or those who are mentally or physically unable to be left alone, and of course, uses pretax money. Health FSAs and Dependent Care FSAs are considered separate accounts, and you may deduct up to $5,000 from your income per year for each account, for a total of $10,000 annually. For a list of allowable Dependent Care expenses and an explanation of each, go to www.aetna.com/fsa/understanding/dependent/dependentcareexpenses.html.

Health FSAs are what is called "pre-funded," meaning that if you designate $5,000 a year to be deducted in 26 pay period increments beginning in January of your work year, and your child needs surgery for a birth defect in February, all $5,000 is available to you at that time, although only a small portion would have actually been deposited to date.

Dependent Care FSAs are not pre-funded, and many require that you pay the first month's childcare fees out of pocket before the plan begins to pay. Because childcare fees are usually accrued and charged monthly, the plan makes sense. Your deduction of pretax money goes in twice a month, and you file a claim for reimbursement each month for payment to your childcare provider.

Not every employer who offers Health FSAs offers Dependent Care FSAs, but the tax savings are so significant that I would recommend that you talk to your employer about the possibility of setting up Dependent Care FSAs as a benefit of your job.

Most employers have an annual open enrollment period when you are invited to make changes in your benefits, as discussed earlier in the section on Health Insurance. It is during this open enrollment period that most employers ask you to determine the amount you'd like to have deducted and set aside for your Health and Dependent Care FSAs. If you are in the adoption process, it may be a good idea to plan ahead for the next 14 ½ months and to begin to save for your new child's expenses.

Adoption, or placement for adoption, is considered to be a "Qualifying Life Event," just as it is for Health Insurance. That means that if you decide to adopt after the open enrollment period is over, but before the next open enrollment period, you can change your benefits within 30 days, including your FSAs.

Claims may be made for reimbursement from your Health FSA for expenses incurred until March 15th for money deposited through December of the previous year. In other words, you save for 12 months, January through December, but may use the money for 14 ½ months, January through March 15th of the next year. It is important to note that FSAs have a "use-it-or-lose-it" rule. Any money not used by March 15th of the following year is lost. The 2 ½ months give you time to arrange all of you and your child's check-ups, should you have a surplus.

Family Medical Leave

Depending upon the age of the child that you decide to adopt, you may want to take some time off from work when you bring the child home. With adoption of an older child from foster care, you've probably been living with and caring for the child for some months. The child is already established in school, daycare, or with a babysitter, and the actual adoption, while an emotionally significant event, doesn't change the day to day workings of your household.

If you are bringing a newborn, toddler or a child from another country into your home, however, life as you've known it will never be the same! Margaret Schwartz, who adopted two toddler boys from Ukraine, arrived home shortly before Christmas and stayed home for months, working on potty training, language, getting to know her kids, and trying to get used to the daily routine of having children.

Other friends of mine, who adopted a six year old girl from Kazakhstan, also arrived home shortly before Christmas, but put her in school the day classes resumed after the New Year. She went to school with an older sister, went to afterschool care with her sister, and came home with her mom as she left work. In this case, there was actually no need for a lot of time off, because it was really in the best interest of the child to be in school and around other children rather than being at home with Mom.

So, obviously this decision is going to be based on the age of the child, where the child is coming from (intercountry, foster care, newborn), and her needs for the first weeks and months that she's in your family. Should you decide to stay home for awhile, however, you should know about the Family and Medical Leave Act of 1993, which requires employers with 50 or more employees to give you at least 12 weeks of unpaid leave to care for a child.

You must have worked for that employer at least 1,250 hours over 12 months, and if "foreseeable," give 30 days notice of your intention to take the leave. You can use Family Medical Leave once every 12 months, should you plan to adopt again! Some employers will require that you use paid leave first, but then you would be eligible for unpaid leave when paid leave is exhausted.

You are also eligible to maintain your health insurance coverage during that time.

State laws vary on how much leave you can take, and even on whether it is paid or unpaid. For instance, California, Minnesota and Washington offer paid family leave, and Tennessee requires companies of 8 or more employees to offer 16 weeks for the birth or adoption of a new child. The National Conference of State Legislatures has published a state-by-state list of laws and requirements, and since they vary widely, go to www.ncsl.org/programs/employ/fmlachart.htm to check out your state's requirements.

School or Childcare

After you've brought your new child into your home, unless you have the luxury of being a stay-at-home parent, you are going to need to arrange for a place for the child to be during the day while you work. Depending upon the age of the child, this may be a babysitter, nanny, or au pair in your home, family daycare in someone else's home, a daycare center, or school. In most cases, unless you have a family member waiting in the wings to help out, you're going to need to start making these arrangements before you bring your child home. Let's look at the basics of each.

If you're adopting a newborn or infant, you probably will want to keep your child at home to try to keep her in a familiar environment and to minimize travel and exposure to illness and weather. A baby is happy with an adult and doesn't yet need the company of other children. This, however, will be your most expensive option.

The fewer children a caregiver is responsible for, the more expensive he or she will be. With only your child, your babysitter will rely on you for her total income. If you know someone who is also looking for childcare who could split the cost with you, it becomes a little more affordable. Depending upon your area of the country and its economy, expect to pay $300-$500 per week for a caregiver who comes to your home every day.

Another in-home option is the au pair. The au pair is usually a 19-25 year old woman from Europe, Scandinavia, or South America who lives in your home for a year, with the option to sign on for a second year. You must provide a separate bedroom, meals, and can only expect her to work a normal work week. If you work during the day, she gets evenings and weekends off, and here in the Washington, D.C. area you pay her about $175 per week. She will want to pursue a social life, meet with other au pairs, especially those from her country, and may date. With most agencies you will be able to interview (by telephone) potential candidates and choose the young woman who feels right for you. If you choose wisely, you may make a lifelong friend for you and your child.

And then there is out-of-home care. This can be a daycare center or a family daycare provider. Both will be licensed by your county or state and have been required to complete training in such things as infant and child CPR. You should be able to find them by going to your county website. You can also go to www.childcareaware.org/en/, find the Childcare Connector, enter your zip code, and find the Childcare Referral Agency in your area. This site is sponsored by the Childcare Bureau of the U.S. Department of Health and Human Services. Expect to pay between $100 and $300 per week, depending upon your area of the country. Your Childcare Referral Agency should be able to provide rates for you.

Finding child daycare can be difficult. Ask your friends about their experiences with different centers and home providers, and if one comes highly recommended, visit it as soon as possible. High-quality child daycare providers can have waiting lists of up to a year or more.

When you visit the childcare center or provider, you will need to ask questions about the ratio of childcare providers to children, level of training of the providers and their rate of turnover each year. You will also want to observe the providers interact with the children – do they seem to enjoy them? Are they patient with the children? Do they actually play with the children, or do they sit with their coworkers and talk? Does there seem to be a variety of toys and activities? Is the facility clean? Is the furniture kid-size? Do the children seem happy?

The American Psychological Association Public Interest Directorate has a list of questions that you may want to ask. You can find them at www.apa.org/pi/cyf/daycare.html. Another website with an excellent article on evaluating daycare can be found at www.daycare.com/news/tips.html. Or go to www.arizonachildcare.org, click on "Parent Resources," then "Quality Checklist."

If your child is 5 or older, you need to think about preparing for school registration. Here in Arlington County, Virginia, children are expected to be in school within days of arriving in the county. You need to check with your school district when you find out that your adoption is imminent in order to prepare the documents necessary for school registration. In general, you will need the following:

1. Proof of the child's age and legal name, usually a birth certificate
2. Proof that the parent or legal guardian of the student lives in the school district, usually a lease or home purchase documents
3. Social Security Number or a Social Security Status Form
4. Official school records from another school system or country, if available
5. Medical information including immunization records, a physical examination and a TB screening done within 12 months prior to starting school
6. An Authorization for Medication if your child will be on any type of medication that would need to be administered during the school day
7. Application for Extended Day (before and/or after school care), if applicable.

If your child has special needs physically or emotionally, doesn't speak English, or has learning disabilities, you will probably need to set up an evaluation with the school district. If you are in a foster-to-adopt or pre-adoptive period, you may not be allowed to sign an Individual Education Plan (IEP) for special education, behavior and/or speech classes. If this is true in your school district, ask about Education Advocates which are essentially appointed school guardians. They will sign off on IEPs until you are legally the child's parent.

You will need to set up a physical examination for your child as soon as you find out when the child will be moving in with you, or as soon as you get word that it's time to go abroad to pick her up. This will make the school registration process possible when you return, and will also give you peace of mind that your child is getting treated for any illnesses that she might have.

Preparing Your Home

At this point you have probably given up your one bedroom apartment for a two bedroom, and have begun to furnish it with a crib, or a youth bed, or furniture for a teenager. You've thought about a circus theme, or wall colors, or accessories that your new child will require. It's fun to think about clothes, toys, or furniture and you probably don't need any help doing that. Your friends and family will more than likely be glad to give you advice, hand-me-downs or even an adoption shower.

You've gone through so much to get a son or daughter, and the last thing you want is for your new child to get hurt or sick or worse once you get them home. This section will alert you to dangers that you may never have considered, with some suggestions on how to remedy them. It will also include some useful websites to help you learn more.

Let's start with childproofing your home for the baby, toddler, or preschooler. These are the ages where your child can move faster than lightning and can imagine "new uses" for household items that would never occur to you. We all know about the obvious: covering electrical outlets, removing breakable objects from low tables, and safety latches on kitchen cabinet doors and drawers. But did you know about window blind cords and how they can hurt a baby or toddler, or that many household and garden plants are toxic to humans?

Here is a list of things that you need to do according to the U.S. Product Safety Commission:

1. Safety latches and locks for cabinets and drawers anywhere that there is something poisonous, such as household cleaners, bleach, medicines, alcohol, or sharp and/or breakable items such as knives, glassware,

barbeque skewers, icepicks, etc. You need to think about all the ways a child could use a tool that would not be its intended use. And about what would happen should he put it in his mouth or bring it towards his face.

2. Safety gates – Do not use pressure gates, that is, the gates that stay in place with springs that tighten them against the walls. Install gates that screw into the wall, and put them at the top of the stairs and in entrances to any rooms that are off-limits. Newer safety gates have certifications from The Juvenile Products Manufacturer's Association.

3. Door knob covers and door locks – Many a parent has left a child in the living room happily playing, only to return to find him gone and outside. We usually realize that a child has learned to turn a doorknob for the first time when he's entered or left a room when he shouldn't have, and you certainly don't want your 2 year old wandering down the street. Put locks on doors to rooms like shops, garages, basements, and sewing rooms to keep your child from having access to expensive or dangerous items.

4. Set your water heater to 120 degrees. Turn away from a toddler in a bath for 5 seconds and the hot water can be turned on, resulting in scalding.

5. Smoke detectors near bedrooms and on every level.

6. Window guards for when windows are open. Screens are not strong enough to contain a child leaning on them. Also, safety netting for balconies and decks, to keep a small child or baby from squeezing through the bars.

7. Corner and edge bumpers for sharp corners on tables and fireplace hearths.

8. Outlet covers and plates, of course.

9. Carbon Dioxide (CO) Detectors near bedrooms, especially if you have an attached garage and oil or gas heat.

10. Window blind cords are a strangulation hazard if your child's crib is near a window, or if the child can reach

the cords from the floor. Window blind cords need to be cut to eliminate potential nooses, so that all cords hang simply with a tassel and inner cord stops. You can do this yourself by going to www.windowcoverings.org/howtorepair.html. You can get free tassels from the Window Coverings Safety Council at the same address.

11. Door stops and door holders. A friend tells me that the first time her son locked himself in the bathroom, she had to take the lock out completely to get him out! A door holder goes near the door hinge to keep it from closing. Disabling a lock, or putting the lock high enough in the door that the child can't reach it also works.

12. Use a cordless phone so that you aren't stuck in one room with your children in another. www.cpsc.gov/cpscpub/pubs/grand/12steps/12steps.html.

Look around for bookcases, aquariums, lamps, entertainments centers, TV stands, even refrigerators (when open) that can be climbed by a rambunctious toddler. They have been known to topple over onto the child and can injure him. These pieces of furniture and appliances may need to be attached or bolted to the wall to prevent such an accident. You can also buy appliance locking straps to make it so that your child cannot open the oven door, the refrigerator, or the dishwasher (sharp knives and glassware again!).

You might want to install knob covers on your stove, so that your child cannot turn on the stove or oven. When cooking, turn pan handles inward so that they can't be reached, and whenever possible, use the back burners rather than the front ones. http://www.pediatrics.about.com.

Plants: I was totally surprised by the number of plants that are toxic to children. Here is a short list of common plants to remove from your home and your yard:

1. Azalea bushes
2. Rhododendron
3. Daffodils
4. Holly bushes

5. Irises
6. Lilies of the Valley
7. Mistletoe
8. Morning Glory
9. Philodendron

For a complete list, go to http://www.poison.org/prevent/plants.asp.

Luckily, some common plants are safe. Notice that the Poinsettia is considered to be safe because it may only cause irritation.

1. Coleus
2. Dandelion
3. Petunia
4. Poinsettia
5. Roses
6. African violets
7. Swedish Ivy
8. Impatiens

Here is one last list of things to consider:

1. Cover trash containers, for obvious reasons.
2. Never carry hot liquid when carrying your child, or when your child is at your feet.
3. Do not use the microwave to heat a baby bottle. Even when it feels comfortable to the touch, it can contain pockets of very hot milk that can burn the baby's mouth.
4. Store plastic bags of all kinds, especially grocery store and shopping bags. They are a suffocation hazard.
5. Use only plastic or paper cups in the bathroom.
6. Keep coins, buttons, etc., out of reach. They are a choking hazard.
7. You may want to install toilet lid locks so that your child can't fall headfirst into the water. Also, use non-slip bath mats and keep appliances far away from the tub.

8. It might be a good idea to stop using tablecloths for awhile until your child is older. You don't want her to pull dishes, vases, etc. over onto her head.

9. And last. Sit on the floor and crawl around your home at your child's eye level. You'll be able to see what she will see and what will look enticing. www.arizonachildcare.org, click on "Provider Resources," then "Safety." Or go to the University of California at San Francisco Patient Education site, www.ucsfhealth.org/childrens/edu/ wellBaby/childproofing.html

Of course, no one expects you to do everything listed above. Most of us grew up with at least one toxic plant in the yard, and came to no harm! I, however, was a plant eater, which tells me that we have to be on the lookout for personality differences, quirkinesses, and temperaments, and react accordingly. You will know soon enough if your child is a climber or an explorer, and hopefully the above list will help you decide what to do at that point.

Resources

- For information about health insurance. www.dol.gov/ebsa/pdf/consumerhipaa.pdf
- For information about state laws and individual policies www.healthguideusa.org/state_insurance_departments.htm
- Application for Taxpayer Identification Number for Pending U.S. Adoptions, along with instructions. www.irs.gov/pub/irs-pdf/fw7a.pdf.
- Life Insurance www.money.CNN.com/, www.Smartmoney.com/insurance/, www.SuzeOrman.com, www.MSN.com
- How much life insurance? www.SuzeOrman.com, www.smartmoney.com/insurance/
- Wills and Trusts www.completetrusts.com/trust_vs_will.html, www.janetdlaw.com
- Flexible Spending Accounts www.irs.gov/publications/p502/index.html, www.irs.gov/publications/p969/ar02.html
- Dependent Care FSAs, www.aetna.com/fsa/understanding/dependent/dependentcareexpenses.html
- Family Medical Leave Act, www.ncsl.org/programs/employ/fmlachart.htm
- Childcare Referral Agency, www.childcareaware.org/en/
- Daycare, www.apa.org/pi/cyf/daycare.html, www.daycare.com/news/tips.html
- Window Blind Cords, www.windowcoverings.org/howtorepair.html
- Childproofing your home, www.cpsc.gov/cpscpub/pubs/grand/12steps/12steps.html, www.pediatrics.about.com, www.arizonachildcare.org
- Poisonous plants, www.poison.org/prevent/plants.asp

Chapter VI

What if Adoption is Not for You?

Well, at this point, if you've read or skimmed through the entire book, you've pretty much seen what is available to you and what it's going to take to adopt. Your gut is either telling you that this is an exciting possibility and you feel, perhaps, scared but eager to move forward. Maybe your gut tells you to do it now, or maybe it says that by next year you'll be ready. Either way, it feels like the right thing for you, when the time is right.

But maybe you are a gay man or a lesbian and live in Florida or Mississippi, or you are straight or gay and in a cohabiting relationship in Utah. You've discovered by reading the book that you are not allowed to adopt in your state, and you don't want to leave home in order to become a parent.

Or maybe your gut is telling you that adoption is just not the right thing for you. You may be feeling that you can't be a parent at all. You may also be feeling that you really only want to raise your own biological child. Or you may be feeling like adoption is just too much to take on, but you'd like to live with a child and take it slowly. Or even just have an ongoing relationship with a child and see what it feels like.

As I noted in the introduction, parenting options that require assisted reproduction – artificial insemination and surrogacy – are discussed in a free document on the book's website. www.adoptionforsinglesbook.com Inclusion in the book, whether in an interview or a directory, does not imply support or endorsement of assisted reproduction.

In this chapter we're going to discuss other options that are open to you. They are:

1. Foster Care
2. Respite Foster Care
3. Mentoring programs such as Big Brother/Big Sister

Foster Care

One very good way of finding out how it feels to parent a child day to day for a long period of time is to become a foster parent. The process is similar to becoming an adoptive parent, but it does not result in permanent custody of the child. Requirements vary from jurisdiction to jurisdiction (for instance, you must be 21 years of age in Arizona, but only 18 in Florida), but are generally as follows:

1. You may be single or divorced.
2. You do not have to own a home, but must have room for the child. Some jurisdictions require a separate bedroom, while some will allow the foster child to share a room with a same-gender child, as long as she has her own bed. No sharing with you.
3. You must be at least 21 in most states.
4. You may work outside the home.
5. You must be able to work with social service, health and school professionals within the system.
6. No one in your home can have a criminal or abuse registry record.
7. You have adequate income to support yourself and your family before the addition of the foster child.
8. Your home must pass a health and safety inspection.
9. You must be a legal U.S. resident.
10. You must be physically and emotionally able to care for a child.

If you think that you would be interested in becoming a foster parent, but are concerned about the costs of parenting a child, check out the following website to see what your state pays for the maintenance of a foster child. www.hunter.cuny.edu/socwork/ nrcfcpp/downloads/foster-care-maintenance-payments.pdf

If you meet the general requirements, the process is:

1. Contact your local county department of social services to indicate your interest in becoming a foster parent.

Some counties also contract out foster care services to private social service agencies, so ask if there is one near your home. Reserve your spot at a regularly scheduled informational meeting, where you will learn the requirements for your locality. You will also need to complete a formal application. Be prepared to supply financial information, a physician's health statement, fingerprinting, references, and a criminal background check.

2. Attend a pre-service training course. This can vary from county to county, but generally consists of 10 3-hour sessions (30 hours) designed to help you understand the role of the foster parent. You will learn about the children who may need your care – their circumstances, what to expect if they've been abused or neglected, and how to parent them given the losses they're experiencing from being taken away from their loved ones. You will need to ask a lot of questions and begin to explore your feelings about what kinds of children you can foster. Some people will realize that they can't deal with abused, older children, and will want to make themselves available for small children and babies only. Some will realize that they can't take on the care of an infant, or will want only girls. You will be encouraged to look at your own limitations and decide whether this is right for you, the right time for you, and where you can be of the most help. You will be introduced to all of the members of the foster care team and learn each person's role in the care of your foster child. These are the people who will support you and be available for day to day advice.

3. Next is the Home Study, which is essentially the same as the Home Study described in Chapter IV. If you didn't read that chapter carefully, let me reassure you that it is not as scary as it sounds! When most of us hear the words "Home Study" we get visions of someone coming into our home with white gloves, looking to eliminate us from consideration because we are not perfect enough! Social workers are not looking

to eliminate us or they would never find enough foster homes for all the kids that need them. This step is simply the most personal and collaborative, the time when the social worker interviews household members, discusses with us our feelings about all the issues these kids can have and which kids we could best parent, and determines whether our home is a safe place for children. It is a very thorough process and could take weeks or even months. You know who you are and whether you can be trusted with a child, but you are an unknown to the foster care system. Imagine the care you would want taken if you were the foster child.

4. After the social worker has completed her study and all the interviews, checked all your references, and the criminal background checks are done, she will submit her report to the Department of Social Services, or in some states, the court. It will include information on what kind of child or children you want to foster, and will recommend that you be certified or licensed as a foster parent. You are now ready for a placement.

Some of you may be concerned about the types of children that are available for foster care. You may be worried that they are all terribly scarred, or difficult, or sick. I'd like to tell you about a grown-up foster child who has recently written a book about her life, where she came from, and the scores of people who held her hand along the way.

Her name is Victoria Rowell, and you may know her as the recently departed Drucilla Winters on the television daytime drama, *The Young and the Restless*, or from her numerous roles in other television shows and feature films. She is also a humanitarian – the founder of the Rowell Foster Children Positive Plan, which provides scholarships in the arts to foster children, and serves as national spokeswoman for the Annie E. Casey Foundation/Casey Family Services, established in 1948 to support public policy and community efforts to help vulnerable children and families. Let me tell you a little bit about Victoria as a child in foster care.

Victoria was born to a mentally-ill white mother and an unknown black father, and with two older sisters, was taken from her mother's custody at birth. As a mixed race baby in the State of Maine in 1959, foster care and adoption by white families was discouraged, and by the age of two, Victoria was placed with a black couple who had already raised ten children. This placement reunited her with her two older sisters, and would turn out to be the most emotionally significant and long term placement that she would have as a foster child. She and her sisters were never available for adoption because at that time birth mothers had the legal right to refuse termination of parental rights. Today, a schizophrenic mother with four children in foster care would eventually have her parental rights terminated when it was determined that her mental illness was intractable and unremitting, and that the likelihood of her ever being able to effectively parent was extremely low.

So Victoria had two strikes against her. A mentally-ill birth mother and no potential for adoption and all the privileges that come with it.

She is included in this section, however, to give you a vivid example of how most of the time it all boils down to the love, support, physical nurturing and expectation of boundless potential in determining the outcome for a foster child. Victoria grew up with gumption, an eager, curious, and obviously gifted child. At age 8, after several years of her foster mother teaching her ballet from a book, Victoria received a scholarship from the Ford Foundation to study at her first ballet school. As an older teenager, she took care of herself in New York City so that she could study at the American Ballet Theatre.

If you are wondering about foster children and what you may be able to give to a child even if you are not an adoptive parent, I strongly encourage you to read Victoria's autobiography, *The Women Who Raised Me*, Harper Collins, 2007. You can buy it at any bookstore or from her website, www.VictoriaRowell.com. It is an astounding story and beautifully and poetically written. If you're thinking of adopting from foster care, read this book to see how resilient and strong foster kids can be. Anyone would have loved to be her mother.

Respite Foster Care

Respite Foster Care is simply foster care that is not full-time. Children in foster care, or children in homes without constant adult supervision are sometimes placed in respite foster homes for a weekend, a few days, or a few weeks to give the parents or regular foster parents a break. The process for becoming a respite foster parent is the same as for regular foster care. If you are not ready to parent a child full-time, but would like the experience of having a child in your home from time to time, consider being a respite foster parent. There is a constant need for them, and you would be helping at the same time that you are trying the role on for size.

Mentoring

The easiest way to start the process of finding out how you feel about spending time with kids is to become a mentor. This may involve spending social time together or becoming a tutor in your local department of education or school district. I'm going to tell you about Big Brothers Big Sisters, probably the best-known mentoring program in the country.

Big Brothers Big Sisters (BBBS) is a national program that is actually very easy to join. You have your choice of school-based matches, where you spend about an hour a week with your "Little" (you are the "Big") at school having lunch, doing homework, reading in the library, or shooting hoops. You can also opt for community-based matches, where you and your "Little" spend time together based upon when you both are free. It is flexible and probably more recreationally based. You can go to a museum, take a ride, listen to music, or do a jigsaw puzzle. Anything that gives you time to talk and get to know each other. The relationship is mostly one-to-one, at least initially until you get to know each other and feel comfortable with each other. You can bring your significant others into the relationship down the road, but it is important at the outset to spend time alone together to bond.

Children are from all socio-economic groups and races and come to BBBS from their schools, churches, or television commercials. All of them are there voluntarily because they desire a relationship and a mentor in an adult of the same gender. All children choose to be in the program. Oftentimes the children have only one parent and desire a relationship with an adult of the gender of the missing parent. All children have the support of their custodial parent to be in the program, and it is important that you partner with that parent in determining the amount of time you spend with the child and what activities you choose.

If this sounds like something that would interest you, go to www.bbbs.org and speak with a match specialist about any questions that you have about the program. You can apply online, after which you will be interviewed by a match coordinator, and a background check will be conducted to make sure that you don't have an abuse registry record. You will supply at least two references who can attest to your ability to be a mentor, and then you'll be matched. Your match coordinator will review the applications of children in your area and determine who might be the best match for you based upon gender and interests. This could happen overnight, or could take some time based upon the kids who are available. It is important to BBBS that matches are well-made to enhance the possibility of a long term relationship. Ideally, you and your Little will know each other for a very long time and grow very close, like brothers or sisters! It is important to know that you will get the final say over whether a match feels right for you.

Once you are matched, you will be assigned to a Match Support Specialist who will be available should you have any questions or need help with any difficult situations. Your MSS will be able to make suggestions about activities, will occasionally invite you both to a ball game or the theater when tickets are donated to the program, and will be there to support you and tell you how important you are!

You will be encouraged to spend as little money as possible with and on your Little. Activities that cost money can be lots of fun, but you will not want to be like the stereotypic weekend parent who always spends a lot of money on the child, becoming the Santa Claus while the custodial parent holds down the fort. The relationship is most important, not what activities you share. Talking and being available to support the child in friendships and at school is the goal. All it takes is time! Again, go to www.bbbs.org to find out if being a big brother or big sister is for you.

Conclusion

Well, now you've read about the process of becoming an adoptive parent. You know what kinds of children are available to you, what it will cost, and what you have to do to become an adoptive parent. You've also been told what other options are available if you decide that adoption is not right for you at this time. You bought this book because you thought that you wanted a child in your life, a child who has a primary relationship with you, and who you can grow to love and take care of.

If you don't already know what is right for you, you probably need to put the book down and go about your life, noticing kids everywhere you go and constantly checking in with yourself about how it feels. There is no right or wrong about whether adults should be parents. Some of us should parent children and some of us should work for the good of society in other ways. I am a psychiatric social worker and a life coach. I could adopt a child, which would take most of my free time, or I could help many others take the steps necessary to decide to parent the orphaned children in the world. Middle age brings in Erickson's stage of Generativity – that is, our need to give back to people and the world. Being a parent is only one way to do that. Now you have the tools you needed to make that decision and it is either right for you or it isn't. God Bless you as make your way in life and decide what way of giving back is best for you. Please stay in touch and let me know if I can be of more help to you. You can reach me by going to "Contact Us" on the book's website, www.adoptionforsinglesbook.com. I'd love to hear how your life turned out.

122

Resources

- Assisted Reproduction and Surrogacy, www.adoptionforsinglesbook.com
- State Foster Care Maintenance Payments, www.hunter.cuny.edu/socwork/nrcfcpp/downloads/foster-care-maintenance-payments.pdf
- *The Women Who Raised Me,* www.VictoriaRowell.com.
- Big Brothers Big Sisters, www.bbbs.org

Chapter VII

In First Person

In this chapter we will interview seven people who are involved in the adoption world in one way or another. The first three interviews are with parents who have adopted – Thesia Garner adopted from China, Margaret Schwartz from Ukraine, and Art Engler and Ron Kolonowski from the foster care system. We will then hear from several adoption professionals – Natalie Newton, a social worker in Fredericksburg, Virginia, who talks about the local adoption scene, Patrick Mason, a doctor who heads up an adoption clinic and talks about medical issues around intercountry adoption, and Rita Soronen, the Executive Director of The Dave Thomas Foundation for Adoption who describes a national organization that recruits adoptive parents and facilitates foster care adoptions.

Thesia Garner
Adopted from China

AFS: When did you decide you wanted to adopt a child as a single person?
TG: I had wanted to be a mom for a long time. I had been in various relationships and for whatever reasons they had not led to marriage. In September 1999 and in November the following year I had two surgeries and I almost died. During recovery I reevaluated my life and what was going on in my life and I asked myself, "20 years from now, what would I regret not doing if I don't do it soon?" The only thing I could think of that I would regret was not having been a mom. So I started looking into ways of becoming a mother. I went to my doctor who thought it was a great idea if I got pregnant. I went to a gynecologist who specialized in complicated pregnancies (since I was over 40 years old) and went through some tests. I tried various options to become pregnant and couldn't. After some time of trying to get pregnant I began to question whether getting pregnant was the way for me to become a mom. I started to attend meetings on adoption. I went to

three adoption agency information meetings. After that I wanted to clear my mind for awhile. It was on a trip to North Carolina with my family when I decided it was important that I become a mom, not how I would become a mom. At that point I decided I would pursue adoption.

AFS: *Once you decided you wanted to adopt, what was the next step?*

TG: In September 2001 I was ready to proceed with the adoption process. I picked an agency; I had been to this agency's information meeting already. I initially tried to adopt from India because when I went to the information meeting the speaker at that meeting suggested that potential adoptive parents consider whether or not you would like to be married to someone from the country that you are adopting from. I knew some friends across the street from me who were from India and I had dated someone from India a few years earlier.

In working with an adoption agency it is necessary to have various forms completed. One of the forms is a medical form. I had submitted this medical form for completion to my primary care physician. On the form he had indicated that I had a decreased life expectancy due to my recent surgeries. The agency said they would not be able to forward my application with this in my medical record and suggested that I check with another doctor if there were questions about my life expectancy. Instead, I contacted the doctor who had done my surgery. He indicated that my life expectancy was clearly increased rather than decreased. With this new medical information in addition to some additional information required by the agency I contacted my agency again and then they told me there was an issue with the orphanage in a particular state in India that this agency dealt with. When I was exploring working with the agency in the summer before I had committed to adoption, the staff told me that they expected the court case to be resolved in the summer. They thought it was to be over in the summer. However, by November 2001 the court case was still not resolved.

I didn't want to continue waiting for the India program to resolve, so I said I would like to be included in the agency's China program. I was told by the agency that they had reached their quota of singles adopting from China. The Chinese government had put a quota on singles adopting from their country that would go into effect December 2001. So, I got on the internet and started checking about other agencies and I called different agencies from Maine to Florida to Oregon to see if I could be included in their singles program. Some of them said that their singles' program to China was closed, while others said the wait was going to be two–three years.

Then I called the director of an agency named CASI (I had also attended one of their information meetings—it was the first informational meeting I had attended). The director sensed my urgency and invited me to come over to her office. I immediately took the Metro and started talking to her and I told her my situation. She said, "We might have some space. We have a very good relationship with the Chinese Center for Adoption Affairs." They thought they might be able to get one more single as part of their quota—the director said she would check with other directors within CASI. However, before I left her office she suggested I should go ahead and fill out the forms. As it turns out, CASI agreed to accept me to their China adoption program as a single.

AFS: Why did you choose to adopt internationally instead of domestically?
TG: I had been warned by various adoption agencies around the country that it would be very difficult for a single woman to adopt a baby in the U.S. The reason being is that many of the children in the U.S. are born to single mothers. Most single moms placing their children for adoption prefer two-parent homes. International adoption was going to increase my chances of becoming a mother of a healthy, younger child (which is what I wanted).

I chose China, too, because China has a tradition of respecting older parents and those with higher education (I have a Ph.D.). Others' previous experience had suggested that the adoption process working with China was relatively straightforward, although the wait was on average longer than other countries at the time.

AFS: What paperwork did you have to fill out?
TG: The next thing I had to do was to identify an organization that would be able to have a social worker conduct a home study for my adoption application (CASI was a new agency and didn't have its own home social worker who could conduct the home study). I still worked with CASI, but used Lutheran Social Services for my home study. I had to be interviewed by the adoption director at Lutheran Social Services for them to accept me. Once I was accepted then they gave me a long list of things I needed to get to them before an appointment could be set up for my first home study: a completed authorized adoption application, medical form, report concerning fertility status (some countries require it), most recent pay stub, last year's federal income tax return, copy of birth certificate, copy of letter sent to FBI, two copies of my fingerprints, a copy of my police clearance, a copy of my INS letter, my child abuse clearance, a color photograph of myself, a statement of financial responsibility (notarized), a discipline policy, an emergency fire evacuation form, a copy of my DC driving record, client rights and responsibility forms, release of information form from a psychologist I had seen about becoming a mom, and four reference letters sent directly to them. I mailed that package to Lutheran Social Services on December 21, 2001.

AFS: Can you please explain the home study process?
TG: The social worker conducting the home study visited me three times. Each visit had a different focus. The focus of one of the visits was my readiness to be an adoptive parent. Another visit focused on safety and lifestyle issues (the social worker looked at my home). Another visit focused on my financial situation (she reviewed the current values of all of my finances). She set up her first appointment in January 2002 and everything was completed by the middle of March 2002. At that point, I had completed all of my paperwork, except I still had not written my letter as to why I wanted to adopt, so I still needed to do that.

AFS: What happened after you completed all of the paperwork and home study?
TG: I began the waiting process. As it turns out the Chinese government announced on the one-year anniversary of my

paperwork being logged in that they were putting a moratorium on Chinese adoptions due to SARS, so the whole process was going to be delayed even further.

On top of the SARS crisis, the Chinese government had misplaced all the dossiers from the people in our group. So the process was delayed another three or four months. It wasn't until August 4, 2003, that I got word a child was available for me. I filed all my paperwork in March 2002 and I didn't hear until August 2003. My little daughter had to wait for me and I had to wait for her.

At the very beginning of the process after I first signed all the paperwork in the CASI office in Washington, DC, I realized that my little girl was in China (I remember exactly what street I was walking on when I had the realization). At that point she hadn't been born, but I just knew that China was where my child would be. I just had a sense of peace.

AFS: *When and how did you get word that a child was available for you to adopt?*
TG: When I first learned about my child I was attending a conference in San Francisco and I got the call on August 4, 2003. The director of the CASI office in Washington called me and told me I would be receiving a picture and other info about my soon-to-be daughter. The agency was going to Fedex the package to me at my hotel—it was supposed to arrive that afternoon but it didn't arrive until the next day around 2 p.m. Once I had the package in hand I wanted to wait and open it so that I could share the experience with my friend who was also attending the conference. But someone from the main CASI office called me and told me to open the envelope right away. So, I asked a stranger who was lying by the pool to take my picture as I opened the envelope. I was very excited and I started crying and he took pictures of me learning about my daughter. The dossier included my little girl's Chinese name, date of birth, basic statistics, medical information, and information about her daily routine. I went into my room and I cried I was so happy. It was really great. That night my friend, her husband, and I went to Chinatown in San Francisco and I bought a small journal that had Chinese symbols on the outside and I began to write my daughter's story.

The package contained a letter that I had to sign, but everything was in Chinese. I didn't have the translation about her medical history yet either. So I went down to the lobby of a large hotel where many of the other conference participants were staying and there were 100 or so what looked to be Chinese in the lobby. I saw a group of three people or so standing together talking and I asked if any one of them could read Mandarin and if they would consider translating some pages in the envelope for me. They all started laughing and said they all knew Mandarin. One of them started to read the letter and saw that it was referring to Hefei where my daughter was from. Another person in the group—an assistant professor at the University of Florida—said he was from Hefei so he started to read the letter. That is the first time I learned about my daughter—how big she was, what her name meant in Chinese, where she was born, what she ate and how much she slept, her temperament. It was so exciting!

When I got back home from the conference I was sent a translation of her medical record and once I had that I had a pediatrician in the Washington area, Dr. Patrick Mason, (See his interview later in this chapter) who specializes in international adoptions look it over. I still wanted someone else to look over it so I sent it to my friend in Denver who had a pediatrician who was from Mainland China look over it as well and his colleague who had adopted international children. They said everything looked fine. I contacted a colleague of mine who had a friend who adopted from that same orphanage. My colleague's friend called the orphanage to talk to the assistant director (who at the time was a medical doctor). The assistant director said that he was very familiar with my little girl and said she was a delight and was very, very, very petite. After a lot of prayer, I went ahead and signed the paperwork to accept the little girl.

AFS: *When did you leave for China?*
TG: I left for China on September 8, 2003, with a friend of mine who went to graduate school with me who went with me for support. It was so wonderful for me that she agreed to go with me. It was especially nice to have her to talk to during the process as well.

My friend and I went over to China a week earlier than was required so that we could see more of the country and this was recommended to us. We flew from Dulles to Los Angeles and from Los Angeles to Guangzhou, China. From there we flew to Xian, China. We landed in Xian on September 10. On September 12 we flew to Beijing where we met up with other adoptive families in our group. There were 25 adoptive families. We toured China with them. From there, four groups of us went to Hefei. There was only one other single mother in our group.

When I finally met my daughter she was put in my arms and she cried—she finally settled down, though. We had our first official family portrait (an official document for the Chinese government) in Hefei. We were told that China has a rule that you have to stay in the place you adopted your child for five business days. Since we arrived on a Tuesday (September 15), we stayed through the weekend which gave me time to be with my daughter there and we got to know each other. We visited the orphanage so that I could see where she had been. It was very nice-looking place and it was clean. I got to see her little crib. We left Hefei the evening of September 22 to go back to Guangzhou. Once we got there, I had to fill out lots more paperwork and my little girl had to have a medical exam and had her footprints and fingerprints taken. She also got her Chinese passport in her Chinese name. We were only in Guangzhou for a couple of days. It was a very hectic time—such a whirlwind!

There was a family that met us at the airport who was from Wuhan, China. I know their son who went to school in the U.S. He had contacted them and told them all about my story. They had a beautiful bouquet of flowers and took us to dinner. I felt totally loved and cared for. They brought some cousins as well. Only one of five people spoke English. One took care of my daughter while I visited with the family, another was a photographer.

After a couple of days we flew back to Los Angeles. Some dear friends met us at the airport.

When I got back to the United States, two to three weeks later I got her green card in the mail and it was so funny because it said she was cleared to work. Once I had all of this I went to apply for her passport. Once I got her passport I could then use that as proof of citizenship so I could register her birth with the District of Columbia government (this is not required by law, but is encouraged). I also applied for her to get a certificate of citizenship. It took a long time—the U.S. government lost her paperwork. I was working through a congressman from Hawaii who helped me get it through. Once I got her certificate of citizenship they took away her green card.

I stayed home from work with my daughter for about a month and a half.

AFS: If you don't mind sharing, how much did the whole adoption process cost you?
TG: In total it cost about $25,000. My fees to the Lutheran Social Services for the home study were $2,250 (that included post-placement services). My flight, travel insurance, and hotel costs (we spent a night in Los Angeles on the way back) cost $7,500 for both of my friend and I and the return flight for my daughter. The agency fees were $100 for the application, $2,000 for the program fee, $2,500 for the dossier processing, $120 for the State Department authentication, $3,000 (a donation to the Chinese orphanage). Once in China it cost about $3,600 –that's what they charge for in-country hotel stay, food, airfare, etc., and then another $3600 additional for additional home studies.

Margaret Schwartz
Adopted from Ukraine

AFS: When did you decide you wanted to adopt children as a single person?
MS: I was engaged to be married and my fiancé broke off our engagement. For the first time in over 15 years I was without a significant other in my life and I realize I needed to spend time by myself to figure out who I was and what would make me happy. I spent almost two years reading self-help books, meditating, and thinking about what I wanted to do in my life. After a lot of thought and reflection I decided at the age of 44 that I wanted to have children in my life. I knew if I didn't adopt then I would regret my decision later in life.

AFS: How did you decide whether to adopt domestically or internationally?
MS: I began the process by conducting research on the Internet, checking out domestic adoption sites with photos of children

available for adoption. Most of the children on these sites were older, part of a larger sibling group, or had disabilities. Many of the sites had descriptions of the children, including lists of their challenges. I was terrified I couldn't cope with these issues. I had decided I wanted to adopt two children and even though it sounds cruel I was not prepared to deal with children struggling with behavioral and emotional issues. I had to be honest about my feelings and understand my limits as a prospective parent. Deciding whether to pursue a domestic or foreign adoption is a difficult and personal choice. Much depends on one's circumstances and the health, age, and gender of the child one wants to adopt.

I didn't want to adopt an infant, but I did want to adopt younger Caucasian children between the ages of two and four. After spending many hours reading websites with personal stories and talking to people about their own adoption experiences it was clear to me that international adoption was the right way for me to proceed.

AFS: *Once you made that decision, what was the first step?*
MS: I had to decide next what country I wanted to adopt from, as that affected my choice of a social worker/agency for my home study. Knowing that I wanted to adopt children who were Caucasian, I looked primarily at Eastern European countries and evaluated their processes and costs. I chose Ukraine for three reasons: first, I wanted children who looked like me—fair skin with hazel eyes and dark blond hair. Second, I wanted to be the one to decide which children I adopted and the process in Ukraine is structured so that no pre-identification takes place. Many countries, including Russia, pre-select children for adoptive parents. It is illegal in Ukraine to do this; instead people go directly to the orphanage and select the child they want. That meant I wouldn't see pictures of available children until I was actually in Ukraine at the National Adoption Center (NAC). Lastly, Ukraine is the only country I am aware of that allows you to adopt children without the use of an agency. This meant I would be able to save a considerable amount of money by doing the paperwork myself and finding a facilitator on my own.

AFS: Please take us through the steps you had to go through during the adoption process.

MS: After my home study was approved, I had to collect/create the following documents:

1) Confirm that I was not on the "Sex Offender and Crimes Against Minors" list
2) Provide a medical form attesting to my state of health
3) Submit an approval letter from the INS (now Homeland Security)
4) Confirm that I did not have a criminal record
5) Create a will, naming my children as heirs

All of these documents had to be notarized, and then stamped by the Virginia state office, the U.S. Department of State, and the Ukrainian Embassy.

AFS: If you don't mind sharing, what was the cost you had to pay for the adoption?

MS: I spent approximately $22,000 in total to complete my adoption, including $1200 for the home study, $3000 in travel fees, and $10,000 in fees and expediting costs in Ukraine

AFS: What was the easiest part of the adoption process?

MS: The easiest part of the adoption process was the day I made the decision to move forward.

AFS: What were some of the major stumbling blocks you experienced?

MS:
1) Waiting for my approval letter from the INS to arrive (this took over two months from mid February until April 28)
2) Waiting for an appointment from the NAC in Ukraine
3) Getting the proper signatures and notary stamps on all the documents
4) Dealing with simple typos or misspelled words that could be enough to have one's dossier rejected

AFS: What has been your experience as a single mom? What are some of the challenges?

MS: The main challenge is feeling like I never have enough time for myself. I always feel I have to multitask when I am with my sons instead of playing with them. I have to work so much harder now to support my children; I have given up some of my hobbies and ability to travel. It's challenging being the nurturer and the disciplinarian. And I feel guilty when I yell at them because I'm tired after working all day.

AFS: How do you balance work and having children as a single person?

MS: One of the smartest things I did was hire an *au pair* to live with us and help take care of the boys. Having some free time in the evenings has allowed me to maintain contact with my friends and enjoy social outings with other adults.

AFS: What are some of the things you enjoy the most about being a mom?

MS: Getting hugs and kisses are a wonderful benefit! Knowing that my children have someone to tuck them in at night and comfort them when they are hurt or tired. Watching them grow and develop their abilities and skills. Feeling unconditional love from another human being. Having the ability to teach my children about the wonders of nature and God and how to be good to others.

AFS: What advice would you give a single person interested in adoption?

MS: Ask yourself if you are ready to make a lot of sacrifices in your life. Are you willing to give up your free time, spend money with no tangible return, and curb your career potential? Are you willing to put your child's needs ahead of your own? If so, then you are ready to be a parent.

Art Engler
Adopted from Foster Care

AFS: Tell me about your decision to become a parent. When did you start thinking seriously about it?

AE: Ron's brother and sister-in-law adopted a baby from China in December 2004, which made us start thinking about it again. We contacted DCF and had a preliminary interview early in January 2005 and Joshua was with us in June of that year.

AFS: Did you consider other ways of becoming a parent, such as surrogacy, partnering with a female friend, or looking for a newborn?
AE: No, we didn't really think of any of those options. We knew about the huge number of kids in foster care available for adoption and really felt that need was so great we had to respond.

AFS: You adopted your son, Joshua, through the foster care system. Did you become a foster parent with the intent of adopting?
AE: Yes, the system in Connecticut is set up so foster parents have to choose to be licensed as "regular" foster parents (meaning, not planning to adopt) or pre-adoptive foster parents (meaning, becoming foster parents with the specific intention of adopting).

AFS: Did you have parameters on the child you would consider adopting, such as gender, race, or age?
AE: No, we were open to whomever God sent to us. We really thought we would become parents of older children as the number of children under 2 is relatively limited. But, as we often say, you can tell Connecticut is a "blue" state because a gay couple "beat out" four straight couples to be awarded care of Joshua!

AFS: How old was Joshua when you got him? What were the circumstances of his placement with you?
AE: Joshua was just 14 months when we met him. We visited with him for three weeks then he came to live with us. He had been in foster care for 9 months before that with a foster mother that was just perfect for a little guy who had spent most of his first five months of life in a homeless shelter with his birth mother. His foster mother was a very nurturing, grandmotherly type of person who gave him just what he needed.

AFS: Was he available for adoption when you got him? If no, did it look like he would be available for adoption at some point? I ask this question because readers of this book are interested in adopting and wonder if the foster care system will honor that from the start.

AE: No, Joshua wasn't legally free for adoption but he was classified as "low risk" because both birth parents had already agreed to voluntarily relinquish their parental rights. So we knew it was going to happen, we just didn't know when. Sadly, at the birth mother's hearing for termination of her parental rights, her major concern was when she could get breakfast.

AFS: What was it like to suddenly have such a small child in your home? How did you manage it?

AE: It was during the summer so I was off from school and home with J most of the time. Ron was doing a summer ministry internship. I managed by being pretty organized and we were both very intentional about sharing childcare time equally. Even with good planning though, about 4 o'clock in the afternoon I would find myself lying on the floor playing with J thinking, "How can I be so tired? He's only 14 months old!"

AFS: What surprised you most about foster parenting? Anything you didn't anticipate?

AE: Although I know the state works slowly, I was and am still surprised by the fact that we have something like 5500 kids in foster care and we still haven't been able to get a 2nd child placed with us. We did just get a call from our social worker yesterday though asking us if we'd like to be considered for a sibling group consisting of a 20-month-old girl and a 7-month-old boy!

AFS: Please tell us about the adoption process. How did it start? Can you walk us through the steps you had to take to finally adopt?

AE:
1. First, we had a preliminary interview at our house for information-gathering. This was conducted by a social worker whose only job is recruiting new foster parents.

2. We then had 19 hours of foster parent training that focused on general parental issues as well as issues specific to foster care and adoption.

3. We had several home visits, got our fingerprints done, had numerous types of background checks, and submitted financial statements, veterinary statements, and physical exams, among other things.

4. The last administrative step before we were awarded custody of Joshua was the Permanency Planning Team meeting at which 4 other families were represented by their social workers and the children were represented by their social workers and lawyers. All families were presented then everyone voted on who should get J and we won!

5. The next day we met him at his foster home. Within just a few minutes he was sitting on my lap reading a book and then Ron was holding him talking about things they saw out the window. His foster mother was crying because they had been worried that J wouldn't "take to" two men as he had been in a household with almost all girls and women.

6. The day after that I picked him up and took him out for a drive, to the park, to say hello at our church, and to meet our dog and cat. A funny aspect of the park visit was that when we were ready to leave I absolutely couldn't figure out how to get his car seat buckled up properly! After about 10 minutes, just when I was ready to swallow my pride and ask some mothers in the park to rescue me, the buckles clicked together and we were set!

7. For 3 weeks we did that, including spending more time with us at our house. He would sleep at his foster home though. His first public outing with us was to a friend's ordination at the Cathedral in Hartford. He was quite a hit with our friends who were there!

8. On June 20, 2006, his social worker, our social worker, and his foster mother brought him to our house – and left him! It's been great ever since.

9. We had monthly visits from his social worker and our social worker until his adoption was finalized on June 15, 2006 – a whole year!

AFS: Any glitches?
AE: No, things have gone exceedingly well in this whole process.

AFS: How long did it take?
AE: From the first social worker's visit in January 2005 to the adoption was finalized was about 1.5 years.

AFS: If you don't mind sharing, what was the cost of the adoption? If possible, could you break it down by expense?
AE: When adopting from the State of Connecticut, you incur absolutely no costs. Not only was the whole process free, Joshua receives a stipend from the State until he's 18 years old, has free state health coverage, and when he's 18 has free college tuition! And we even get paid for mileage and childcare for trainings! It's absolutely sensational!

AFS: I understand that you'd like to adopt another child. Have you started that process? Would you like to adopt from foster care a second time?
AE: We'll definitely adopt from DCF. I'm not sure why it's taken so long, but we did just get a call from our social worker about being considered for two siblings: a 20-month-old girl and her 7-month-old brother.

AFS: Did your state allow you to adopt together, or did you need a second-parent adoption?
AE: I adopted Joshua first then gave permission for Ron to adopt him seconds later.

AFS: What is the best part about being a parent?
AE: The best part for me is seeing him grow, giving him new experiences, feeling the richness that comes with sharing life so intimately with another human being.

AFS: What are the stresses?
AE: The biggest stress is scheduling childcare responsibilities although compared to the joy have being parents, it's nothing.

AFS: What advice would you give a single person who is interested in adopting a child?
AE: Definitely consider the state system. In Connecticut, it's completely free, as I said, plus J gets a stipend every month until he's 18 (I think it's about $900 now), he gets free health care until he's 18, and free college tuition!

Art's partner, Ron Kolonowski

AFS: I hear that you have some new additions to the family?
RK: Yes, we do! We got Benjamin and Anna in the middle of December [2007].

AFS: How did this come about?
RK: Well, being older parents, we realized that Joshua was going to spend a chunk of his life without us around. It was important for him to have siblings, so we stayed in the foster care program in the state of Connecticut. We were only open to children who were on the path to adoption. As you know, you have to foster until they are adopted. In the state of Connecticut they've tightened up the system so that it's better for the kids, so there's a 90 day window where the social workers have to come to the court with a plan. With the twins, they knew immediately that they wanted them to be placed at birth.

AFS: So the social workers knew that the babies couldn't go home with the birth mother? What was the situation there?
RK: We try not to say too much out of respect for the family, but they have other children who've had to be placed. The family had broken down.

AFS: So how did this happen and when did you find out?
RK: We found out the week before my ordination that these children were being born and that there was a chance that we would be teamed for these children. Our social worker contacted us and said that there were newborn twins who were going to be

139

born 7 weeks premature. They needed to go straight from the ICU to a home. The teaming process is a transparent process in the Department of Children and Families, where they put out a statewide bulletin that these children are coming into the system. All foster care social workers get the bulletin. Our social worker saw this and thought we would be great for these babies. Two other families entered the process through their social workers. As soon as the three families were identified, the social workers, medical people, and the babies' social worker met and went through this case to review all the factors. They also review all the families and independently score how they would be with the kids. They try to create a level playing field and get the best possible home for the children. They then offer the children to the family with the highest score.

AFS: So you're asked by your social worker if you're interested, but it doesn't mean anything until the teaming happens?
RK: Yes. We thought the teaming would be the first week in December, but we didn't get a call.

On Tuesday before I was going to be ordained (December 15), our social worker arrived at our house with two stuffed animals and said, "Congratulations, Dads!" We had to get ready for two babies and we didn't even have a crib in the house anymore. Art was at school teaching, so I went to the neighbors, told them we had twelve hours, and asked if they would they make a list of everything we would need. I needed a list that I could use to go shopping because I knew that I would go to the store and just stand there. They not only made the list within two hours, but also did the shopping and got us everything we needed to start – bottles, diapers, clothes, everything.

Benjamin came home to us on Wednesday. Family arrived on Thursday, and then on Friday, two hours before 30 people were coming over for dinner, I missed my ordination rehearsal because I went to pick up Anna. So when people began arriving for dinner, they saw a house full of baby supplies and two new babies!

AFS: What's it been like?
RK: It's been great and exhausting. Twins are not just one plus one equals two. They were preemies so they needed to be fed

every two hours. It's just now at three months that they are going a little longer between feedings. They were 45 minute feedings, so you would have an hour and a half and you would have to start all over again. We couldn't leave the babies with the au pair until they were 3 months old, so we decided who would be on duty through the night based on what each of us had the next day. The church was very lenient with me and Art was just beginning Christmas break.

AFS: What does Joshua think of this?
RK: He's had to cede a great deal. When we were in New Zealand this time last year and had to come back to the United States, we thought we were coming home to get a child that they had ready for us. We decided to say no because we needed to allow Joshua to settle in. He had had his first school experience in New Zealand and I was getting ordained to the deaconate the next month. It's very, very important to decide when the next child comes. Joshua has had to cede a huge amount of ground to these babies. We get a lot of holding time with the babies at night, but when Joshua is awake we make sure to spend as much time as possible with him. We had to make sure that the timing was good for him and that we were able to provide more attention to him. I try to make sure that I'm not holding a baby when he gets up so that he can go right into my arms and I rock him. He likes to snuggle, and it's important that I'm available to him and not always with a baby when he's around.

AFS: That's really thoughtful.
RK: It really takes a lot of thought and planning to make it work. We have thought about how to make it work for Joshua and each of us. We have elaborate schedules on the refrigerator as to who's on duty when. With two babies instead of one, it's much more complicated. Like last night, Art was on and I took over at 5 a.m., he got some sleep and the au pair came on at 7:30. So it's not only who's on duty when, but scheduling for recovery time, too.

AFS: What else would you like to tell prospective adoptive parents who read this book?
RK: The one thing that is very important is that there are pluses and minuses to every form of adoption. In the state, we continue

to be in the support system. As long as they are in the foster care system, there is a stipend and WIC pays for formula. Our au pair is going to be on vacation during Holy Week, and we get two weeks of respite care. We get help with whatever we need from the social workers. You get as much information as the state has on the birth family. We know medical, drug, family, and mental illness histories about the parents that you don't get with foreign adoptions. With Joshua's family we have generations of history.

The biggest down side and the most difficult is that there is risk. Some children are not free and clear for adoption, and with Joshua it took about a year to plow through the system. There is always, until it's over, a chance that those babies will not become yours. So one thing that is really important is to be clear about what level of risk you're willing to take. We realized that we wouldn't take children that were high risk. There is always a chance, even after a year of living with us that the court would decide to reunite them with their family. In this case, the state has filed to terminate the rights of the mother, and she has a history that will make it easier. But there is a new father, and that will make it take longer. Joshua had 5 months with his birth mom, 9 months in foster care, and then came to us at 14 months.

We're moving forward with a closed adoption, which means that we will not maintain contact with the birth family. That choice is ours. With an older child, although the choice is yours, looking at the best interests of the child makes it a totally different ballgame. That child may need some level of contact with that parent – they're already in a relationship on some level. So it gets more complicated.

Our twins have twice-weekly court-ordered visitation with the birth parents. The social worker comes to our house and takes the babies to her office and the parents come there. They get to document whether they miss visits and how they are with the babies. The parents have rights because they are their parents. But they are unable to parent. It's part of the level of transparency that everyone gets a chance. The babies have their own social worker and she's the one who's walking this thing through the courts. Our social worker is there if we need her, but we have more contact with the babies' social worker and lawyer right now. We have no legal hold over the kids right now. We are only licensed by the state to provide care until they are available for adoption. On a day to day basis, we function as these children's parents. Understanding all of that up front is really, really important. We've been in it for 3 years, so we kind of understand it and have low anxiety about it all.

But, there are a lot of kids in the system who are free and clear, meaning that their parents' rights have been terminated and they are free to be adopted.

AFS: What was the oldest child you were willing to consider?
RK: We were looking at under 5. There were times when we thought about teens, as well. That's where our heads were when we started. We never dreamed that we would get a baby. When they presented Joshua to us, we were stunned. Our social worker said that we needed to have a baby. And we did.

When you go through the training it's as much discernment as training. You learn what level of risk, sickness you're willing to tolerate. There are a whole lot of reasons that families can't sustain their kids. I think people should take a serious look at adopting through their state. Connecticut alone has about 7,000 kids in the system. I think there's a stigma about these kids that they're broken. No, the truth is that their family has broken down. Older teens have issues, but they are able to appreciate that they adopted.

[Author's note: Connecticut is somewhat unusual in terms of having families compete for children – or "teaming" as Ron described it. In most states the child is placed with a family or single person and other families are not considered unless the first placement does not work out.]

Natalie M. Newton
Senior Social Worker
Fredericksburg City Department of Social Services

AFS: Please tell us your title and a short description of your job.
NMN: I am a senior social worker and I specialize in adoptions. Once a child's parental rights have been terminated, I take over the case. I will place the child in an adoptive home and will prepare the child for adoption.

AFS: Because this book is for singles who are interested in adopting, the majority of my questions will be geared toward this

subject. Can singles adopt a child through the Fredericksburg City Department of Social Services?

NMN: Singles can adopt a child through the Fredericksburg City Department of Social Services, but we require that they foster our children first before pursuing adoption. Our foster parents often foster a number of children before they foster the child they eventually are able to adopt. This happens for a few reasons: the child may return home, may go to live with a family member, the family may not be able to meet the child's needs, or the child may be at an age of discretion and wish to not be adopted. Because our agency uses the PRIDE (Parent's Resource for Information, Development and Education) model to train our foster/adoptive parents, once a child is placed in one of our homes it is not likely that they will have to move into another home to be adopted. Therefore, here in Fredericksburg, it is very likely that the child a family fosters will be the child they end up adopting.

AFS: What is (roughly) the percentage of singles who adopt a child through your division?

NMN: 20% of our adoptive families are singles. The majority of single adopters are women and we do have men who adopt.

AFS: Are the majority of children available for adoption through the foster care system defined as special needs? If so, what is the definition of special needs that you use? Is that definition the same nationwide?

NMN: Yes, the majority of the children available for adoption fall into the special needs category. We have six different categories within special needs—if a child meets at least one of these six criteria that child would be defined as *special needs.*
The categories are:

> If the child has a physical, mental or emotional disability
> If the child has a hereditary or congenital problem or birth injury
> If the child is over six years old
> If the child is of a minority race
> If the child is a member of a sibling group; and

If the child has significant emotional ties with the foster parent with whom the child has resided for at least 6 months.

AFS: Why do the majority of kids end up in the foster care system? Are all of them up for adoption? If not, why are some and others are not? (Does this depend on parental rights? Can a child be put up for adoption before parental rights are terminated?)

NMN: Most of the kids in our foster care system come into our care due to abuse or neglect. Some children that come into our care are classified as CHINS (Child in Need of Supervision). In CHINS cases, a parent may not have abused or neglected the child but it's been brought to our attention that the child needs extra supervision. Sometimes we serve as just an extra set of eyes and ears in the home to help parents take care of their children.

AFS: How much does it cost to adopt a child through the system? What costs are associated with the process? Do adopters get monetary assistance? Would a single individual get more assistance? Do adopters receive any other financial breaks—tax? State? Medical assistance?

NMN: Foster parents receive a monthly stipend. The amount varies depending on the child's age. Foster parents fostering a child between ages 0–4 receive $326; 4–12 receive $381; 14+ receive $383. All children get Medicaid. Some foster parents qualify for additional help if they are fostering a sibling group, for example. It doesn't happen a lot that the foster family needs extra money beyond what they receive. We had one child that required a lot of transportation for doctor appointments so we provided the foster family extra monetary assistance for that. When families are fostering we don't want to have them delve too much into their own pocket to care for the children.

Once it comes to adoption we do help with legal fees (attorney fees) up to $2,000. In our agency/locality the legal fees for adoption usually run no more than $1100. Once the child is adopted, we do talk with the parents about a subsidy before they sign papers. The parents are eligible to continue to receive a monthly stipend plus Medicaid, but sometimes the adopted families refuse the monthly stipend. Sometimes they're eligible for special service fees—we agreed in one case, for example, to pay daycare for the adopted child. Another kind of subsidy we provided is called a *conditional subsidy,* which is given to the adoptive parents if the child has any issues or special needs that are not present at the time of adoption but are caused by things that happened before the adoption (birth injury or separation anxiety).

AFS: What types of things are you looking for when you are matching an adopter to an adoptee/vice versa?
NMN: We look at the needs of the child. If the child is of age we will ask the child what they want in an adoptive family. Both the adoptive family and the child have to take part in the placement. We ask both what they feel they would want…what they best can handle.

AFS: The children's emotional/physical health is known by the state. How are the children evaluated—school reports? Foster parent reports? Medical reports?
NMN: When children first come into care, we refer them to the Child Development Center through the health department. Our child development center services other areas besides Fredericksburg. There the child is evaluated in a number of ways (educational, IQ, hearing, vision, etc.). A lot of our kids are not learning-disabled, but are ED (emotionally disturbed). We do try to get our foster parents to get copies of every doctor's appointment and ask them to keep a file of everything.

AFS: Do you adopt to single men?
NMN: Yes.

AFS: Are the majority of children up for adoption part of a sibling group?
NMN: I wouldn't say that the majority are sibling groups. They may have siblings, but not are always up for adoption.

AFS: If a single person is interested in adopting can you walk him/her through the steps? What is the first thing he/she should do? How long does the process usually take? Who should he/she contact?

NMN: The first step a single person or a family interested in adopting should do is to contact our resource parent coordinator. We are a small agency but we hold resource parent training twice a year, which trains the parents on fostering to adopt. The training is an eight-week course and runs three hours each week. During the training we conduct a home study and complete background checks. We also evaluate the person or family's financial situation.

Once the training is complete and the background checks have been approved, we try to figure out what kind of child would best suit the person or family as well as what kind of child they can handle—what behaviors they can handle and what they can't handle. Once a child is placed with the person or family, the child has to live in the home for six months. Again, we require all of our potential adopters to foster a child first for at least six months. This foster-to-adopt requirement ensures that the match is a good fit for both child and parent.

Patrick Mason, M.D., Ph.D
Director and Founder of the International Adoption Center
INOVA-Fairfax Hospital

AFS: What kind of services does your center provide and how did you become interested in working with internationally adopted children?
PM: I'm a pediatric endocrinologist. I became interested in international adoptions when parents starting bringing their children (adopted mainly from Romania and Russia) to see me because the children were showing signs of early puberty. I put together an international adoption clinic in Atlanta and about seven years ago my family and I moved up to Northern Virginia and I started the International Adoption Center. I've been working with international adoptions for about 13 years now.

Our center helps individuals interested in adoption through the entire international adoption process. We meet with them early in the process to help them determine which countries to consider. Then, after a referral is made (when the adoption agency tells the parents a child is available), we review the referral information with them (telling them what it potentially means for the family and child). During the adoption process I also make myself available to the adopter or adoptive family—they can call me from the country when they are traveling to tell me what they are seeing. With Russian adoptions, the adopter takes two trips overseas and I counsel them on what they should look for.

After a child has been adopted and brought home to the States, our center works with the child's pediatrician. We let the pediatrician handle all the general pediatric concerns. Children who are adopted may be at risk for a number of diseases. Our center may talk with the adopter about sleep transition from an orphanage to an adopted family or discuss feeding and nutrition. We also conduct a developmental screening and assessment on the child. We do a complete medical evaluation on the child to determine the child's growth points and what the child's development level is at the time of the evaluation.

AFS: What is one of the first things you discuss with someone who is interested in international adoption?
PM: The first thing I always like to talk about with a person or a family interested in adoption is country of origin. A growing number of studies indicate that a child adopted from a country that relies on a foster care system (in general) does better. Guatemala and Korea both rely on a foster care system. I had a conversation today with a single mother who couldn't tolerate a lot of risk in her adoption (meaning that she was not comfortable trying to care for a child with high risks). I counseled her that there is a risk with every child (adopted or biological)…they can always develop health issues down the road.

But overall, I've found that the children coming from Guatemala are in better health upon arrival. The children from Guatemala tend to be adopted at a younger age. And a child that is out of foster care or an orphanage at 2–3 months of age has better chances of not having as many health issues as a child who has been in a foster care situation or orphanage for 2–3 years.

AFS: How do you know the health status of the child you are adopting?
PM: Each country has a very different process. The one consistent thing about international adoption is there is nothing consistent about international adoption. Russia recently has been changing the amount of information they provide on the health of a child.

Some regions in Russia do not provide any information, but others do. It also depends on the region or even the orphanage director; some will provide a lot of health information while others will provide none. It really depends on a lot of factors.

China gives quite a bit of health information. The accuracy of the information is somewhat suspect, though. Sometimes the health records from China indicate that a child has developmental skills above what they should. I've seen medical records that indicate a 12-month-old is speaking in full sentences, which we know isn't true.

Guatemala has a very good Western-based medical system and I trust their medical records more. The problem is, though, that the majority of children adopted from Guatemala are young and you can't really evaluate the long-term aspects of their health at such a young age. From Guatemala, though, the adopter should expect to get updates, often monthly. Most of the children from Guatemala are adopted before they are a year old.

AFS: At what point in the process do perspective parents come to you?

PM: I would say the vast majority will come in when they have a referral from a country indicating that a child is available for adoption. They want help with evaluating the health of their child from the medical records. We would like to, in some situations, see them sooner than that so that we can steer them in directions to help them adopt a child who more closely matches their parenting desires. I'm always happy to see happy families and successful adoptions.

AFS: Do you conduct physicals on babies once they arrive in the U.S.? Do you recommend pediatricians that specialize in working with children adopted from other countries?

PM: I generally find that I don't recommend pediatricians that specialize in working with adopted children. That's why I'm here—I can help with specifics of a child from various countries. The families just need a good pediatrician because soon the child will not be an adopted child, just a child that happens to be adopted.

We can take care of the initial health issues specific to internationally adopted children. For instance, the American

149

Academy of Pediatrics (AAP) suggests certain lab studies, stool studies, and growth points that measure development.

Within the last nine years AAP has recognized international adoptions as a subsection. I'm on the executive committee, so I'm one of the leaders of that group. The Academy publishes the Red Book, the infectious disease bible for pediatricians. The most recent book (2006) just came out and includes a section on international adoption that lists recommended tests—stool studies and lab studies. Screening tests recommended by AAP for internationally adopted children include tests for Hepatitis B, Hepatitis C, syphilis, HIV, a blood count looking for anemia, stool studies for eggs and parasites, and specific antigens looking for Giardia and Cryptosporidium. They also recommend a skin test for TB. Other things that generally are recommended include an evaluation for thyroid problems, a test for lead levels, and recommendations for hearing and vision screening. The book also includes a section on immunizations (many of us are a little skeptical on whether or not children have received certain immunizations in their countries). But most of us doctors are getting away from starting the immunization process in children all over again once they arrive in the U.S. We've found, when looking into it, that many of the kids have received their vaccines. It also depends on the country.

AFS: What are some of the health issues that you would consider "red flags"?
PM: The one thing that gives me the most concern is when I hear that the biological mother drank alcohol. We know that alcohol does nothing good to the developing brain. In fact, it is devastating. In Eastern Europe we're more concerned about whether or not the mother was an alcoholic. That's the number one thing that I never want to see.

The next red flag would be if a child was taken away for significant abuse or neglect. I'm always concerned about the long-term implications of that. Many children are resilient, but many are not.

The other thing I really look out for is the child's growth and development. If I see in the medical records that a child is not growing well or not developing well it does send up a red flag for me.

AFS: How much reactive attachment disorder (RAD) do you see? How big of a problem is it and what is its prognosis? What are the chances of adopting a child with reactive attachment disorder? Do the medical records indicate psychological issues such as reactive attachment disorder? Are there ways to determine how severe it is before you adopt the child? Do you treat it in your clinic?

PM: We are not really seeing RAD as a big issue. I do not have the exact number, but my guess is that it would be less than 1% of all of the children who are adopted. I also do not think that it is something that can be improved. If the family feels that they will just be able to adopt a child and be "attached" immediately they have not really done their homework. Some studies suggest that attachment can take up to a year to fully occur. In my opinion, it is really the very rare child who will not be able to make improvements with attachment with time. Which countries may offer the greatest risks? I would say those in which children are being adopted at an older age and those that rely on an orphanage system (Eastern Europe and China, for instance).

There are a number of hot topics with big catch phrases that become popular. This is one of the mixed blessings of the internet—many families are learning about disease, etc. There is a lot of misinformation on the internet about attachment, though. Half the people that are writing on the internet about attachment disorder don't know what they are talking about. Some kids do have attachment problems. Every single child who is adopted has an attachment problem. Most of these kids coming from an orphanage have never had a parent. They all have some degree of attachment issues because they never had a parent to attach to. But we do not see many cases of severe forms of attachment disorder.

AFS: How about other diseases— Giardiasis, HIV, Hepatitis C? What diseases are most common?

PM: Fortunately, the diseases you mention are not very common. We test for all of these infections and find that not many of the children have them. We do see an increase in Giardia (an intestinal parasite). This may sound really terrible but is generally very easy to treat. Most of the kids have some degree of developmental delays. The most common issue is speech delay. It

Victoria Solsberry

is very common to observe some sort of speech delay in an internationally adopted child.

The second most common delay is motor delay. This seems to be a big issue in Guatemalan children, for instance. In Guatemala, children are carried by their foster parents all of the time and the children do not have a lot of opportunities to crawl and develop their motor skills.

AFS: Who conducts the physicals in the foreign countries? Government-appointed physicians?
PM: This varies by country. In Russia and China, doctors go around to the orphanages and evaluate the children or sometimes the director of the orphanage is a doctor. In Guatemala, though, the people who run the adoption process are lawyers, so they contract out to doctors. The foster care mothers will take the child to the pediatrician's office to get examined and then the pediatrician will send out the medical information and records to adopters.

AFS: This book is for a national audience, not a local one. How would someone from Oregon who is interested in adopting find a center like yours? Are there others in the country—is this a trend?
PM: The number of centers is growing around the country. The number of people who have identified themselves as adopted-interested experts has been growing. There are probably 10–20 centers around the country that are like ours.

The American Academy of Pediatrics maintains a list on their web site that has doctors who are members who are also members of the Section for Adoption and Foster Care (www.aap.org/sections/adoption/default.cfm). In addition, a number of other centers around the country offer lists of people on their websites. One of the best lists is on the University of Minnesota International Adoption Clinic's website.

AFS: Does your center employ the use of mental health professionals?
PM: No, we refer our patients to mental health professionals and other specialists (social workers, psychologists, family therapists, speech therapists). We get together monthly for conferences and

discuss common patients, interesting cases we've seen, and we review medical literature, etc. We do have a number of professionals that we work with and refer to in this area.

AFS: *What issues do you cover in your training sessions?*

PM: We do offer parenting classes that we provide to the families several times a year (we rely on a lot of the people I just mentioned in the previous answer to help with the teaching and classes). We cover issues related to adopting a child. For instance, a speech and language person might talk about transitioning the child from another language to English. An occupational therapist might discuss normal motor development and how to know when a child has development issues and how to play with a child and help with their motor development. We also talk about general parenting issues. Many new parents wonder how to change a diaper. So we discuss general health and parenting issues, too. We have older parents who have adopted come back and talk about their experience.

AFS: *Can you give us your thoughts on some of the most common countries to adopt from and briefly touch upon common illnesses, syndromes, and developmental problems?*

PM: I will try to touch on the countries briefly. In China, the girls adopted are generally delayed on arrival but most do well with time. We have seen a number of language issues that may persist with children adopted from China.

In Russia, Ukraine, Bulgaria, Kazakhstan (all about the same), there is more risk of developmental delay and I am always concerned about alcohol exposure (about the same risk in each country). I have more concerns about development and attachment from here than most countries and the risks seem to be greater with older children.

Guatemala and Korea are both very good countries with good reliable medical systems and the children are generally healthier on arrival. Children adopted from these countries may have more motor delays because in those countries children are carried around a lot. Both countries have good medical systems with more reliable records. The upside is that children there are so young when they are adopted, which means they are home with their new family earlier. The downside to that, though, is that they are so young that we won't know much about their risks and development at the time of their adoption.

We are seeing more children being adopted from Ethiopia. The children we have seen so far have done well. The children generally have delays on arrival but have improved with time and with hard work by the children and their families. The problem for the new family is that when they review the information there is generally very little information and the process goes very fast.

Rita Soronen, Executive Director
Dave Thomas Foundation for Adoption

AFS: Okay, let's say, hypothetically, that I'm a 45-50 year old single man or woman and I'm just beginning to think about adoption. I have concerns about whether I can do it. Can you answer some questions for me?
RS: I'd be happy to.

AFS: Can singles adopt from the foster care system? How about gays and lesbians?
RS: Yes, singles can and do adopt from the foster care system. In fact, during the last reporting year (Adoption and Foster Care Analysis and Reporting System, U.S. Dept. of HHS; as of September 2006), 27% of the children adopted from foster care were adopted by single women and 3% were adopted by single men. Every state, by law, allows single parent adoption.

Today, by law, two states – Mississippi and Florida have banned gay and lesbian adults from adopting. Utah does not allow unmarried co-habiting couples to adopt.

Law, of course, can differ from practice. In many agencies there may remain a bias against single parent adoption or gay/ lesbian parent adoption. Additionally, single males may face more skepticism and scrutiny in the application process.

AFS: Are there lower and upper age limits for prospective adoptive parents in foster care adoption?
RS: The states differ on the lower age limits for adopting – in six states one can be 18 and adopt, in four states the age is 21, and two states set the minimum age to adopt at 25. Some states specify age

relative to the child to be adopted; for example, in six states, the adopting parent must be at least ten years older than the person being adopted, and in one state, the parent must be at least 15 years older. Typically, there is no upper age limit for adopting non-infants. Of course, state laws frequently change, but generally speaking, there are few age limits for prospective parents in foster care adoption.

AFS: How much do I have to earn to be eligible to adopt?
RS: In general, the only income constraint for prospective parents in the foster care system is the ability to provide a safe and nurturing home for a child. Individuals engaged in the home study process, a requirement prior to adoption, will be asked to show some sort of income verification, which may be a tax return, paycheck stub or W-2 form.

AFS: What are the costs associated with foster care adoption? If I can't afford it, is it still possible?
RS: Children in foster care are in the custody of the state or county and frequently defined as special needs (older youth, siblings, children of color and/or children with physical or emotional challenges) in which they are being served. As a result, there are few or no costs associated with the process of adopting out of foster care. The kind of costs that may be incurred include legal fees, if the prospective parent chooses to hire an attorney ($1,000 - $6,000) and in some situations, the cost of the home study (the cost can range from $0 - $3,000). Frequently, these expenses are reimbursable through a number of options, detailed below.

AFS: I understand that foster parents receive monthly stipends to care for the child. If I'd like to adopt but would have difficulty supporting the child, is there any financial aid?
RS: There are many public and private supports in place for individuals choosing to expand their family through foster care adoption. For example, since 2003, parents who adopt children who have special needs from the U.S. foster care system (and whose annual adjusted gross income is less than $190,000) have been able to claim up to $11,390 in tax credits or exclusions to offset adoption costs *without* documenting adoption expenses (www.irs.gov/instructions/i8839/).

155

Additionally, a parent who adopts a child with special needs may be eligible for a federal or state adoption subsidy to help offset the short- and long-term costs associated with adopting children who need special services. In general, children adopted from the custody of state or county child welfare agencies (or private agencies under contract with the state that provide services for foster children) are eligible for adoption assistance benefits. Benefits available through subsidy programs vary by state, and may include monthly cash payments, medical assistance, social services and/or one-time expenses. It is critical to discuss subsidies with the caseworkers involved in the adoption during the process and learn as much as possible about the guidelines and process (www.nacac.org/adoptionsubsidy/adoptionsubsidy.html).

A growing number of workplaces are including adoption benefits in their human resource packages, in order to provide support for families who adopt. This kind of assistance can include paid or unpaid leave (5 weeks, average), over and above that provided by FMLA, and/or financial assistance for adoption expenses ($5,000, average). Adoption-Friendly Workplace, a signature program of the Dave Thomas Foundation for Adoption works to both encourage employers to include adoption benefits in their workplace packages and celebrate those who do through the annual 100 Best Adoption-Friendly Workplace list (www.adoptionfriendlyworkplace.org).

Finally, parents may also consider low-interest flexible loans and insurance loans, or contact adoption organizations that provide financial assistance (National Adoption Foundation, www.nafadopt.org; Fore Adoption Foundation, www.foreadoption.com; Shaohannah's Hope, www.shaohannahshope.org; Gift of Adoption Fund, www.giftofadoption.org).

AFS: I might be interested in adopting an older child, but I don't have savings to pay for college. Is that okay?
RS: We frequently hear that one barrier to a parent considering adopting an older child is that they have not had time to save for college. Tuition assistance through vouchers, waivers or scholarships is increasingly available through federal legislation enacted at the state level and through a growing number of private non-profit organizations.

The Promoting Safe and Stable Families Amendments of 2001 added a new category of assistance. It created education and training vouchers for youth aging out of foster care and includes provision for young people adopted from foster care at the age of 16 or greater. Eligible youth may receive up to $5,000 in vouchers per year, and may be eligible until they are age 23. For more information, see the National Resource Center for Youth Development fact sheet at www.nrcys.ou.edu/yd/etv.htm. Information about other sources for tuition assistance can be found at the Child Welfare Information Gateway (www.childwelfare.gov/adoption/postadoption/assistance/college.cfm).

AFS: It would be very expensive to change from single to family health insurance coverage at work. Is there any way to get other health coverage for the child?
RS: The Adoption and Safe Families Act of 1997 is federal legislation that is intended to help foster children find placement in permanent homes by tightening timelines associated with the adoption process, assuring that a child's safety is a paramount and by providing financial assistance to families. It dovetails with similar legislation at the state level. Among other provisions, the federal act "extends Medicaid or state funded health insurance to children with non-federal (state funded) adoption subsidy agreements, if the children are determined to have 'special needs for medical or rehabilitative care.' Under the Title IV-E adoption assistance program, Medicaid coverage transfers with the child to any new state of residence."

For families who do choose to stay with their employer-based health care coverage, it is important to note that Federal law requires that group health plans that provide coverage for "natural" children must provide the same coverage for adoptive children, *to begin when children are placed for adoption* (Section 609(c) of the Employee Retirement Income Security Act of 1974/ERISA).

AFS: Do I have to own my own home to adopt?
RS: Absolutely not. As long as your home is safe and can provide a nurturing environment for the child, you can adopt.

Victoria Solsberry

AFS: What kind of home is required for foster care adoption?
RS: A home full of joy for children, patience, humor, tolerance, knowledge of the dynamics of adoption and particularly adoption from foster care, strength, resourcefulness and an indefatigable belief that children deserve a loving environment (no matter what challenges are encountered) and a permanent family, is a home ready for foster care adoption.

AFS: I've heard that some countries are cutting off prospective adoptive parents with any physical problems. Am I allowed to have any chronic health issues to be considered for adoption?
RS: In the United States, caseworkers take great care to determine the best possible placements for children. Chronic health issues can cover a wide range of medical circumstances and no single issue necessarily or automatically disqualifies a parent from adopting. For all the right reasons, the adoption agency and the court will consider medical or psychological issues that may prevent the potential parent from being able to provide a safe and nurturing home.

I am not expert in the area of international adoption and the ever-changing policies and practices in countries other than the U.S.

AFS: What is the range of ages of children available for adoption from foster care?
RS: Children in foster care available for adoption range in age from birth to 18, although the average age of the waiting child is 8.6 years, and 57% of the children available for adoption from the United States foster care system are age 7 or older.

AFS: Can you walk me through the steps for adopting a child from foster care?
RS: Foster care adoption can appear daunting at times – paperwork, classes, legal issues and delays. But life is full of each of those challenges, and the effort is worth the end result. The first best step is to do a self-assessment and ask; Am I ready to adopt? Am I willing to change my lifestyle in order to accommodate a child in my life? Do I understand that children from foster care have special needs and challenges? What age child am I interested in adopting? Would I consider a sibling group, a child with

158

medical or emotional needs or a child from a different race or culture?

If an individual is comfortable moving forward then the following steps should occur:

1. Learn all you can about foster care adoption – books, online, calls to adoption agencies.
2. Explore adoption expense issues and assistance.
3. Search for an appropriate adoption agency in your community and let them know you are ready to start the process.
4. Complete an adoption application.
5. Complete a home study.
6. Attend adoption/parenting classes.
7. Begin the search for a child or sibling group.
8. Commit to a child or sibling group to adopt.
9. Prepare your home for the child.
10. Have the child placed in your home for 6 - 12 months prior to finalization.
11. File a petition with the court to adopt.
12. Finalize the adoption in court – and celebrate!

There are professionals who guide prospective adoptive parents through each step of the process. Call the Dave Thomas Foundation for Adoption at 1-800-ASK-DTFA and ask for a free copy of *A Child is Waiting: A Beginner's Guide to Adoption*, or order online at www.DaveThomasFoundationForAdoption.org.

AFS: How would a specific child be matched up with me?

RS: The matching process is a unique collaboration between the agency caseworker and the adoptive parent. Based on the parent's wishes and requirements for a child, the caseworker will work to find a child whose needs make a good match. This is accomplished through a variety of methods, including through the parent's search of websites, agency materials, match events and discussions and the caseworker's thorough knowledge of the children available.

Before agreeing to adopt any child or sibling group, learn as much as possible about the child, including prenatal care and exposure to drugs or alcohol, birth parents' medical histories, attachments to foster families or other relatives, foster care placements, relationships with siblings, interests and talents, etc. Most agencies want adoptive parents to get to know children before agreeing to adopt. If the child has certain medical conditions or other disabilities, decide if your family is prepared to address issues that may arise from the child's situation.

At this stage of the process, parents need to stay in close contact with the agency and help continue to move the process forward.

AFS: I went on the website, Adoptuskids.com, and looked at pictures of children from all over the country who are waiting to be adopted. If I were interested in a child from out of state, how would that work?

RS: The Internet has played a major role in the increased number of children adopted across state lines. Interstate adoptions are affected by two agreements between the "sending" and "receiving" states. These agreements carry the force of law and include the Interstate Compact on Adoption and Medical Assistance (ICAMA), and the Interstate Compact on the Placement of Children (ICPC). Children's and parents' adoption workers, agencies, or attorneys will generally prepare the necessary paperwork, but placing and adopting parents should be aware of the Compacts, their provisions, and whether one or both apply.

AFS: Do I need to foster the child before I can adopt him or her?

RS: One does not have to be a foster parent prior to adopting. The value in foster parenting as a first step, though, is in having the experience of the systems that surround the child (legal, social, medical, educational); the multitude of professionals who have managed the child's case (social workers, attorneys, therapists), the issues impacting the child's life (abuse, neglect, and/or abandonment) and the networks available to foster and adoptive parents (parent support groups, training sessions). Last year about 60% of the adoptions from foster care occurred by their foster parents. An individual wishing to simply apply to be an adoptive parent can learn as much as possible by researching on-line, through literature and by calling the county, state or private adoption agencies in the community and asking for information.

AFS: Who would I contact if I'm interested in learning more about foster care adoption?
RS: There are many excellent programs that can provide information, links to resources and answers to questions. One source is the Dave Thomas Foundation for Adoption (1-800-ASK-DTFA;   www.DaveThomasFoundationForAdoption.org). The Foundation provides free of charge *A Child is Waiting: A Beginner's Guide to Adoption* that details the steps to adopting and connects the reader to multiple national and local resources. The Foundation will also link interested individuals to the Wendy's Wonderful Kids recruiter in their community. This is a skilled adoption professional who spends 100% of his or her day matching children in foster care with families wanting to adopt. There are more than 100 Wendy's Wonderful Kids recruiters in all 50 states and the District of Columbia dedicated to helping families come together through foster care adoption.

APPENDIX A

INTERCOUNTRY ADOPTION DIRECTORY

On December 12, 2007, the United States ratified the Hague Convention on Protection of Children and Cooperation in Respect of Intercountry Adoptions. What that means is that we have agreed to follow the rules of a treaty governing adoption processes meant to protect children – among the rules, to promote transparency and prevent trafficking, to ensure that children being adopted abroad are indeed orphaned or have had their parents' rights terminated, and that mothers are not being paid to relinquish those rights. The U.S. signed the treaty in 1994, Congress passed the Intercountry Adoption Act of 2000 (PL 106-279) consenting to the ratification and implementation of the rules, and as noted above, full ratification happened in December 2007. The rules went into effect on April 1, 2008.

This appendix will list the countries that you may consider when you think about adoption. Some are included just to inform you that you cannot adopt from that country. The reason will be given – either the country does not adopt to singles, or they adopt only to their citizens, or now that the Hague Convention has been ratified by the U.S., we can no longer adopt from that country. Some countries will have travel alerts issued by the State Department. To check for updates on travel alerts for specific countries, go to http://www.travel.state.gov/travel/travel_1744.html, and click on "Travel Warnings" on the right menu.

Also included in this list is information about the availability of children in the country; if available, recent U.S. immigration visa statistics (which indicates how many children were adopted to U.S. citizens in that year); age and civil status requirements for prospective adoptive parents, document requirements for that country, approximate in-country costs, and any special information pertinent to that country. The list is in alphabetical order.

The following is a short list of terms and definitions:

- I-600 Petition: Petition to Classify Orphan as an Immediate Relative --Used to grant a U.S. visa when the parent has identified a specific child to be adopted (i.e., a family member).
- I-600A Petition: Application for Advance Processing of Orphan Petition --Used to grant a U.S. visa when the parent has not identified a specific child, usually when the parent intends to go abroad to find a child for adoption.
- I-171H: Notice of Favorable Determination Concerning Application for Advance Processing of Orphan Petition. The I-171H basically says that you have been approved by the U.S. government to find and adopt a child abroad. It remains in effect for 18 months.
- FD-258 Fingerprint Chart: Used to determine criminal record of prospective adoptive parent and every adult 18 and up living in the household.
- Article 5 Letter: Issued by the Consular Officer at the U.S. Embassy to the local adoption authorities stating that the prospective adoptive parent is "suitable" and that the child will be allowed to enter the United States to be adopted.
- IR3 Immigrant Visa: For a child adopted abroad in a Non-Hague country
- IR4 Immigrant Visa: For a child to be adopted in the U.S. from a Non-Hague country
- IH3 Immigrant Visa: For a child adopted abroad in a Hague country
- IH4 Immigrant Visa: For a child to be adopted in the U.S. from a Hague country
- Authentication: Many countries require that civil documents such as birth certificates (also divorce and death) not only bear the seal of the issuing state, but also be "authenticated" by the U.S. government. This service costs $7 (Check or money order) per document and can be done at the U.S. Department of State Authentication Office, 518 23rd Street, N.W., State Annex 1, Washington, DC 20520. Telephone: (202) 647-5002.

Special Note: This directory is a snapshot of policies in January, 20010. Because of the quickly changing world of intercountry adoptions, use the links provided to see if changes have occurred. The URL provided for each country should take you directly to the country page. If that doesn't happen, go to www.adoption.state.gov, click on "Country Info." on the top menu, then go to "Please Select a Country" to get an alphabetized list of countries with updates.

* * * * * * * * * *

ALGERIA

- **Availability of children for adoption:** In fiscal year 2009, 3 immigrant adoption visas were issued, up from 1 in 2007. However, prospective adoptive parents must hold citizenship in Algeria, although they do not have to reside there. Only abandoned children may be adopted in Algeria. If a parent is known but unable to care for the child, he or she must be cared for by a family member.

- **Age and civil status requirements:** Singles are permitted to adopt, but must be Muslim. Men cannot be over 60 years of age, and women over 55 years of age.

- **Document requirements:**

  - Written request for a "Kafala", or legal guardianship
  - Birth certificate of prospective adoptive parent
  - Medical certificate
  - Criminal record directly from authorities in prospective adoptive parent's home country
  - Proof of work and income
  - Pay stubs for the last 3 months

- Copy of consular registration form
- Proof of citizenship of prospective adoptive parent
- Recent photo ID
- Proof of ownership or lease of residence

- www.adoption.state.gov/country/algeria.html

ANGOLA

- **Availability of children for adoption:** Only 1 immigrant adoption visa has been issued in the past 5 years. However, it may take years to identify a child for adoption, and once that happens it takes an Act of the National Assembly to approve the adoption.

- **Age and civil status requirements:** Singles are permitted to adopt in Angola, but must be at least 16 years older than the child.

- **Document requirements (translated into Portuguese):**

    - Letter stating intention to adopt, identifying information about the prospective adoptive parent and prospective adoptive child
    - Criminal background check and clearance
    - Medical examination
    - Proof of income
    - Birth certificate
    - If possible, birth certificate of child or statement from institution that cared for the child
    - Divorce certificate, if applicable
    - If possible, consent biological of parent of child

- http://www.adoption.state.gov/country/angola.html

ARGENTINA

- **Intercountry Adoptions are not permitted in Argentina.**

- www.adoption.state.gov/country/argentina.html

ARMENIA

- **Availability of children for adoption:** In fiscal year 2009, 20 immigrant adoption visas were issued. There were 32 issued in fiscal year 2007 and 46 in fiscal year 2006.

- **Age and civil status requirements:** Singles are permitted to adopt in Armenia, but must be at least 18 years older than the child.

- **Document requirements:**

  - Copy of passport
  - Home study
  - Letter verifying work position, salary, and 3 related letters of reference
  - Copy of most recent federal tax return
  - Copy of divorce decree or spouse's death certificate, if applicable
  - Medical report confirming no psychological condition, HIV, alcoholism or drug abuse, active TB or other infectious diseases
  - Local police clearance
  - Child's consent if the child is over 10 years of age
  - If child's biological parents are alive, a written statement releasing the child for adoption

- http://adoption.state.gov/country/armenia.html

AUSTRALIA

- **Only Australian citizens and permanent residents may adopt.**

- www.adoption.state.gov/country/australia.html

AUSTRIA

- **Availability of children for adoption:** Two immigrant adoption visas were issued in 2002, with none since that time. There are very few Austrian children available for intercountry adoption. Prospective adoptive parents must be legal residents of Austria.

- http://www.adoption.state.gov/country/austria.html

THE BAHAMAS

- **Availability of children for adoption:** No immigrant adoption visas have been issued in the past five years.

- **Age and civil status requirements:** Single adoption is permitted and there are no age requirements. The prospective adoptive child must be abandoned, orphaned, or released by the birth mother.

- **Special Information:** Because the number of available children is very small, Bahamian citizens and legal residents are given preference in adopting children. Blood relatives are given first preference. A lawyer is required to take the adoption through the country's Supreme Court. The approximate cost for the lawyer is between $1,000 and $3,000.

- http://www.adoption.state.gov/country/bahamas.html

BAHRAIN

- **Adoption is not permitted at all in Bahrain.**

BANGLADESH

- **Availability of children for adoption:** Adoption is not permitted at all in Bangladesh, but American citizens and residents who are also citizens of Bangladesh may apply for guardianship in Bangladesh and complete the adoption process in the U.S. In fiscal year 2009, 12 immigrant adoption visas were issued, down from 16 in 2006. It is unclear whether singles are permitted to adopt in Bangladesh, but they make no statement against it.

- http://adoption.state.gov/country/bangladesh.html

BARBADOS

- **Availability of children for adoption:** In fiscal year 2009, one immigrant adoption visa was issued. The last visa issued before 2009 was in 2004, and there have been only 6 issued in the past ten years.

- **Age and civil status requirements:** Singles are permitted to adopt in Barbados. If related to the child, prospective parent must be at least 18 years old. Otherwise, prospective parent must be 25 years old and at least 18 years older than the child.

- **Document requirements:**

  - Birth certificate
  - Divorce documents, if applicable
  - Medical report
  - Police report

- Three personal references known for at least five years, and not related
- Statement of income

- **Special information:** Must use a local attorney to take you through adoption process, which will cost approximately $3,000.

- http://www.adoption.state.gov/country/barbados.html

BELARUS

- **Availability of children for adoption:** Adoptions were suspended in Belarus in October of 2004, and although the procedures were changed in 2005, adoptions have not resumed at this time. In 2004, there were 202 immigration visas issued for adoptions, 21 in 2005 (to finish adoptions already in process). The following requirements are expected to apply when Belarus reopens adoptions to Americans. The State Department has taken the Belarus page down, but check the site (www.adoption.state.gov) or call the State Department if you have a reason for wanting to adopt from that country.

- **Age and civil status requirements:** Single adoption was permitted. Prospective parent must be at least 16 years older than the adoptive child. Single parents are allowed to adopt children of either gender.

- **Special information:** Adoption can cost between $18,000 and $25,000 in Belarus. Children adopted from that country remain citizens of Belarus until their 16th birthday.

BELGIUM

- **Belgium is not a country of origin for intercountry adoptions. All children available for adoption are adopted in-country.**

BELIZE

- **Availability of children for adoption:** In fiscal year 2009, 6 immigrant adoption visas were issued, 7 in 2007, 9 in 2006, and 14 in 2005.

- **Age and civil status requirements:** Single adoption is permitted. Prospective adoptive parent must be a minimum of 25 years of age and at least 12 years older than the child. Single men may not adopt girls. Americans may adopt if they do not have a criminal record and have a current recommendation as to their suitability to be a parent from a welfare officer or social worker in their home country.

- **Document requirements:**

  - Home study
  - Police report
  - Approved I-600 or I-600A

- **Special information:** Prospective adoptive parents must live with the child for at least 12 months before the adoption is finalized. This can happen either in Belize, or an interim adoption decree can be issued to take the child back to the United States. Attorney's fees in Belize range from $1,500 to $3,000.

- http://adoption.state.gov/country/belize.html

BOLIVIA

- **Availability of children for adoption:** With the ratification of the Hague Convention and its implementation on April 1, 2008, adoptions have reopened in Bolivia. In fiscal year 2007, 4 immigrant visas were issued for children adopted by American citizens who were also citizens or legal residents of Bolivia. By contrast, before the moratorium on U.S. adoptions because of our noncompliance with the Hague Convention, 35 immigrant visas were issued in 2001. As part of the Hague Convention requirements, Bolivia is required to set up agencies in-country to aid American adoption agencies in finding Bolivian orphans for adoption. The Bolivian government has not yet done this, making intercountry adoption almost impossible.

- **Age and civil status requirements:** Single people are permitted to adopt, but must be between the ages of 25 and 50 and 15 years older than the adoptive child.

- **Document requirements:**

  - Birth certificate of prospective adoptive parent
  - Home study
  - Physical and psychological health certificates
  - Financial and employment certifications
  - Two or three personal references
  - Police record
  - Participation in and completion of a parenting workshop in the U.S.

- **Special information:** A Bolivian attorney is required, and will cost between $5,000 and $7,000. Direct adoptions are prohibited (as in when the birth mother directly releases a child to the prospective parents) and all children adopted must be abandoned, and thus, chosen for the prospective adoptive parent by the Bolivian government.

- http://adoption.state.gov/country/bolivia.html

BOSNIA-HERZEGOVINA

- **Availability of children for adoption:** Bosnian law requires that there be "overwhelming justification" for adoptions to foreigners, and that such adoptions can only happen when the child cannot be adopted by a Bosnian family, and if it is in the "best interest of the child." Only 3 immigrant visas were issued in fiscal year 2005 and the State Department no longer publishes a web page for adoptions from Bosnia.

- **Age and civil status requirements:** Prospective adoptive parents must be between 25 and 45 years of age, and that the parent be at least 18 years older than the child. In exceptional circumstances, the adoptive parent may be older than 45, but the age difference between the prospective parent and the child cannot be more than 45 years. Although single adoption is permitted, in practice, adoptions are made only to married couples. It is believed that special needs children can be adopted by singles in extreme cases.

- **Document Requirements:**

  - Birth certificate
  - Medical certificate of good health
  - Copy of passport
  - Police certificate proving no criminal record
  - Court certificate stating that prospective adoptive parent is not under investigation for any reason
  - Proof of employment, resume, signed letter from employer
  - Proof that prospective adoptive parent has never been charged with abuse or neglect of a child
  - Proof of income and ownership of property, if applicable
  - Home study

- **Prohibited from adopting in Bosnia:**

  - Prospective adoptive parents who have had parental rights stripped in the U.S.
  - Those with limited or no ability to work
  - Those who cannot promise to raise the child "correctly"
  - Mentally ill, retarded or physically ill in a way that would endanger the child

- **Special information:** There are no government fees to adopt in Bosnia. No American adoption agencies operate in Bosnia, so prospective parents my contact the U.S. Embassy in Sarajevo for a copy of a list of local attorneys to help with the adoption process. If the prospective parent does not have a specific child picked out, he/she can contact the Center for Social Work to inquire about children eligible for adoption. As stated above, however, it is extremely unlikely that a child who is not a relative would be available for adoption.

BRAZIL

- **Availability of children for adoption:** Until the U.S. ratified the Hague Convention for Intercountry Adoption, U.S. citizens were not given preference in adoptions for children under the age of 5. Single, healthy children over the age of 5, sibling groups of any number and age, and special needs children of all ages were generally available to U.S. citizens. Since the U.S. ratified The Hague Convention on December 31, 2007 and it went into effect on April 1, 2008, all children are available for adoption at this time. In fiscal year 2009, 32 immigrant adoption visas were issued.

- **Age and civil status requirements:** Singles are permitted to adopt, but must be over the age of 21, and must be at least 16 years older than the adoptive child.

- **Residency requirements:** The prospective parent must live with the adoptive child in Brazil for at least 15 days if the child is under 2, and 30 days for older children.

- **Document requirements:**

  - Home study
  - Psychological evaluation
  - Medical examination
  - Certificate of residence (proof of home ownership or lease, including pictures of the home, inside and out)
  - Pictures of prospective adoptive parent and if possible, grandparents

- http://adoption.state.gov/country/brazil.html

BULGARIA

- **Availability of children for adoption:** Currently there are very few children on the waiting list, so it can take many months or even years before a child is offered by the government for adoption. Children approved for intercountry adoption must have been turned down by three Bulgarian families, and usually have serious medical conditions. Preference is given to prospective parents willing to adopt a child with handicaps. In fiscal year 2009, 15 immigrant visas were issued, down from 296 in 2001.

- **Age and civil status requirements:** Single adoption is permitted. Prospective adoptive parents must be at least 15 years older than the adoptive child, but not more than 45 years older.

- **Special information:** Because children offered to U.S. prospective parents have special medical and/or physical needs, when a child is offered, adoptive parents have two months to accept or decline the adoption. If the child is declined, another child will be offered if there is a child in need. The government of Bulgaria focuses on finding the appropriate parent for each child, not on finding a child for prospective parents.

- **Document requirements:**

    - Application prepared by American adoption agency (history, financial data, personal information)
    - An FBI fingerprint clearance to determine if prospective adoptive parent has ever had parental rights terminated
    - Home study
    - Medical examination
    - Police record
    - I-171H (approval of U.S. Immigration)

- http://adoption.state.gov/country/bulgaria.html

BURKINA FASO

- **Singles are not permitted to adopt in Burkina Faso.**

BURMA

- **Americans are not permitted to adopt from Burma.**

BURUNDI

- **Availability of children for adoption:** Burundian law states that the only children who are eligible for intercountry adoption are those unable to be placed locally. Four immigrant adoption visas were issued in 2009.

- **Age and civil status requirements:** Singles are permitted to adopt in Burundi, but must be at least 30 years old and 15 years older than the child.

- **Document requirements:**
    - Copy of passport
    - Medical report
    - Psychological report
    - Financial statement
    - References attesting to good behavior and family composition

- http://adoption.state.gov/country/burundi.html

CAMBODIA

- **Availability of children for adoption:** Adoptions of Cambodian children were suspended on December 21, 2001, because of concerns about fraud, trafficking and the absence of a local legal framework to protect the children. Since that time the U.S. government has urged the Royal Government of Cambodia to repair their system, and the first step was taken in March, 2007, when their government began the accession to the Hague Convention. The State Department is hopeful that the necessary changes will be made and that adoptions will once again be possible for American prospective adoptive parents in Cambodia. For updates, check the web address below.

- http://adoption.state.gov/country/cambodia.html

CAMEROON

- **Cameroon does not adopt to singles.**

CANADA

- **Canada is not a country of origin for intercountry adoptions. American adoptions of Canadian children are extremely rare, and are permitted only for children who are related to American prospective adoptive parents.**

CHILE

- **Chile does not adopt to singles.**

CHINA

- **Availability of children for adoption:** In December, 2006, China closed adoptions to single adults from any country. Singles that were in process at that time were allowed to complete their adoptions.

- http://adoption.state.gov/country/china.html

COLOMBIA

- **Availability of children for adoption:** Private adoption is not legal in Colombia, that is, children may only be adopted through the Colombian government and approved adoption agencies. Therefore, children are not permitted to be brought back to the United States to be adopted, so the adoption process must be complete before leaving the country. 306 immigrant adoption visas were issued in fiscal year 2008.

- **Age and civil status requirements:** Single adoptions are permitted, but only for children over the age of 7. Prospective parents must be at least 25 years of age.

- **Special information:** Parents receiving immigrant visas reported spending from $12,000 to $20,000 for the entire adoption process.

- **Document requirements:**

  - Application form for adoption (www.icbf.gov.com)
  - Birth certificate of prospective adoptive parent
  - Medical examination
  - National Law Enforcement clearance
  - Birth certificates of children previously adopted
  - Financial certificate – proof of employment, salary in U.S. dollars, length of tenure
  - If self-employed, certified document regarding finances or last tax return
  - Social and psychological study (Home study)
  - If previously married, proof of divorce or death certificate of former spouse
  - Notarized statement regarding any name changes – NOTE: In Colombia, women do not change their last names when they marry, so Colombian agencies are not used to birth certificates, marriage/divorce certificates and identification (Driver's license) having different last names.

- http://adoption.state.gov/country/colombia.html

COSTA RICA

- **Availability of children for adoption:** Adoptions reopened on April 1, 2008, when The Hague Convention on Intercountry Adoption went into effect. In fiscal year 2008, only 1 adoption immigration visa was issued. The Costa Rican government prohibits the adoption of any child under the age of 5 unless he or she is part of a sibling group or has special needs.

- **Age and civil status requirements:** Single persons are permitted to adopt. Prospective adoptive parents must be at least 25 years of age, and not older than 60 years of age.

- **Special information:** Private adoptions are no longer legal in Costa Rica. All adoptions must go through the Costa Rican Central Authority for the Hague Convention, the Patronato Nacional de la Infancia (PANI). PANI now requires that American prospective adoptive parents use an accredited American adoption agency. Adoptive parents should plan on two trips to Costa Rica, one for as long as 30 days to sign consent papers and start the adoption process, and at the end to finish the process and obtain immigration papers from the U.S. embassy.

- **Document requirements:**

  - Prospective parent's birth certificate
  - If previously married, certified copy of divorce decree or death certificate
  - Medical certificate
  - Certificate of "good conduct" or police certificate from local police department. FBI report is also acceptable
  - Verification of employment and salary
  - Two letters of reference
  - Property deeds, if applicable
  - Home study

- Bank statements
- Family letter of desire to adopt, including preferences for gender, age, etc.

- http://adoption.state.gov/country/costarica.html

CYPRUS

- **Cyprus is not a country of origin for intercountry adoption. Cypriot children who are related to American singles may be considered for adoption, but prospective adoptive parents must be permanent residents of Cyprus.**

THE CZECH REPUBLIC

- **Availability of children for adoption:** Until April 1, 2008, adoption was impossible for Americans living in the United States because the U.S. had not yet ratified and implemented the Hague Convention. It is now possible to adopt from the Czech Republic, although it is extremely difficult. Because the birth rate has gone down in the country, and because parents must release the child for adoption (which rarely happens), only 25-30% of all adoption applications to the country result in an actual adoption. Even then, it takes 2-5 years to bring a child home. The State Department no longer maintains an adoption web page for The Czech Republic. In 2005, the last year reported by the State Department, 2 immigrant adoption visas were issued.

- **Age and civil status requirements:** Single persons are permitted to adopt. The prospective adoptive parent can be no more than 40 years older than the adoptive child.

- **Special information:** There are no adoption agencies in the Czech Republic. Once adoptions for Americans resume, prospective adoptive parents locate adoptable children by contacting local Czech social service agencies, or by engaging a local attorney experienced in Czech adoptions. There are no fees for adoptions. Czech officials often require 3-24 months of preadoption care of the child by prospective parents.

- **Document requirements:**

  - Prospective parent's birth certificate
  - Police clearances from all countries where the prospective parent has resided
  - Medical certificates
  - Proof of employment and financial status
  - Home study

DENMARK

- **Availability of children for adoption:** There is a long waiting list of Danish citizens wanting to adopt very few available children. Only Americans legally resident in Denmark are eligible to adopt. Exceptions can be made for the adoption of relatives. There have been no immigrant adoption visas issued in the last 5 years.

- **Age and civil status requirements:** Singles are permitted to adopt, must be at least 25 years of age, and cannot be more than 40 years older than the adoptive child.

- http://adoption.state.gov/country/denmark.html

DOMINICA

- **Availability of children for adoption:** Although there were 36 American adoptions of Dominican children in 1993, there were none for many years after that, and only 2 immigrant adoption visas were issued in 2008. It is unclear whether singles are permitted to adopt from Dominica.

- http://adoption.state.gov/country/dominica.html

DOMINICAN REPUBLIC

- **The Dominican Republic does not adopt to singles**.

ECUADOR

- **Availability of children for adoption:** All adoptions must be facilitated by American adoption agencies licensed to deal with Ecuadorian adoption agencies or private attorneys. In fiscal year 2008, there were 26 immigrant adoption visas issued.

- **Age and civil status requirements:** Single persons are permitted to adopt, but except in special circumstances, the child must be the same gender as the prospective adoptive parent. Exceptions are made in terms of gender, but the age difference can be no more than 30 years in those cases.

- **Special information:** Prospective adoptive parents are required to reside in Ecuador for 4-5 weeks to complete the adoption.

- **Document requirements:**

  - Certified copies of birth certificate of adoptive parent
  - Certified proof of termination of previous marriage(s), or death certificates, if applicable
  - Certified copy of state law regarding adoption from home state
  - Home study
  - A sealed certificate of no criminal record from local police or FBI
  - Proof of employment and salary
  - Notarized letter of authorization from home adoption agency
  - Certificate of physical and mental health
  - Photocopies of passport

- http://adoption.state.gov/country/ecuador.html

EGYPT

- **Singles are not permitted to adopt from Egypt.**

EL SALVADOR

- **Availability of children for adoption:** The adoption process for foreign prospective adoptive parents can be quite lengthy and complicated, and one person's experience can be quite different from another. Most complicating is that the prospective parent needs to reside in El Salvador as a foster parent to the child for at least a year before the adoption. Even so, in fiscal year 2008, 21 immigrant adoption visas were issued.

- **Age and civil status requirements:** Single persons are permitted to adopt, although they must be at least 25 years of age and at least 15 years older than the adoptive child. If the child is under 1 year of age, however, the prospective adoptive parent can be no older than 45.

- http://adoption.state.gov/country/elsalvador.html

ESTONIA

- **Availability of children for adoption:** There are very few children available for adoption in Estonia, and Estonian citizens are given first priority for adoption. One exception is for children with medical need that could be provided in the United States. In fiscal year 2008, 11 immigrant adoption visas were issued, down from 21 in 2007. At this point in time, about 20 children a year are adopted by foreigners.

- **Age and civil status requirements:** Single persons are permitted to adopt, but be at least 25 years of age. If the prospective adoptive parent is divorced, the ex-spouse must give permission for the adoption.

- **Document requirements:**

  - Home study
  - Health certificate
  - Proof of financial status
  - Photocopies of prospective parent's passport
  - Any other information that might prove useful: ties to Estonia, letter of reference, etc.

- http://adoption.state.gov/country/estonia.html

ETHIOPIA

- **Availability of children for adoption:** The much-publicized adoption by Angelina Jolie of an Ethiopian child in 2005 has brought attention to the staggering numbers of children awaiting adoption in this country. Some estimates put the number of orphans at 5 million, and adoption agencies in Addis Ababa have doubled in the last few years. In fiscal year 2004, 289 immigrant adoption visas were issued to Americans, with 440 in 2005 and 731 in 2006. 1724 immigrant adoption visas were issued in 2008, showing a strong trend toward American adoption in Ethiopia. American prospective adoptive parents are required to use an American adoption agency approved for adoptions by the Ethiopian government.

- **Age and civil status requirements:** Although the Ethiopian government prefers to place children with married couples, singles are permitted to adopt if they are over 25 and not openly gay or lesbian. Exceptions have been made, however, in all these categories. There is no upper age limit, although the government prefers that adoptive parents be no more than 40 years older than the child they plan to adopt.

- **Special information:** It is common for the Ethiopian government to require that a child live in an orphanage for 3 months before being eligible for adoption. Children with two HIV/AIDS-infected parents, or one infected living parent are declared orphans by the state. All Ethiopian adoptions are final. To read one parent's story about adopting from Ethiopia, go to www.veronicasstory.org to learn about Tracey Neale, former CBS news anchor in Washington, DC, and her two adorable babies. Click on "Meeting my Kids" in the left menu. The State Department recommends that prospective adoptive parents choose an American adoption agency carefully. Some Americans trying to adopt in Ethiopia have had many more difficulties than others using different agencies. Check references and talk to parents about their experiences before choosing an agency.

- **Document requirements:** All documents must be translated into Amharic.

  - Written statement about why an Ethiopian child is desired
  - Original birth certificate of prospective adoptive parent
  - Ethiopian police clearance for prospective adoptive parent
  - Medical certificate for prospective adoptive parent
  - Home study
  - Proof of financial status including letter from employer, salary, position in company, tenure, bank statement, life insurance certificate, proof of other assets
  - Three letters of reference from relatives, friends, church
  - Two passport pictures
  - Signed certificate from home adoption agency agreeing to required home visits after the child returns to parent's home (3 months, 6 months, 1 year)
  - Verification by adoption agency of child's qualification for citizenship under parent's home state law

- http://adoption.state.gov/country/ethiopia.html

FIJI

- **Singles are permitted to adopt in Fiji, but must be a permanent resident.**

FINLAND

- **Finland does not allow out-of-country adoptions.**

FRANCE AND MONACO

- **Availability of children for adoption:** The number of children in France that are available for adoption is so small that most French citizens desiring to adopt go overseas. Only 2 immigrant adoption visas have been issued in the past 5 years. In the event that an American citizen wants to adopt a specific child (relative, etc.), requirements will be given.

- **Age and civil status requirements:** Single persons may adopt, but must be at least 28 years of age, and there is no upper age limit. Prospective adoptive parents must be at least 15 years older than the child.

- **Special information:** If you have identified a French child to adopt, such as a family member, and need an attorney in France, you can go to http://france.usembassy.gov/consul/acs/guide/Attorneys.pdf to find legal help.

- http://adoption.state.gov/country/france.html

THE GAMBIA

- **Availability of children for adoption:** Non-citizens of Gambia are allowed to adopt only in exceptional circumstances, and must be resident in Gambia for 6 months before applying. Only one immigrant adoption visa has been issued in the past 5 years.

- **Age and civil status requirements:** Single persons are permitted to adopt and must be between the ages of 21 and 60. They must also be at least 15 years older than the child, and cannot adopt a child of the opposite gender.

- **Special information:** Between the time of applying for adoption and the adoption itself, the prospective adoptive parent must foster the child for 36 months, which can take place in the U.S., but must be supervised by a local social service agency. The State Department no longer maintains an adoption web page for The Gambia.

GEORGIA

- **Availability of children for adoption:** In August of 2006, the Georgia Ministry of Education informed the U.S. government that a very limited number of children were available for adoption. Previously, only children who are unable to be placed in Georgia were adopted out of country. Information about available children may be obtained by calling Ms. Tamar Golubiani, who speaks English, at 955-32-95-17-68. In fiscal year 2006, 9 immigrant adoption visas were issued, down from 128 in 2003.

- **Age and civil status requirements:** Single persons are permitted to adopt and must be at least 16 years older than the child.

- **Document requirements:** If and when adoptions open again:

  - Copy of passport
  - For single and divorced prospective adoptive parents, a sworn statement notarized by the local U.S. Embassy
  - Certificate of health, including psychiatric
  - Proof of employment and salary
  - Bank statements
  - Police record
  - Home study
  - References

- **Special information:** Children must be classified as orphans for at least 6 months to qualify for out-of-country adoption, and the adoption takes 3-9 months. The State Department no longer maintains an adoption web page for Georgia.

GERMANY

- **Availability of children for adoption:** There are very few children available for adoption in Germany, and more and more German prospective adoptive parents are adopting out-of-country. In the event that a relative is available for adoption, requirements are given.

- **Age and civil status requirements:** German law requires that prospective adoptive parents be married and at least 25 years of age, but exceptions can be made in specific cases.

- http://adoption.state.gov/country/germany.html

GHANA

- **Availability of children for adoption:** Children are available for intercountry adoption only when the child cannot be adopted in Ghana, or when the child requires care that cannot be provided in that country. In addition, prospective adoptive parents must reside in Ghana for 3 months before the adoption. Even with those restrictions, 97 immigrant adoption visas were issued in 2008, up from 22 in 2005.

- **Age and civil status requirements:** Single U.S. citizens are permitted to adopt in Ghana only if they also citizens of Ghana. They must be at least 25 years of age and at least 21 years older than the child.

- **Document requirements:**

  - Copy of birth certificate
  - Medical report and clearance
  - Copy of divorce decree, if applicable
  - Evidence of financial stability
  - Proof of employment

- http://adoption.state.gov/country/ghana.html

GREECE

- **Availability of children for adoption:** In fiscal year 2006, 1 immigrant adoption visa was issued. Children may only be adopted by residents of Greece, and U.S. citizens who live in Greece must be of Greek origin. Exceptions are made for Greek children with health problems.

- **Age and civil status requirements:** Single persons are permitted to adopt, and must be between the ages of 30 and 60, and at least 18 years older but not more than 50 years older than the adoptive child.

- **Special information:** Although there is no religion requirement in Greece, preference is given to prospective adoptive parents who are Greek Orthodox.

- **Document requirements:**

  - Application notarized by Greek police or by International Social Service
  - Birth certificate and baptism certificate
  - Medical certificate and separate mental health certificate
  - Proof of financial status
  - Two letters of recommendation from friends, family, church

- "Penal record" – proof of "conviction-free" background. FBI record will suffice.
- Home study

- http://adoption.state.gov/country/greece.html

GRENADA

- **Availability of children for adoption:** U.S. citizens may adopt in Grenada, but only if they are resident of and live in Grenada. Four immigrant adoption visas were issued in 2008.

- **Age and civil status requirements:** Single persons are permitted to adopt, but must be at least 25 years of age and at least 21 years older than the child.

- **Document requirements:**

  - Copy of passport
  - If divorced, copy of court decree
  - Naturalization papers
  - Birth certificate
  - Bank statements
  - Medical history

- http://adoption.state.gov/country/grenada.html

GUATEMALA

- **Availability of children for adoption:** Guatemala has been an extremely popular source of adoptive children for U.S. citizens for a number of years. Guatemala ratified the Hague Convention on December 31, 2007, but they have not yet adopted the practices required by the Convention. The Social Services Agency Bienestar Social was named the Central Adoption Authority for Guatemala at the end of 2007, but the agency has not yet put into place processes approved by the Hague Convention on Intercountry Adoption. These processes are extremely important, because there has been evidence that some children put up for adoption in Guatemala in the past have, in fact, not been available for adoption – i.e., they may have been stolen or bought. According to the State Department, Hague Convention rules and procedures came into force for the United States on April 1, 2008, and that means that all countries that are out of compliance with the Hague Convention have to be put on hold until they come into compliance. In fiscal year 2007, 4,728 immigration adoption visas were issued, and in 2008, 4121, so there is pressure for Guatemala to come into compliance as soon as possible. The following information applied before April 1, 2008, and is expected to apply again once adoptions reopen.

- **Age and civil status requirements:** Singles are permitted to adopt from Guatemala, and must be at least 18 years old.

- **Special information:** Until now, adoptions in Guatemala have been handled by private attorneys, which accounts for the relatively high cost of adoption from that country. Although most U.S. citizens use American adoption agencies with relationships with Guatemalan attorneys, some prospective adoptive parents have hired Guatemalan attorneys directly with good outcomes. This should only be done with a solid, positive referral from someone with direct knowledge of the attorney's adoption work. Guatemala has had arguably the most complicated adoption process in all of the countries Americans choose, and there is something to be said for hiring an experienced American adoption agency to reduce your risks and to support you through the process. Guatemalan adoptions cost an average of $27,000, and now include a second DNA test before leaving the country with the child (beginning in August 2007) to determine if the woman who claims to be the baby's mother is in fact its mother. This also adds about 2 weeks to the adoption process once you arrive in Guatemala.

- Check this address to find out if adoptions have reopened in Guatemala: http://adoption.state.gov/country/guatamala.html

GUINEA

- **Availability of children for adoption:** There are two kinds of adoption in Guinea – simple and pleniere, or full adoption. Only pleniere adoption severs ties with the biological family permanently and is the only form of adoption that qualifies the child for immigration to the United States. There are no adoption agencies in Guinea, but the American Embassy in Conakry maintains a list of attorneys that practice adoption law in Guinea and who can assist with the legal system in the country. According to the State Department, at times missionaries can help identify children who are eligible for adoption. In fiscal year 2008, 3 immigrant adoption visas were issued.

- **Age and civil status requirements:** Singles are permitted to adopt, but must be at least 30 years of age and at least 15 years older than the adoptive child.

- **Document requirements:**

  - Written justification for the adoption
  - Identification
  - Certificate of domicile verifying prospective adoptive parent's place of residence

- http://adoption.state.gov/country/guinea.html

GUYANA

- **Availability of children for adoption:** The only U.S. citizens that may adopt from Guyana are those who are "domiciled" in Guyana or who are former citizens of Guyana. Guyanese children may also be adopted by Guyanese nationals living in the United States. In fiscal year 2008, 25 immigrant adoption visas were issued.

- **Age and civil status requirements:** Singles are permitted to adopt, but must be at least 25 years of age and must be at least 21 years older than the adoptive child (18 years older if the child is a relative).

- **Document requirements:**

  - Certified copy of birth certificate of prospective adoptive parent
  - Bank statements
  - Proof of employment
  - Police record
  - Home study

- http://adoption.state.gov/country/guyana.html

HAITI

- **Availability of children for adoption:** In fiscal year 2008, 301 adoption visas were issued, down from 355 in 2004.

- **Age and civil status requirements:** Singles are permitted to adopt, but must be at least 35 years of age. Requests for a waiver of the age requirement can be submitted to the IBESR (Institut du Bien Etre Social et de Recherches), and are sometimes granted.

- **Document requirements:**

  - Birth certificate of prospective adoptive parent
  - Child's birth certificate
  - Death certificates of parents of adoptive child, if applicable
  - Tax returns
  - Police clearances
  - Health, both physical and mental, reports on prospective adoptive parent and child

- **Special information:** Although Haitian law does not require that the prospective adoptive parent reside in Haiti, the child must be adopted in Haiti before they can leave the country. To get through the adoption process quickly and efficiently, the services of a Haitian attorney are necessary. The U.S. Consulate in Port-au-Prince maintains a list of Haitian adoption attorneys, which can be found at http://portauprince.usembassy.gov/adoption.html. The total approximate cost to adopt a Haitian child is $3,000, not counting travel.

- **Document requirements:**

  - Birth certificate of prospective adoptive parent
  - Statement of plan to adopt a child in Haiti
  - Three photos of prospective adoptive parent
  - Report from home state authorizing adoption
  - Financial documents, tax returns, notarized bank statements, copies of deeds and mortgages – Form I-864 Affidavit of Support
  - Police report showing absence of criminal record
  - Medical evaluation
  - Psychiatric evaluation
  - Two letters of reference

- http://adoption.state.gov/country/haiti.html

HONDURAS

- **Availability of children for adoption:** In fiscal year 2008, 11 adoption visas were issued, down from 22 in 2008. Policies regarding the process and time frame are currently being reevaluated by the Honduran Family Court.

- **Age and civil status requirements:** Previously, singles were able to adopt if there were at least 25 years of age and at least 15 years older than the adoptive child. The following information may be changed once the Honduran Family Court issues its new rulings. Check the web address below for updates.

- **Document requirements:**

  - Form I-171H
  - Photographs of prospective adoptive parent and family
  - Copy of prospective adoptive parent's passport
  - Birth certificate of prospective adoption parent
  - Results of physical examination, including urine, stool, blood tests and HIV status
  - Police clearance
  - Proof of employment, including specific position, salary, tenure and benefits
  - Copy of adoption law in prospective adoptive parent's home state
  - Two recent photos of prospective adoptive parent's home and neighborhood
  - Three letters of reference from prospective adoptive parent's local community (government, school or church officials)
  - Bank statements
  - Certified copy of title to property
  - Home study

- "Follow-up certification" from home adoption agency, agreeing that reports will be filed on well-being of child until s/he is 14 years of age
- Proof of licensure of adoption agency
- Written certification from local Honduran consulate that prospective adoptive parent has met all state adoption requirements

- **Special information:** You must use an American adoption agency that is registered with the IHNFA (Instituto Hondureno del Nino y la Familia), which will hire a local Honduran attorney to present your adoption petition to the courts. As soon as your application and required documents are reviewed and approved, you are put on a list of applicants until a child is found for you. This can take up to a year. When a child is found, you may only refuse for "acceptable" reasons, and if you refuse a second child, you are taken off the list. Adoptions cost between $3,000 and $10,000.

- http://adoption.state.gov/country/honduras.html

HONG KONG

- **Availability of children for adoption:** In fiscal year 2006, 25 immigrant adoption visas were issued.

- **Age and civil status requirements:** Singles are permitted to adopt, but must be over 25 years of age, and are not "preferred" unless they have "special parental skills such as social work or nursing, financial ability and support from family." It is easier for a single adult to adopt a special needs or older child, especially if they already parent a special needs child. It is also easier for ethnic Chinese Americans to adopt.

- **Document requirements:**

  - Copy of prospective adoptive parent's passport
  - Copy of divorce decree, if applicable
  - Proof of income
  - Transcripts from degree programs (proof of education)
  - If any prior adoptions, documentation
  - Home study
  - Medical examination report

- **Special information:** U.S. citizens in the United States may apply to bring a child to the United States through the International Social Service in Hong Kong under the International Adoption Program. ISS has an office in the U.S. at 700 Light Street, Baltimore, Maryland 21230 (tel: 410-230-2734).

- http://adoption.state.gov/country/hong%20kong.html

HUNGARY

- **Availability of children for adoption:** The State Department no longer offers information on adoption from Hungary. In fiscal year 2008, 11 immigrant adoption visas were issued. If you have a specific reason to adopt from Hungary, contact the United States Embassy in Budapest. www.hungary.usembassy.gov

- **Age and civil status requirements:** Singles are permitted to adopt, but must be under 45 years of age. There is a "strongly held opinion" in Hungary that children should be raised in tradition, two-parent family, but Hungarian law permits single adoption. It is decided on a case-by-case basis.

- **Document requirements:**

  - Home study
  - Proof of income
  - Psychological evaluation of prospective adoptive parent, done by psychologist
  - Proof of citizenship
  - Written statement by prospective adoptive parent about expectations and motivation for adoption
  - Certified copy of home adoption agency license, if applicable
  - Statement from prospective adoptive parent consenting to registration on national register

- **Special information:** The Ministry of Youth, Family and Social Affairs in Hungary prefers to work with American adoption agencies that have registered with them and are known to them.

ICELAND

- **Availability of children for adoption:** Prospective adoptive parents must be resident in Iceland or "have a special connection to Iceland" to adopt. In fiscal year 2006, one immigrant adoption visa was issued.

- **Age and civil status requirements:** Singles are permitted to adopt only in special circumstances and "if the adoption benefits the welfare of the child." Prospective adoptive parents must be at least 25 years of age and no older than 45 years of age.

- http://adoption.state.gov/country/iceland.html

INDIA

- **Availability of children for adoption:** In fiscal year 2008, 308 immigrant adoption visas were issued. Adoption is not legal for foreigners or non-Hindus, Sikhs, Jains or Buddhists in India, but prospective adoptive parents are granted guardianship to take the child out of the country for adoption. India allows adoptions through not-for-profit adoption agencies only.

- **Age and civil status requirements:** Single adults aged 30 to 45 may adopt, and should be at least 21 years older than the child. Exceptions can be made for older children, sibling groups, or children with special needs. The prospective adoptive parent cannot be divorced.

- **Document requirements:**

  - Approved I-600A
  - Birth certificate for child
  - Abandonment certificate for the child
  - "No Objection" Certificate from Central Adoption Resource Agency

- http://adoption.state.gov/country/india.html

INDONESIA

- **Indonesia adopts to married couples only.**

- http://adoption.state.gov/country/Indonesia.html

IRAN

- **Adoption is not permitted in Iran at this time.**

IRAQ

- **Foster care in-country only. No adoptions possible, and children cannot immigrate to the United States.**

IRELAND

- **Availability of children for adoption:** Only 4 immigrant adoption visas have been issued in the last 5 years.

- **Age and civil status requirements:** The only single adults allowed to adopt from Ireland are widows and widowers, unless the prospective adoption parent is a relative. Prospective adoptive parent must have lived in Ireland for the past year. There is no upper age restriction nationally, but adoption agencies have maximum age requirements.

- http://adoption.state.gov/country/ireland.html

ISRAEL, WEST BANK, GAZA

- **Availability of children for adoption:** Adoption in Israel by non-Israeli citizens is rare. Single adults may adopt under special circumstances, i.e., when the child has special needs and an Israel family cannot be found to take the child. Prospective adoptive parent must be the same ethnicity and religion as the child. Prospective adoptive parent must live in Israel for the duration of the adoption, at least 6 months.

- www.adoption.state.gov/country/israel,%20west%20bank, %20and%20gaza.html

ITALY

- **Italy adopts to married couples only.**

JAMAICA

- **Availability of children for adoption:** There were 39 immigration adoption visas issued in 2008, down from 62 in 2005.

- **Age and civil status requirements:** Jamaica allows adoption by singles who are at least 25 years of age. There are no requirements on age difference between prospective adoptive parent and child.

- **Special Information:** There are two types of adoption in Jamaica. *Adoption Licenses* are issued to non-residents of Jamaica, have no residency requirements, and typically take about 4 months. An *Adoption Order* is issued to residents of Jamaica, and typically takes longer. In both cases, the Child Development Agency is the only legally authorized adoption agency in Jamaica. Prospective adoptive parents should expect to travel to Jamaica at least twice during the adoption process.

- **Document Requirements:**

  - Application form provided by Child Development Agency
  - Home Study
  - Medical examinations of both prospective adoptive parent and child
  - Letter from home adoption agency that they will supervise the placement between the time the prospective adoptive parent and child return home and the completion of the adoption
  - Bank statement

- Employment letter regarding nature of employment and salary

- http://adoption.state.gov/country/jamaica.html

JAPAN

- **Availability of children for adoption:** In fiscal year 2008, 35 immigrant adoption visas were issued. Children available for adoption may be found through either the Child Guidance Center in each Japanese city, or through religious institutions or local adoption agencies. The prospective adoptive parent must show evidence of long-term residence in Japan.

- **Age and civil status requirements:** Singles are allowed to adopt in Japan, but only on a case-by-case basis. The prospective adoptive parent must be at least 25 and must show evidence of "long-term residence in Japan".

- **Document requirements (translated into Japanese):**

  - Birth certificate
  - Copy of passport of prospective adoptive parent
  - Copy of U.S. military ID, if applicable
  - Divorce or death certificate of spouse, if applicable
  - Medical examination
  - Certificate of foster parent certification, if applicable
  - Criminal report issued by home or state police
  - Report of employment, salary, and legal address
  - Copies of bank statements and property deeds, if applicable
  - Biography of prospective adoptive parent
  - Statement of consent to adoption by child's guardian/parents

- Statement of intent to adopt by prospective adoptive parent
- Pictures of prospective adoptive parent
- Home Study

- http://adoption.state.gov/country/japan.html

KAZAKHSTAN

- **Availability of children for adoption:** In fiscal year 2008, 380 immigrant adoption visas were issued, down from 835 in 2004. There are no preselections of children in Kazakhstan. Prospective adoptive parents must arrive in Kazakhstan, choose a child, and petition the court for adoption of that child. Information about the child, including medical information, is available at the orphanage housing the child. In March 2008, the U.S. Embassy in Kazakhstan announced that the local government was conducting a review of intercountry adoption policies. Although no new adoption dossiers were to be accepted until the review was completed, it has been reported that some cases have been accepted. Please check the web address below to find updates on the review process.

- **Age and civil status requirements:** Although legally, singles are allowed to adopt in Kazakhstan, many have found it difficult to do so. The prospective adoptive parent must be at least 16 years older than the child.

- **Special information:** Prospective adoptive parents should expect to live with the child for at least 14 days, in the child's place of residence to fulfill the adoption requirements. This typically means a stay of 30-60 days in Kazakhstan. In 2005 - early 2006, waits for court times increased, and stays increased to as much as two months. In addition, prospective adoptive parents should expect to file Post Placement Reports on the child every year until the child turns 18. The State Department notes that this is extremely important, and failure to do so can jeopardize the future of American adoptions in Kazakhstan.

- **Document requirements:**

    - Letter of intent to adopt the child
    - Commitment to adhere to Kazakhstani law, i.e., post-placement reports until the child is 18, maintenance of child's Kazakhstani citizenship until the age of 18, and "allowing Kazakhstani officials to visit as often as twice a year until the child is 18.
    - Home Study
    - Commitment from home agency to file post-placement reports yearly until child is 18.
    - Letter of recommendation from home agency
    - Home agency must file "Certificate of Approval" concurring with home study
    - Notarized copy of license of home agency
    - Commitment from prospective adoptive parent to follow-up visits from Kazakhstani officials
    - Commitment from prospective adoptive parent to post-placement reports
    - Commitment from prospective adoptive parent to register child with Kazakhstani government before leaving the country
    - Notarized copy of prospective adoptive parent's passport
    - FBI background check
    - Medical examination
    - Letter from employer (must be officer) attesting to employment, including annual salary. If self-employed, letter must be from accountant
    - Notarized financial statement
    - Letter from prospective adoptive parent's bank, attesting to the existence of bank accounts in good standing

- Notarized statement of home ownership, if applicable
- Notarized copies of I-171H or I179C
- Power of attorney for prospective adoptive parent, if applicable
- Pictures of prospective adoptive parent

- **Special note for single prospective adoptive parents:** Singles must also submit notarized copies of birth certificate, and notarized letter indicating who would become the child's guardian should something happen to the adoptive parent. The appointed guardian must also submit a notarized letter accepting this responsibility.

- http://adoption.state.gov/country/kazakhstan.html

KENYA

- **Availability of children for adoption:** In fiscal year 2008, when 24 immigrant adoption visas were issued. Kenyan courts have historically been biased against cross-racial adoptions, but recently have been taking a more liberal view.

- **Age and civil status requirements:** Kenya allows adoptions to singles, although single men are just beginning to be allowed to adopt in Kenya. The prospective adoptive parent must be resident in Kenya, and have custodial care of the child for at least 3 months preceding the adoption. The prospective adoptive parent must be at least 25 years old, unless they are related to the child, in which case they must be at least 21 years old. In addition, the prospective adoptive parent must be at least 21 years older than the child.

- **Document requirements:**

    - Home study
    - Recent photographs of prospective adoptive parent
    - Medical report
    - Proof of financial status, including report on employment
    - Income tax records
    - Bank references
    - Statement of willingness to adopt child
    - Proof of residence, home ownership, if applicable

- http://adoption.state.gov/country/kenya.html

KOREA (SOUTH)

- **Singles are not allowed to adopt in Korea.**

- http://adoption.state.gov/country/south%20korea.html

KYRGYZSTAN

- **Availability of children for adoption:** In fiscal year 2008, 78 immigrant adoption visas were issued, up from 4 in 2005.

- **Age and civil status requirements:** Singles are allowed to adopt in Kyrgyzstan, although homosexuals are not allowed to adopt in the country. Single prospective adoptive parents may have to swear that they are not gay or lesbian.

- **Special information:** Once the dossier of the prospective adoptive parent has been accepted by the Krygyz authorities, a child will be chosen and presented for adoption. If the prospective adoptive parent decides to accept the referral, he or she will travel to Krygyzstan and will live with the child for at least a week. During that time they will be observed by a psychologist who will monitor the relationship between the prospective adoptive parent and the child and determine whether enough of a bond has developed to recommend adoption.

- **Document requirements:**

  - Written statement of intent to adopt the child
  - Copies of prospective adoptive parent's passport
  - Home study
  - Medical and psychological examinations
  - Statement of employment, including salary
  - Reports certifying that the prospective adoptive parent has not been denied parental rights or had parental rights terminated, and is not incapable of parenting for mental or physical reasons
  - Copy of I-600A as proof of no criminal activity and that the child will be allowed to enter the U.S.
  - Statement from the Kyrgyz Republic from the child's guardian that there is no objection to the child's adoption
  - Letter stating that the child will be educated and medically cared for
  - Statement of guarantee that the home adoption agency will submit reports on the child's welfare until he or she turns 14

- http://adoption.state.gov/country/kyrgyzstan.html

LAOS

- **Availability of children for adoption:** When the first edition of this book was written, Laos had suspended intercountry adoptions. But on July 26, 2008, the National Assembly of Laos passed a revised Family Law, allowing for adoptions to recommence. Because there are no official orphanages in Laos, prospective adoptive parents must work with religious groups or hospitals in Laos to identify abandoned babies and children available for adoption. The adoption process in Laos can be lengthy because of the necessity of verifying orphan status. Three immigrant adoption visas were issued in 2008.

- **Age and civil status requirements:** Singles may adopt in Laos, and must be at least 18 years old and 18 years older than the child.

- **Special information:** The adoption process in Laos is as follows:

  - Work with an American adoption agency to find a child to adopt
  - Prospective adoptive parent must send a letter indicating a desire to adopt to the Lao Embassy in the United States (2222 S Street, NW, Washington, DC 20008, (202) 667-0076, 9 a.m. to noon only). The documents listed below must be attached. An interview may be required.
  - Adoption must receive approval from both the Minister of Foreign Affairs and the Minister of Justice.
  - The Office of the Prime Minister approves and the Minister of Justice issues a Final Agreement.

- **Document requirements:**

  - Child's home birth certificate
  - Custody certificate of Lao guardian
  - Residential certificate of Lao guardian
  - Criminal record of Lao guardian
  - Financial statement of Lao guardian
  - Letter from village chief explaining why child is available for adoption
  - Medical report for child and Lao guardian

- Copy of household book of child and Lao guardian
- Six 4 x 6 cm. photos of child
- Biographic information on Lao guardian
- If the child is 10 or older, letter of agreement to be adopted
- Birth certificate of prospective adoptive parent
- Proof of residence
- Criminal record of prospective adoptive parent
- Medical report on prospective adoptive parent
- Financial statement
- Copy of passport
- Letter stating why prospective adoptive parent wants to adopt
- Six 4 x 6 cm photos of prospective adoptive parent
- Biographic information
- "Guarantee Statement" from prospective adoptive parent
- Adoption application

- http://adoption.state.gov/country/laos.html

LATVIA

- **Availability of children for adoption:** In fiscal year 2008, 38 immigrant adoption visas were issued, up from 15 in 2004.

- **Age and civil status requirements:** Singles are allowed to adopt in Latvia and must be at least 25 and at least 18 years older than the child.

- **Special Information:** There are very few infants and younger children available for adoption in Latvia. Public opposition to foreign adoption in Latvia now means that children available for intercountry adoption are usually sibling groups of 3 or more, or over the age of 9, or with health problems. Prospective adoptive parents are required to share a household and take care of the child until the courts have determined that a parent-child relationship has developed, not to exceed 6 months. The following is a list of American adoption agencies approved by the Latvian government for adoption:

- About a Child
- Child Adoption Associates, Inc.
- Lutheran Social Services of New York
- One World Adoption Services, Inc.
- The Open Door Adoption Agency, Inc.
- World Links International Adoption Agency

- **Document requirements:**

  - Application to adopt a child, including information about the age, gender, and religion that prospective adoptive parent is interested in adopting
  - If applicable, copy of divorce decree
  - Statement about housing to be provided for the child
  - Autobiography of prospective adoptive parent
  - Medical examination
  - Home study
  - Police clearance

- http://adoption.state.gov/country/latvia.html

LEBANON

- **Availability of children for adoption:** In fiscal year 2008, 11 immigrant adoption visas were granted, down from 16 in 2002. In Lebanon, adoption is a religious institution and only Christian organizations recognize adoption legally. Islam does not recognize the practice of adoption, so adoptions in Lebanon must be handled through church institutions. Prospective adoptive parents must have no other children.

- **Age and civil status requirements:** Singles are allowed to adopt in Lebanon, but the prospective adoptive parent must be at least 40 years old and the age difference between the prospective adoptive parent and the child must be at least 18 years, 15 years for Armenian Orthodox adoption. To adopt from a Catholic institution, the prospective adoptive parent must be Catholic.

- **Document requirements:**

  - Certificate of good behavior, delivered by the priest or bishop of the prospective adoptive parent
  - Medical report for both Catholic and non-Catholic parents stating reasons for not having their own child
  - Home study
  - Photocopy of official ID, passport, etc.

- http://adoption.state.gov/country/lebanon.html

LESOTHO

- **Availability of children for adoption:** Intercountry adoptions were suspended in Lesotho on June 4, 2007. The Ministry of Health and Social Welfare believed that trafficking (buying and selling) and abuse of children had occurred. The Government of the Kingdom of Lesotho lifted the ban in November 2008, and by the end of 2008, one immigrant adoption visa had been issued.

- **Age and civil status requirements:** Singles are allowed to adopt in Lesotho, and must be at least 25 years old and 21 years older than the adoptive child. Openly gay men and lesbian women are not permitted to adopt.

- **Special information:** Currently, prospective adoptive parents must live in Lesotho for two years prior to adoption, although courts do allow intercountry adoptions under special circumstances. The General Assembly is debating a revised child welfare bill, which would allow intercountry adoptions (meaning that the two year residency rule would be lifted). Adoptions take approximately 6 months, and prospective adoptive parents must apply directly to the Department of Social Welfare and request gender, age, special needs

- **Document requirements:**

    - Request for adoption to Department of Social Welfare
    - Home study
    - Financial statements
    - Police record
    - Medical certificate
    - Letters from relatives of prospective adoptive parent stating their support for the adoption and willingness to care for the child should anything happen to the prospective adoptive parent

- http://adoption.state.gov/country/lesotho.html

LIBERIA

- **Availability of children for adoption:** In fiscal year 2008, 254 immigrant adoption visas were issued, up from 29 in 2003. **On January 26, 2009, the Government of Liberia suspended adoptions to investigate corruption in the adoption process. Check the web address below for updates on when adoptions recommence. The requirements given below were in effect before the suspension.**

- **Age and civil status requirements:** Singles may adopt in Liberia and there are no age requirements for prospective adoptive parents.

- **Special information:** Since October, 2004, prospective adoptive parents must obtain a letter from the Liberian Ministry of Health approving the adoption of a specific child. This means that a social worker has thoroughly investigated the child's circumstances and believes that adoption is in the best interest of the child. The Minister's office then reviews the adoption paperwork and approves the adoption. The American Embassy in Monrovia will not sign off on immigration status for the child until they receive the letter. **On March 18, 2008, adoption agency employees with three children were stopped from leaving the country. At this time, the use of escorts (non-adoptive parents) to bring adoptive children home is being investigated in Liberia. The prospective adoptive parent should plan to go to Liberia to bring the adoptive child home.**

- **Document requirements:**

  - Petition for adoption, including identifying information about the prospective adoptive parent (name, resident, marital status), identifying information about the child (name, age, place of birth), information about how the prospective adoptive parent obtained the child, and a request for a name change for the child.
  - Formal letter of relinquishment of parental rights (necessary for American Consulate to declare immigrant status)
  - Copy of passport
  - Copy of birth certificate of prospective adoptive parent

- http://adoption.state.gov/country/liberia.html

LITHUANIA

- **Availability of children for adoption:** In fiscal year 2008, 16 immigration adoption visas were issued, down from 70 in 1998.

- **Age and civil status requirements:** Singles are allowed to adopt only in special circumstances, such as when the child has severe health issues, or when the prospective adoptive parent has resided in Lithuania and provided foster care, or if the child is over age 8 and difficult to place. The prospective adoptive parent must be at least 18 years older than the child, and not more than 50 years old.

- **Special information:** Until April 1, 2008, because the U.S. had not yet implemented the Hague Convention on Intercountry Adoption, prospective adoptive parents had to be represented by an American adoption agency and that agency had to present its credentials for working in intercountry adoption. American adoption agencies will no doubt be pursuing relationships with Lithuania now that the U.S. is in compliance with the Hague Convention.

- **Document requirements:**

  - Letter of interest from Prospective Adoptive Parent, submitted through American adoption agency, asking to be placed on waiting list for an adoptive child
  - Information that might enhance the chance of adopting, such as ties to Lithuania, family heritage, letters of reference
  - Home study
  - Medical examination
  - Photocopies of passport
  - Financial statements
  - Police certificates

- Copy of birth certificate of prospective adoptive parent
- Copy of approved DHS I-600A

- http://adoption.state.gov/country/lithuania.html

LUXEMBOURG

- **Only married couples can adopt in Luxembourg**

MADAGASCAR

- **Only married couples may adopt in Madagascar.**

MALAWI

- **Availability of children for adoption:** In fiscal year 2008, 2 immigrant adoption visas were issued.

- **Age and civil status requirements:** Singles may adopt in Malawi, must be at least 25 years old, and at least 21 years older than the child.

- **Special information:** Prospective adoptive parents must be resident in Malawi to adopt, and a pre-adoption foster care period of at least 18 months is required.

- http://adoption.state.gov/country/malawi.html

MALAYSIA

- **Availability of children for adoption:** Only 15 immigration adoption visas have been issued in the past ten years because adoption is very uncommon in Malaysia.

- **Age and civil status requirements:** Singles may adopt in Malaysia and must be at least 25 years old.

- **Special information:** Prospective adoptive parents must live and work in Malaysia for at least two years prior to an application for adoption, and must foster the child for at least 3 months before the adoption.

- http://adoption.state.gov/country/malaysia.html

MALI

- **Availability of children for adoption:** Seven immigrant adoption visas have been issued in the past five years.

- **Age and civil status requirements:** Single men may not adopt from Mali, and single women must be at least 30 years old. Preference is given to prospective adoptive parents that reside in Mali and who have no other children.

- **Document requirements:**

  - Birth certificate of prospective adoptive parent
  - Police record
  - Home study
  - Medical and psychological examination
  - Residence certificate (if resident in Mali)
  - U. S. Passport
  - Tax records and pay statements indicating employment, salary and residence

- Notarized statement indicating adult who will care for the child in the event of the prospective adoptive parent's death
- Agreement to provide an annual report on the child's welfare
- Four letters of reference

- http://adoption.state.gov/country/mali.html

MARSHALL ISLANDS

- **Availability of children for adoption:** In fiscal year 2008, 6 immigration adoption visas were issued.

- **Age and civil status requirements:** Singles are permitted to adopt in the Marshall Islands, and must be at least 21 and 15 years older than the child. Although they don't specifically disallow gays and lesbians from adopting, gays and lesbians living with a same sex partner are not permitted to adopt.

- **Document requirements:**

  - Home study
  - Education and any future plans for education
  - Job history and any possible changes in the future
  - Income and any possible changes in the future
  - Information about prior marriage(s) and reasons for divorce, if applicable. If child support is being paid, how much.
  - Extracurricular activities of prospective adoptive parent, especially religious and civic.
  - Criminal background search
  - Child abuse search report
  - Certified copy of birth certificate of prospective adoptive parent

- Certified copy of marriage certificate and divorce certificate
- Medical report
- Psychological report
- Copy of passport

- http://adoption.state.gov/country/marshall%20islands.html

MAURITANIA

- **Only blood relatives may adopt in Mauritania, and may not move the child out of the country.**

MAURITIUS

- **Availability of children for adoption:** No immigrant adoption visas have been issued in the past five years. The Mauritian National Adoption Council does not match orphans with prospective adoptive parents. Children must be located through personal contacts in Mauritius.

- **Age and civil status requirements:** Singles may adopt in Mauritius.

- **Document requirements:**

  - Application for adoption filed at the NAC
  - Four photos of child endorsed by adoption lawyer
  - Birth certificate of child
  - Two medical examinations by two unaffiliated doctors
  - Birth and marriage certificate of biological parent
  - Divorce decree of biological parents, if applicable
  - Medical examination of prospective adoptive parent

- Two recent passport photos of prospective adoptive parent
- Birth certificate of prospective adoptive parent
- Home study
- Financial certificate attesting to ability to care for child
- If applicable, proof of home ownership
- Police report
- If applicable, medical certificate documenting inability to have a child
- Statement of adult who will care for child if anything happens to the prospective adoptive parent
- Progress report on any other children adopted in Mauritius, a one-time report

- http://adoption.state.gov/country/mauritius.html

MEXICO

- **Availability of children for adoption:** In fiscal year 2008, 105 immigrant adoption visas were issued. Mexican officials make every effort to place children with relatives before placing the child for adoption.

- **Age and civil status requirements:** Singles may adopt in Mexico, and must be at least 25 years old and at least 17 years older than the child.

- **Special information:** The DIF (Desarrollo Integral de la Familia) suggests that the prospective adoptive parent be prepared to spend three months in Mexico prior to the adoption. The prospective adoptive parent must foster the child for one to three weeks during this time.

- **Document requirements (translated into Spanish):**

  - Certified copy of prospective adoptive parent's birth certificate
  - Statement from employer indicating position, years of employment and salary
  - Copy of most recent bank statement and proof of financial holdings
  - Two letters of recommendation
  - Police report
  - Home study
  - One 3x3 color photo of prospective adoptive parent
  - Two 3x5 photos of prospective adoptive parent on an outing or at home

- http://adoption.state.gov/country/mexico.html

MICRONESIA

- **Availability of children for adoption:** Adoptions from Micronesia are very rare. There was one immigrant adoption visa granted in 2005, and one in 2006.

- **Age and civil status requirements:** Singles are permitted to adopt on a case-by-case basis. By law, prospective adoptive parents must live in Micronesia for 3 years before initiating the adoption process, although this has not held up in court.

- http://adoption.state.gov/country/micronesia.html

MOLDOVA

- **Availability of children for adoption:** In fiscal year 2008, 33 immigrant adoption visas were issued, down from 77 in 2000. Children must be placed for adoption in Moldova for at least six months before they are eligible for intercountry adoption. Children with health or developmental problems are considered exceptional cases.

- **Age and civil status requirements:** Singles may adopt in Moldova, must be at least 25 years old and no older than 50.

- **Document requirements:**

    - Adoption application which includes the following information:
        - name
        - date of birth
        - information about adoptive child and child's family
        - reasons for adoption
        - request to change child's name and birth certificate to reflect new parent

        - copy of birth certificate of prospective adoptive parent
        - divorce decree, if applicable
        - medical examination showing no evidence of HIV, psychological and behavior conditions, drug addiction, alcoholism, chronic disease, cancer, viral hepatitis
        - statement of employment stating title of position and salary
        - proof of lease or ownership of home
        - police report
        - proof of U.S. approval to adopt

- http://adoption.state.gov/country/moldova.html

MONGOLIA

- **Availability of children for adoption:** In fiscal year 2008, 9 immigrant adoption visas were issued.

- **Age and civil status requirements:** Singles are permitted to adopt in Mongolia, but must be no more than 60 years old.

- **Document requirements:**

    - Cover letter
    - Copy of driver's license
    - Copy of highest level diploma
    - Copy of passport
    - Bank statements no more than 2 months old
    - Tax returns for latest year
    - Medical report not more than 2 months old
    - Lab report on HIV/AIDS status
    - Police clearance
    - Home study
    - Copy of license of social worker who performed home study
    - Copy of adoption agency license
    - Letter from prospective adoptive parent on why s/he wants to adopt
    - Photos of prospective adoptive parent

- **Adoption agencies that work in Mongolia:**

    - Lutheran Social Services in Mongolia – may-lss@mbox.mn
    - Lutheran Social Services Adoption Services – http://www.lsswis.org
    - Small World in Mongolia – surenhuu@yahoo.com
    - Small World – http://www.swa.net

- http://adoption.state.gov/country/mongolia.html

Victoria Solsberry

MONTENEGRO

- **Singles are not permitted to adopt in Montenegro.**

MOROCCO

- **Availability of children for adoption:** In fiscal year 2008, 12 immigrant adoption visas were issued.

- **Age and civil status requirements:** Singles are permitted to adopt, but must be Muslim. Interestingly, the State Department says that the prospective adoptive parent "can easily convert to Islam while in Morocco. They can obtain a conversion document from any court notary (Adul) office."

- **Document requirements:**

  - Islam conversion document of prospective adoptive parent
  - Copy of birth certificate
  - Medical report from doctor in Morocco
  - Work and salary reports
  - Home study
  - Photos (the type of photos required may vary)

- http://adoption.state.gov/country/morocco.html

NEPAL

- **NOTE: The State Department issued a Travel Warning for Nepal on February 25, 2008. The State Department remains extremely concerned about road travel by U.S. citizens because of the threat of Americans being targeted.**

- **Availability of children for adoption:** The Napali Ministry of Women, Children and Social Welfare reopened intercountry adoptions on January 1, 2009, after suspending intercountry adoptions on May 8, 2007. In fiscal year 2005, 62 immigrant adoption visas were issued. At the time of the suspension, adoptions were in process, so 42 immigrant adoption visas were issued in 2007 and 54 in 2008.

- **Age and civil status requirements:** Single men are not permitted to adopt in Nepal, and single women must be between the ages of 35 and 55. The prospective adoptive parent must be at least 30 years older than the adoptive child and if the prospective adoptive parent already has a child or children, the adoptive child must be the opposite sex.

- **Special information:** The Nepalese government recommends that Americans wishing to adopt in Nepal use U.S. adoption agencies with ongoing relationships with Nepalese orphanages. Orphanage adoptions are not regulated by the government, and as a result, fees vary from $3,000 to $17,000, depending upon the orphanage. Adoptions of children over the age of three are typically completed in the shortest time periods, but adoptions often take up to two years. Specific document requirements were not given by the State Department

- http://adoption.state.gov/country/nepal.html

NETHERLANDS

- **Availability of children for adoption:** Adoption of Dutch children by Americans is extremely rare, and the State Department reports that they have not issued an immigrant adoption visa in 25 years.

- **Age and civil status requirements:** In the unlikely event of an American adoption, singles are allowed to adopt and must be under 45 years of age.

- http://adoption.state.gov/country/netherlands.html

NEW ZEALAND

- **Availability of children for adoption:** Foreign adoption is very rare in New Zealand, with only 7 immigrant adoption visas issued in the past 10 years.

- **Age and civil status requirements:** Singles are permitted to adopt in New Zealand and must be at least 25 years old. However, prospective adoptive parents must be permanent residents of New Zealand, and must have lived in the country for at least two years before applying for adoption.

- http://adoption.state.gov/country/new%20zealand.html

NICARAGUA

- **Availability of children for adoption:** In fiscal year 2008, 10 immigrant adoption visas were issued. According to Nicaraguan law, prospective adoptive parents must be either Nicaraguan citizens or permanent residents of Nicaragua. However, in the case of U.S. citizens, this law is typically waived.

- **Age and civil status requirements:** Singles may adopt in Nicaragua, and must be between the ages of 25 and 40, although Nicaraguan authorities have been known to be flexible on a case-by-case basis.

- **Special information:** Prospective adoptive parents must work directly with the Nicaraguan government, specifically the Ministry of Family (Mi Familia), which can be contacted at the following address: De ENEL Central, 100 mts. Al sur, Managua. The telephone number is (505) 278-1837.

- **Document requirements:**

  - Original authenticated I-171H issued by USCIS.
  - Home study
  - Psychological evaluation
  - Birth certificate
  - Letter of employment
  - Police record
  - Certified copy of child' birth certificate, indicating names of biological parents, if known
  - Death certificates of biological parents, if applicable

- http://adoption.state.gov/country/nicaragua.html

NIGER

- **Singles are not permitted to adopt in Niger.**

NIGERIA

- **Availability of children for adoption:** In fiscal year 2008, 149 immigrant adoption visas were issued, up from 33 in 2007.

- **Age and civil status requirements:** Singles are permitted to adopt in Nigeria, but only a same-sex adoptive child. The prospective adoptive parent must be at least 25 years old and 21 years older than the child.

- **Special information:** Nigerian law requires that a parent-child relationship be established before the adoption is complete, which may require the prospective adoptive parent to reside in Nigeria for up to a year, depending upon the state in which the adoption takes place. It is recommended that U.S. citizens interested in adopting in Nigeria use an American adoption agency familiar with different state requirements. For instance, Nigerian law states that foreigners wishing to adopt from Nigeria must be of "Nigerian Heritage," but like the one-year residency requirement, this law is interpreted and applied differently from state to state. American adoption agencies that work in Nigeria know which states are the easiest for Americans wishing to adopt.

- **Document requirements:**

  - Birth certificate of prospective adoptive parent
  - Divorce decree, if applicable
  - Other documents as required by each state

- http://adoption.state.gov/country/nigeria.html

NORWAY

- **Singles are permitted to adopt in Norway, but American adoption is very rare, with only 2 immigrant adoption visas issued in the past 10 years. The only children available to foreign prospective adoptive parents are relatives.**

PAKISTAN

- **Availability of children for adoption:** In fiscal year 2008, 47 immigrant adoption visas were issued. There are no adoption agencies in Pakistan, so private attorneys must be used.

- **Age and civil status requirements:** Singles may adopt in Pakistan and there are no age requirements.

- **Document requirements:**

  - Proof of U.S. citizenship
  - Divorce decree, if applicable
  - Fingerprint cards for prospective adoptive parent and all members of household
  - Home study
  - $525 application fee

- http://adoption.state.gov/country/pakistan.html

PANAMA

- **Availability of children for adoption:** In Fiscal year 2008, 4 immigrant adoption visas were issued, down from 20 in 2005.

- **Age and civil status requirements:** Although State Department and Panamanian Embassy information does not state directly that singles can adopt, it is implied in the usage of "prospective adoptive parent(s)" in describing eligibility requirements. There must be an 18 year age difference between the prospective adoptive parent and adoptive child.

- **Special information:** Panamanian citizens are given preference in adoptions, which typically take 18-24 months. Siblings are not separated, so if an adoptive child has siblings, all are required to be adopted together.

- **Document requirements:**

  - Birth certificate of prospective adoptive parent
  - Medical examination

- Police report
- Letter from employer stating position and current salary. There is no minimum income requirement.
- Two passport photos of prospective adoptive parent
- Two reference letters
- Home study
- Psychological evaluation

- http://adoption.state.gov/country/panama.html

PARAGUAY

- **Only Paraguayan citizens and legal residents are permitted to adopt in Paraguay, and must remain in the country with the child.**

- http://adoption.state.gov/country/paraguay.html

PERU

- **Availability of children for adoption:** In fiscal year 2008, 30 immigrant adoption visas were issued.

- **Age and civil status requirements:** Singles are permitted to adopt in Peru, but must be between 35 and 50 years old, and can only adopt children age 5 and older.

- **Special information:** All adoptions of Peruvian children must be coordinated by Peruvian-approved U.S. adoption agencies. Prospective adoptive parents should expect to stay in Peru for 8 weeks or longer before the child is placed for adoption.

- **Document requirements:**

    - Birth certificate of prospective adoptive parent
    - Home study
    - Physical and psychological health certificates
    - Financial and employment certifications
    - Police report
    - 600-A approval process, in order to assign a child

- http://adoption.state.gov/country/peru.html

THE PHILIPPINES

- **Availability of children for adoption:** In fiscal year 2008, 292 immigrant adoption visas were issued. Some American adoption agencies report that only Americans from The Philippines can adopt, but State Department sources do not confirm that. Check the link below for updates.

- **Age and civil status requirements:** Singles are permitted to adopt in The Philippines, and must be at least 27 years old, as well as 16 years older than the adoptive child.

- **Document requirements:**

    - Home study
    - Birth certificate of prospective adoptive parent
    - Divorce decree or proof of annulment, if applicable
    - Written consent to the adoption by all children over the age of ten living with prospective adoptive parent
    - Medical examination
    - Latest income tax return
    - Three character references (clergy person, employer, non-relative)

- - 3x5 pictures of prospective adoptive parent taken in past 3 years
  - Certificate of attendance at preadoption seminars

- http://adoption.state.gov/country/philippines.html

POLAND

- **Availability of children for adoption:** In fiscal year 2008, 77 immigrant adoption visas were issued, down from 114 in 2002.

- **Age and civil status requirements:** Singles are permitted to adopt, and there are no legal requirements as to age for adopting Polish children, although prospective adoptive parents need to be no more than 40 years older than the child.

- **Document requirements:**

  - Application to the Public Adoptive-Guardian Center asking permission to adopt a Polish orphan and stating your reasons for wanting to adopt from Poland. You are asked to specify age, gender, or which type of special needs you desire.
  - Birth certificate
  - Financial statements, tax returns, deeds to property, letter from employer attesting to salary and length of service
  - Copy of passport
  - Medical examination
  - Psychiatric examination
  - Home study
  - "Good conduct police certificate" – criminal report
  - Approved I-600A petition

- **Special information:** It is customary to make a donation to the orphanage that has cared for the child, usually $300 - $1,000, and a similar amount to the National Adoptive-Guardian Center, the Friends Society or Catholic Adoptive-Guardian Center. The adoption process in Poland may take up to a year, and the prospective adoptive parent can expect to be in Poland for four to six weeks. Two trips to Poland may be necessary.

- http://adoption.state.gov/country/poland.html

ROMANIA

- **Availability of children for adoption:** Foreign adoptions in Romania closed on January 1, 2005, except in the case of "close relatives" of a Romanian child. Romania has ratified the Hague Convention, and closing adoptions is counter to an important policy of the Hague Convention which states that adoption is a "legitimate option" for children who are unable to be placed in their home country. Keeping thousands of Romanian children in orphanages is then a violation of the Hague Convention. Prior to the closing of adoptions in Romania, the U.S. government was concerned about the lack of transparency in Romanian adoptions, and reports that foreign parents were able to go to Romania and adopt directly from the biological parents without a process that provided "child welfare protections." The last update published by the U.S. Department of State was in October 2008. Check the site below for updates.

- http://adoption.state.gov/country/romania.html

RUSSIA

- **Availability of children for adoption:** In fiscal year 2008, 1,857 immigrant adoption visas were issued, down from 5,862 in 2004.

- **Age and civil status requirements:** Singles are permitted to adopt in Russia and must be at least 16 years older than the adoptive child.

- **Special information:** Russia requires that an orphaned child be placed in local, regional and federal databanks for 8 months before being placed for adoption. Prospective adoptive parents must expect to travel to Russia at least twice before taking the child home. In addition, prospective adoptive parents are not permitted to choose a child from an orphanage. Rather, a child is preselected and if the prospective adoptive parent does not bond with that child, they can request that another referral be made. All existing medical records will be available.

- **Document requirements:**

    - Application to regional Ministry of Education for permission to adopt
    - Application to adopt after meeting and choosing specific child
    - Statements on the following issues:
    - Prospective adoptive parent has been informed of health conditions and accept them
    - They will register the child with the Ministry of Foreign Affairs
    - They will provide the MFA with periodic post-placement reports at 6 months, 12 months, 24 and 36 months.
    - Other documents as required by the region

- http://adoption.state.gov/country/russia.html

RWANDA

- **Availability of children for adoption:** In fiscal year 2008, 17 immigrant adoption visas were issued, up from 5 in 2007.

- **Age and civil status requirements:** Single women are permitted to adopt in Rwanda. The prospective adoptive parent must be under the age of 35, but in special circumstances, this can be waived by a judge. The prospective adoptive parent must have 2 or fewer children.

- **Document requirements (in French):**

  - Birth certificate of prospective adoptive parent
  - Original birth certificate of adoptive child
  - Waiver of age limit, if applicable
  - Home study
  - Authorization letter for departing Rwanda
  - Legal Judgment Document (formalizing adoption)

- http://adoption.state.gov/country/rwanda.html

SAMOA

- **Availability of children for adoption:** In fiscal year 2008, only 1 immigrant adoption visa was issued, down from 45 in 2003. Samoan law requires that prospective adoptive parents be citizens of Samoa.

- **Age and civil status requirements:** American singles are permitted to adopt in Samoa, but only after it has been determined that there are no suitable relatives in the country and that no Samoan family is available to adopt the child.

- **Document requirements:**

    - Original birth certificate of prospective adoptive parent
    - Proof of American citizenship, i.e., copy of passport
    - Proof of ownership of home and of adequate room for the child

- http://adoption.state.gov/country/samoa.html

SIERRA LEONE

- **Availability of children for adoption:** In fiscal year 2008, 10 immigrant adoption visas were issued, down from 55 in 2003 because of changes in residency requirements. Policies allowing waivers of 6 month residency requirements for prospective adoptive parents have been eliminated, although the law is under review and could change at any time. Until further notice, prospective adoptive parents should plan to live in Sierra Leone for 6 months. **Note: On May 29, 2009, the government of Sierra Leone suspended adoptions because of worries about the welfare of the adoptive children. The Ministry has established an interagency committee to determine new laws and procedures. The U.S. Department of State expects that the Sierra Leone government will vote on the new bill in 2009. Check the site below for updates.**

- **Age and civil status requirements:** Singles are permitted to adopt in Sierra Leone and there are no age requirements.

- **Document requirements:**

    - Petition for adoption
    - Written consent of living parents of adoptive child, if applicable

- Bank statements, job letters, and other evidence of financial status of prospective adoptive parent
- Other documents as required by the High Court

- http://adoption.state.gov/country/sierra%20leone.html

SAUDI ARABIA

- **Adoptions are not permitted in Saudi Arabia under Islamic law.**

SLOVAKIA

- **Availability of children for adoption:** Because the U.S. had not implemented the Hague Convention on Intercountry Adoption, American prospective adoptive parents had to be resident in Slovakia to adopt. With the recent U.S. ratification of the Hague Convention, adoptions opened once again on April 1, 2008, although with the long residency requirement (at least 6 months), adoption from Slovakia will be difficult for most American singles. Only one immigrant adoption visas was issued in 2005, the last year reported by the State Department.

- **Age and civil status requirements:** Singles may adopt in Slovakia. There are no age limits, and although they have not stated required age differences, it is believed that the prospective adoptive parent must be at least 15 years and no more than 45 years older than the child.

- **Document requirements:**

  - Home study
  - Police report
  - Proof of financial situation

Victoria Solsberry

- Medical examination
- Psychological test

- http://adoption.state.gov/country/slovakia.html

SOMALIA

- **Because it is almost impossible to determine orphan status for children needing homes from Somalia, adoption is not possible at this time. Check the following site for updates from the State Department.**

- http://adoption.state.gov/country/somalia.html

SOUTH AFRICA

- **Availability of children for adoption:** In fiscal year 2008, 7 immigrant adoption visas were issued, but only to Americans living in South Africa. Because the U.S. does not have an adoption agreement with South Africa, American citizens living in the U.S. may not adopt from South Africa. There is a five year residency requirement for adoption.

- http://adoption.state.gov/country/south%20africa.html

SOUTH KOREA

- **Singles are not permitted to adopt in South Korea.**

SPAIN

- **Availability of children for adoption:** Foreign adoptions are extremely rare in Spain, as there are not enough children available for Spanish prospective adoptive parents. Therefore, a citizen of the U.S. may adopt only if they are a legal resident of Spain.

- **Age and civil status requirements:** Singles may adopt in Spain, but must be at least 14 years older than the adoptive child.

- http://adoption.state.gov/country/spain.html

SRI LANKA

- **Single adoption is not permitted in Sri Lanka.**

- http://adoption.state.gov/country/sri%20lanka.html

ST. KITTS & NEVIS

- **Availability of children for adoption:** According to State Department figures, no immigrant adoption visas have been issued since 2005.

- **Age and civil status requirements:** Singles may adopt in St. Kitts and Nevis, but must be resident and domiciled there (i.e., one is not permitted to adopt for the purposes of bringing a child back to the U.S. to live). The adoption of a female child is not permitted by a single man unless they are related.

- http://adoption.state.gov/country/st.%20kitts%20and%20nevis.html

ST. LUCIA

- **Availability of children for adoption:** In fiscal year 2008, 1 immigrant adoption visas was issued.

- **Age and civil status requirements:** Singles are permitted to adopt in St. Lucia, and must be at least 21 years older than the adoptive child. Unless the prospective adoptive parent is a St. Lucian citizen, he or she must reside in St. Lucia for at least six consecutive months before applying for adoption.

- **Special information:** There are no adoption agencies in St. Lucia, so prospective adoptive parents are required to retain an attorney for adoption proceedings. A list of attorneys can be obtained through the U.S. Embassy website at http://bridgetown.usembassy.gov/.

- http://adoption.state.gov/country/st.%20lucia.html

ST. VINCENT & THE GRENADINES

- **Availability of children for adoption:** In fiscal year 2009, 12 immigrant adoption visas were issued.

- **Age and civil status requirements:** Singles are permitted to adopt in St. Vincent & The Grenadines, and there are no residency requirements.

- **Special information:** Prospective adoptive parents interested in adopting from St. Vincent & The Grenadines should contact the adoption authority directly for information on the process: The Adoption Board, c/o the Labor Department, Murrays Road, Kingstown, St. Vincent and the Grenadines. Telephone: 1 (784) 456-1111.

- http://adoption.state.gov/country/st.%20vincent%20and%2
0the%20grenadines.html

SUDAN

- **Availability of children for adoption:** In a statement issued by the State Department in June 2006, adoptions are generally not possible in Sudan at this time for many reasons, but mostly because of the inability to determine the orphan status of children who may be separated from their families. It is suggested that donations be made to American non-governmental organizations working in Sudan.

- http://adoption.state.gov/country/sudan.html

SURINAME

- **Availability of children for adoption:** In 2008, the last fiscal year reported by the State Department, there were 2 immigrant adoption visas issued.

- **Age and civil status requirements:** Singles are permitted to adopt in Suriname, but male prospective adoptive parents must be no more than 50 years older than the child, and female prospective adoptive parents must be no more than 40 years older than the adoptive child.

- **Special information:** Interested prospective adoptive parents should contact the Bureau of Family Rights and Affairs directly at: Bureau Voor Familierechtelijke Zaken, aan Postbus 67, Suriname. Telephone numbers: (597) 478759 and (597) 475763. They may also be contacted at bufazsur@hotmail.com or bufazsur@yahoo.com.

- **Document requirements:**

  - Home study
  - Proof of residency in U.S. including lease, proof of home ownership, or tax returns.
  - Birth certificate of prospective adoptive parent
  - Medical examination
  - Job letter from employer
  - Statement from home country stating that prospective adoptive parent has permission to bring child into country
  - Statement from home country saying that prospective adoptive parent has permission to adopt

- http://www.adoption.state.gov/country/suriname.html

SWAZILAND

- **Availability of children for adoption:** In 2009, 11 immigrant adoption visas were issued, up from one in 2008.

- **Age and civil status requirements:** Singles are permitted to adopt in Swaziland, but must be at least 25 years older than the adoptive child.

- **Special information:** There are no adoption agencies in Swaziland, so interested prospective adoptive parents should contact the Department of Social Welfare, Ministry of Health and Social Welfare, Box 5, Mbabane, Swaziland. Telephone: +268-404-2431. Fax: +268-404-2092.

- **Document requirements:**

  - Request for adoption to the Department of Social Welfare
  - Home study

- ID of prospective adoptive parent
- Other documents as requested as adoption proceeds

- http://adoption.state.gov/country/Swaziland.html

SWEDEN

- **Availability of children for adoption:** Children available for adoption are very rare in Sweden, so it is not considered a country of origin for intercountry adoptions. In rare cases, U.S. citizens resident in the United States may be allowed to adopt a family member.

- **Age and civil status requirements:** Singles are permitted to adopt.

- http://www.adoption.state.gov/country/sweden.html

SWITZERLAND

- **Availability of children for adoption:** Switzerland is not considered a country of origin for adoptive children. In the rare case of a prospective adoptive parent resident in Switzerland and wishing to adopt a family member, he or she should contact the Cantonal Central Authority in the Canton where they live.

- **Age and civil status requirements:** Singles are permitted to adopt in Switzerland if they are at least 35 years old and 16 years older than the adoptive child.

- http://www.adoption.state.gov/country/switzerland.html

SYRIA

- **Syrian law does not permit adoption.**

- http://www.adoption.state.gov/country/syria.html

TAIWAN

- **Availability of children for adoption:** In 2009, 253 immigrant adoption visas were issued, up from 48 in 2002. Unlike other adoption origin countries, in Taiwan it is not legal to adopt a child who is directly related by blood or marriage.

- **Age and civil status requirements:** Singles are permitted to adopt in Taiwan, but must be at least 20 years older than the adoptive child and not older than 55.

- **Documents requirements:**

  - Home study
  - Taiwan household registration of child
  - Certified statement from prospective adoptive parent indicating under which provision of U.S. law the child is being adopted
  - Notarized contract between adoptive parent and biological parents, if applicable
  - Power of attorney if prospective adoptive parent is not going to appear

- http://www.adoption.state.gov/country/taiwan.html

TANZANIA (including ZANZIBAR)

- **Availability of children for adoption:** Singles are permitted to adopt in Tanzania, although they must be residing in the country. In 2009, 4 immigrant adoption visas were issued.

- **Age and civil status requirements:** The prospective adoptive parent must be at least 21 years older than the child, and single men may only adopt female children under court order, which is unusual.

- http://adoption.state.gov/country/tanzania.html.

THAILAND

- **Thailand does not permit adoption to singles.**

- http://www.adoption.state.gov/country/thailand.html

TOGO

- **Availability of children for adoption:** In fiscal year 2008, 2 immigrant adoption visas were issued.

- **Age and civil status requirements:** Singles may adopt in Togo provided they do not already have biological children and are at least 35 years old.

- **Special information:** Adoptions are arranged directly through the high court of Togo. Prospective adoptive parents interested in adopting a child in Togo should write to the President of the High Court of Lome, B.P. 342, Lome, Togo. Telephone: (228) 221-56 39.

- **Document requirements:**

  - Police record
  - Birth certificate of prospective adoptive parent
  - Medical examination

- Proof of financial resources (pay slips, bank statements)
- I-600A
- Home study
- Photographs of prospective adoptive parents and home
- Letters of recommendation from family, friends

- http://www.adoption.state.gov/country/togo.html

TRINIDAD AND TOBAGO

- **Availability of children for adoption:** In 2009, 2 immigrant adoption visas were issued.

- **Age and civil status requirements:** Singles are permitted to adopt in Trinidad and Tobago, but must be at least 21 years older than the adoptive child.

- **Special information:** In order to adopt in Trinidad and Tobago, the prospective adoptive parent must be resident and permanently domiciled in the country. Custody/guardianship is possible for non-Trinidad and Tobago residents, meaning that the prospective adoptive parent can gain custody to bring the child to the U.S. for adoption. However, in Trinidad and Tobago, children available for custody/guardianship are not necessarily orphans, possibly making them ineligible for adoption in the U.S.

- http://www.adoption.state.gov/country/trinidad%20and%20 tobago.html

TUNISIA

- **Tunisia does not permit adoption to singles.**

TURKEY

- **Availability of children for adoption:** Turkey is not considered a country of origin for intercountry adoptions. In fiscal year 2009, one immigrant adoption visa was issued.

- **Age and civil status requirements:** Singles are permitted to adopt in Turkey, and must be at least 35 years old and 18 years older than the adoptive child.

- **Special information:** Under Turkish adoption law, the prospective adoptive parent is given custody of the adoptive child for one year, a period called the "Care Contract." Turkey allows the child to reside outside the country during that year, but the U.S. will not grant an immigrant visa until the child is released for adoption. Essentially, unless the prospective adoptive parent plans to go to another country, he or she must remain in Turkey until the adoption is finalized in a year. It is difficult for U.S. officials to issue a tourist or student visa to the child because of the inability of the child to prove that he or she will eventually go home. Immigrant adoption visas are only issued to children who have been adopted in the foreign country, or who are coming to the U.S. to be adopted. Prospective adoptive parents must have full custody to apply for this visa, and the Care Contract indicates only provisional custody, that is, it can be revoked. Prospective adoptive parents interested in adopting a specific child from Turkey should contact the State Department for updates on adoption law in that country.

- http://www.adoption.state.gov/country/turkey.html

TURKMENISTAN

- **Availability of children for adoption:** Intercountry adoption in Turkmenistan is rare. The U.S. Embassy in Ashgabat has issued only one immigrant adoption visa in the past five years. Prospective adoptive parents who are interested in adopting a specific child from Turkmenistan should contact the State Department for updates on adoption law in that country.

UGANDA

- **Availability of children for adoption:** In fiscal year 2009, 69 immigrant adoption visas were issued.

- **Age and civil status requirements:** Singles are permitted to adopt in Uganda, but must be at least 25 years old, 21 years older than the child, and may not adopt a child of the opposite gender without special permission.

- **Special information:** American prospective adoptive parents must live in Uganda for at least three years and foster the child for at least three years to be eligible for adoption. Exceptions have been made in cases where the courts determined that it was in the best interest of the child.

- **Document requirements:**

  - Police clearances
  - Proof of financial stability – tax returns and bank statements
  - Home study
  - Adoption order from the High Court of Uganda

- http://www.adoption.state.gov/country/uganda.html.

UKRAINE

- **Availability of children for adoption:** In 2007, 606 immigrant adoption visas were issued.

- **Age and civil status requirements:** As of April 24, 2008, singles who are not Ukrainian citizens can no longer adopt from Ukraine. The President of Ukraine signed this change into law on April 21, 2008.

- http://www.adoption.state.gov/country/ukraine.html

THE UNITED KINGDOM

- **Availability of children for adoption:** In fiscal year 2005, the last year reported by the State Department, five immigrant adoption visas were issued.

- **Age and civil status requirements:** Singles are permitted to adopt in the United Kingdom, and while there is no national upper age limit, local authorities have the right to impose upper age limits in their jurisdictions.

- **Special information:** England, Wales, Scotland and Northern Ireland are not countries of origin for intercountry adoption. Most intercountry adoptions are of family members.

- **Document requirements:**

  - Home study
  - Medical examination
  - Police record

- http://www.adoption.state.gov/country/united%20kingdom.html

UNITED ARAB EMIRATES

- **Islamic law does not allow for adoption in the United Arab Emirates.**

URUGUAY

- **Availability of children for adoption:** A special commission in Uruguay has recently issued new guidelines for adoption in their country, and has defined two types of adoption – "Simple" and the "Adoption Legitimating Process." Simple adoption is available to singles, but does not relinquish all parental rights. This form of adoption may not fulfill the U.S. requirements for issuing an immigrant adoption visa. The Adoption Legitimating Process requires that prospective adoptive parents be married.

- http://www.adoption.state.gov/country/uruguay.html

UZBEKISTAN

- **Availability of children for adoption:** In fiscal year 2009, 5 immigrant adoption visas were issued, down from 19 in 2008.

- **Age and civil status requirements:** Singles are permitted to adopt in Uzbekistan, as long as the prospective adoptive parent is at least 15 years older than the adoptive child.

- **Special information:** Adoption is extremely difficult in Uzbekistan. Prospective adoptive parents can expect to have many roadblocks, as adoption is a culturally sensitive issue, and many Uzbek officials are opposed to it.

- http://www.adoption.state.gov/country/uzbekistan.html

VENEZUELA

- **Availability of children for adoption:** With the recent ratification of the Hague Convention by the United States, and its start date of April 1, 2008, adoption in Venezuela has recently reopened. In fiscal year 2008, 2 immigrant adoption visas were issued. .

- **Age and civil status requirements:** Adoption is permitted for singles The prospective adoptive parent must be at least 18 years older than the child.

- **Special information:** It is extremely difficult to adopt in Venezuela without a pre-existing family connection. Prospective adoptive parents who wish to adopt from Venezuela should work closely with the U.S. Embassy in that country, and

- http://www.adoption.state.gov/country/venezuela.html

VIETNAM

- **Special Note:** The following information is included to show what has happened with intercountry adoption in Vietnam in the past few years. As noted, adoption has opened and closed several times during that time. Adoption requirements are included in the event that adoptions reopen in Vietnam.

- **Availability of children for adoption:** In fiscal year 2009, 481 immigrant adoption visas were issued, down from 766 in 2002. After a 2 ½ year hiatus, the United States and Vietnam signed a bilateral agreement that again allowed for intercountry adoptions (September 1, 2005), and on January 25, 2006, the U.S. Embassy in Hanoi issued the first immigrant adoption visa. However, a special warning was issued by the U.S. Department of State on January 28,

2008, stating that the Memorandum of Agreement between the U.S. and Vietnam authorizing adoptions between the two countries expires on September 1, 2008. Adoptions begun now cannot be finished before September 1, and there is no assurance that a new agreement will be reached before that date. It is a priority to both countries, though, that adoptions remain open between the U.S. and Vietnam, and the State Department has offered to do all that it can to help Vietnam attain transparency in its adoption processes. There have been some concerns that adoptions in Vietnam have occurred irregularly – that is, with forged signatures and even without the consent of the biological parent. The following information applied to adoptions in the past 2 years, and will probably apply when adoptions reopen. **Note: On April 25, 2008, the U.S. Embassy in Hanoi issued a report that said that the adoption process in Vietnam was corrupt, that babies were being purchased, and that American agencies in Vietnam were paying orphanage directors up to $10,000 per baby. In response, Vietnamese authorities stated that their country had been insulted and "accused" and on April 28, 2008 announced that adoptions would be closed to Americans who did not have their applications filed by July 1, 2008.**

- **Age and civil status requirements:** Singles are permitted to adopt in Vietnam, as long as the prospective adoptive parent is at least 20 years older than the adoptive child. Vietnamese law prohibits adoption by homosexual individuals and couples.

- **Special information:** Vietnam requires that prospective adoptive parents work with U.S. adoption agencies licensed by the Vietnamese Ministry of Justice's Department of International Adoptions (DIA). See the adoptions page on the American Embassy website for a list of licensed adoption agencies in the United States.

- http://www.adoption.state.gov/country/vietnam.html

YEMEN

- **Islamic law does not allow for adoption.**

YUGOSLAVIA (former)

- **See Serbia**

ZAMBIA

- **Availability of children for adoption:** In fiscal year 2009, 8 immigrant adoption visas were issued, down from 27 in 2007. Adoptions were closed from December, 2007 until May 2008, and since they have reopened, authorities in Zambia are working with the United States embassy to meet Hague-related requirements for adoption.

- **Age and civil status requirements:** Singles are permitted to adopt in Zambia, but single men may only adopt a girl if the court is satisfied that there are special circumstances for the adoption. Both men and women must be at least 21 years older than the child.

- **Special information:** By Zambian law, prospective adoptive parents must live in Zambia for a year to adopt a Zambian child, and may be required to foster the child for three months. For U.S. Citizens, however, often an approved I-600 or I-600A, with a completed home study, will be accepted in lieu of the year of residency and three-month fostering requirement.

- **Document requirements:**

  - Home study
  - Birth certificate of prospective adoptive parent

- Copy of passport
- Approved I-600A

- http://www.adoption.state.gov/country/zambia.html

ZIMBABWE

- **Availability of children for adoption:** In fiscal year 2009, 2 immigrant adoption visas were issued.

- **Age and civil status requirements:** Single women over the age of 25 may adopt with special permission of the Minister of Labor and Social Welfare. Single men may only adopt family members and must also be approved by the Minister.

- **Special information:** Prospective adoptive parents must be either citizens or legal residents of Zimbabwe, although this requirement may be waived by the Minister of Labor and Social Welfare. In addition, Zimbabwe has a strong preference for same-race adoptions interracial adoptions require special permission from the Minister. Caucasian prospective adoptive parents can expect more difficulty in adopting in Zimbabwe.

- http://www.adoption.state.gov/country/zimbabwe.html

APPENDIX B

ADOPTION AGENCIES

The following is a password for a document that can be found on the book's website —www.adoptionforsinglesbook.com. This document contains 81 adoption agencies in 33 states prescreened for experience with or a desire to work with single prospective adoptive parents. If your state does not have agency referrals, it means that no agencies in your state responded to the internet survey. This directory lists the name of the agency, its location, web and/or email address, and a contact person. It will also indicate what type of adoptions the agency facilitates. If the agency is not gay-friendly, that will be noted.

The password is: Joshua.

INDEX

Adoption for Singles Second Edition

CPSIA information can be obtained at www.ICGtesting.com
Printed in the USA
LVOW061712290212

271003LV00005B/86/P